Impeached

NUMBER 126
*Centennial Series of the Association of Former Students,
Texas A&M University*

Impeached

The Removal of Texas Governor James E. Ferguson

EDITED BY
Jessica Brannon-Wranosky and Bruce A. Glasrud

With John R. Lundberg, Kay Reed Arnold, Rachel M. Gunter,
Leah LaGrone Ochoa, Mark Stanley, Kyle G. Wilkison,
Katherine Kuehler Walters, Judith N. McArthur,
and Ricky Floyd Dobbs

TEXAS A&M UNIVERSITY PRESS • COLLEGE STATION

Copyright © 2017
by Jessica Brannon-Wranosky and Bruce A. Glasrud
All rights reserved
First edition

This paper meets the requirements of
ANSI/NISO Z39.48–1992 (Permanence of Paper).
Binding materials have been chosen for durability.
Manufactured in the United States of America

LIBRARY OF CONGRESS CATALOGING-IN-PUBLICATION DATA

Names: Brannon-Wranosky, Jessica, 1976– editor, compiler. | Glasrud, Bruce A., editor, compiler. | Lundberg, John R., author. | Lundberg, John R. Great Texas "bear fight."
Title: Impeached : the removal of Texas Governor James E. Ferguson / edited by Jessica Brannon-Wranosky and Bruce A. Glasrud ; with John R. Lundberg, Kay Reed Arnold, Rachel M. Gunter, Leah LaGrone Ochoa, Mark Stanley, Kyle G. Wilkison, Katherine Kuehler Walters, Judith N. McArthur, and Ricky Floyd Dobbs.
Description: First edition. | College Station : Texas A&M University Press, [2017] | Series: Centennial series of the Association of Former Students, Texas A&M University ; number 126 | Includes bibliographical references and index.
Identifiers: LCCN 2016046713 (print) | LCCN 2016048215 (ebook) | ISBN 9781623495275 (hardcover-printed case : alk. paper) | ISBN 9781623495282 (ebook)
Subjects: LCSH: Ferguson, James Edward, 1871-1944—Impeachment. | Texas—Politics and government—1865-1950. | Texas—Politics and government—1865-1950—Sources. | Women—Suffrage—Texas—History—1846-1950. | Trials (Impeachment)—Texas—Austin.
Classification: LCC KFT1626.45 .F47 2017 (print) | LCC KFT1626.45 (ebook) | DDC 342.764/062—dc23
LC record available at https://lccn.loc.gov/2016046713

FRONTIS PHOTO: *Governor James Ferguson (far left in the window) watches from the Texas State Capitol Building as the May 28, 1917, anti-Ferguson rally reached and gathered on capitol grounds. 1917. Photograph courtesy of Prints and Photographs Collection, di_06864, Dolph Briscoe Center for American History, University of Texas at Austin.*

Contents

Acknowledgments *vii*
Introduction: James Edward "Farmer Jim" Ferguson's
   Impeachment and Its Ramifications
   Jessica Brannon-Wranosky and Bruce A. Glasrud   *1*

Part I: Studies

Chapter 1: The Great Texas "Bear Fight": Progressivism
   and the Impeachment of James E. Ferguson
   John R. Lundberg   *13*
Chapter 2: "Think of the Lives That Might Be Saved":
   James Ferguson, Women's War Work, and the University of Texas
   Kay Reed Arnold   *53*
Chapter 3: "Without Us, It Is Ferguson with a Plurality":
   Woman Suffrage and Anti-Ferguson Politics
   Rachel M. Gunter   *85*
Chapter 4: In the Public Eye: Texas Governor James Ferguson's
   Fight with the Press
   Leah LaGrone Ochoa   *110*
Chapter 5: Fergusonism, Factionalization, and Thirty Years
   of Texas Politics
   Mark Stanley   *135*
Chapter 6: The Texas Governor's Impeachment in Historical
   Memory
   Jessica Brannon-Wranosky   *158*

Part II: Documents

Document 1: Ferguson's Texas Farm Tenant Law
   Comment by Kyle G. Wilkison and Katherine Kuehler Walters   *168*
Document 2: Minnie Fisher Cunningham to Carrie Chapman
   Catt Letter
   Comment by Judith N. McArthur   *175*

Document 3: Pat M. Neff to William Pettus Hobby Letter
Comment by Ricky Floyd Dobbs   *179*

Ferguson's Impeachment: A Selected Bibliography
Jessica Brannon-Wranosky and Bruce A. Glasrud   *185*

Index   *191*

Acknowledgments

Planning and completion of this anthology has been a true experience in community from the beginning. As the centennial of Ferguson's impeachment started to approach, discussion increased for the need of a concise compilation that took into consideration newly available archival sources and public sentiment transitions over the last hundred years. As interest started to build, we, the volume editors, sat discussing the project over lunch and post–Texas State Historical Association annual meeting exhaustion after the conference in the hotel restaurant. As we talked, a number of the authors who specialize in this era walked by and started to gather as folks do as part of the last hurrah at the end of a long academic weekend. As a number of them grabbed a chair at the table, eagerness started to build over plans to bring a centennial examination/recognition of the impeachment to fruition. Over the following year, we narrowed the list of potential contributors and perspectives, and we extended invitations to authors who could bring individualized attention to some of the key aspects and players of the impeachment and subsequent events.

The editors and authors worked together closely during this entire project, sometimes in virtual meetings and many times in person. At points, different groups met at archives to go through materials with and for each other to tighten each individual perspective and still make sure each chapter built on another. This volume would not have been successful without the long hours, hard work, and genuine collegiality expressed by the wonderful contributors; huge thanks goes to John R. Lundberg, Kay Reed Arnold, Rachel Michelle Gunter, Leah LaGrone Ochoa, Mark Stanley, Kyle G. Wilkison, Katherine Kuehler Walters, Judith N. McArthur and Ricky Floyd Dobbs. A special debt of gratitude goes to Elaina Friar Moyer for her patience and help in a number of the chores of compilation, including her photography skills, and to Patrick Cox for assistance in a number of ways regarding media and sources for pieces of the content of the book.

We are especially appreciative of all the time and effort so many archivists, reference librarians, and other information science professionals contributed to this project, including, but not limited to, those at the Dolph Briscoe Center for American History at the University of Texas, Texas Collection at Baylor University, Austin Public Library Austin History Center, University of Houston Special Collections, Texas State Library and Archives Commission Lorenzo de Zavala State Library and Archives, Texas Christian University Archives and Special Collections, and the Missouri History Museum. Additionally, thank you to the two outside readers who provided encouragement and suggestions to make the book stronger.

Importantly, without whose support this book would not exist, we vociferously thank Texas A&M University Press editor-in-chief, Jay Dew. Your encouragement throughout and your friendship overall is more invaluable than we can both express. Two individuals expeditiously took our manuscript and produced a book, copyeditor Dawn Hall and Texas A&M University Press associate editor Patricia A. Clabaugh. Thanks Dawn and Pat.

Finally, we wish to express enormous thanks for the unending support provided by our spouses, Michael Wranosky and Pearlene Vestal Glasrud. Additionally, thank you to Samantha Wranosky for understanding when work just has to happen.

What we have assembled herein is not the end of the conversation, but we hope more of a continuation. All in all, this has been a team experience that we will look back on and share, and for which we are enormously grateful.

—Jessica Brannon-Wranosky and
Bruce A. Glasrud

Impeached

Introduction

James Edward "Farmer Jim" Ferguson's Impeachment and Its Ramifications

Jessica Brannon-Wranosky and Bruce A. Glasrud

In late 1913, a virtually unknown businessman from Temple, Texas, entered the Democratic primary for the position of governor of the Lone Star State. James E. Ferguson, soon to be referred to as "Farmer Jim" and later as "Pa," appeared to be a long shot, but he readily won the Democratic primary and then the general election and took office as governor in 1915. Charming, charismatic, persuasive, and a moderately successful lawyer, businessman, and bank president, Ferguson won the election by opposing any type of liquor or prohibition legislation, campaigning as a successful businessman, appealing to the downtrodden and previously ignored tenant farmers of the state, claiming an affinity with organized labor, and favoring aid to education. He also opposed woman suffrage; of course, that was before Texas women could vote.

A convincing campaigner, Ferguson carefully addressed his speeches and his character to the less well-educated majority of Texas voters, the small farmers of the state. That focus worked and continued to do so for a second term. Ferguson, with a little more difficulty, won reelection in 1916 and began his second term in 1917, after which his political fortunes plummeted. In that same year he was impeached by forces led by the alumni, faculty, and administrators of the University of Texas, clubwomen, woman suffragists, prohibitionists, the Texas press, and other groups united by their antipathy for his sometimes unjust, demagogic, and even unconstitutional actions. Ferguson was convicted and not only removed from the governor's office but also barred from holding any office in Texas in the future. He thus became the only governor of Texas to be impeached.

What precipitated Ferguson's fall? Essentially, "Farmer Jim" Ferguson, although no worse than a few other Texas governors, offended the wrong individuals, but he did so without a solid support structure. He precariously balanced between the two conservative camps of the Texas Democratic Party—the leftovers of the Bourbon Democratic machine, who were wealthy, landed, and funded by machine-backed business endeavors, and the economically disenfranchised farmers whom this machine relied upon for votes but kept poor for the dependency. As a rural banker and lawyer of moderate previous success, Ferguson did not fit in with either the landed Bourbons or the poor farmers.

Even so, he had enough knowledge of both groups to successfully adopt the rhetoric of the subjugated farmers and leverage the rural support to gain the attention of the Bourbon machine after surpassing their chosen candidate in the 1914 state primary election. Faced with a choice between Ferguson and Thomas Ball, the progressive, urban, prohibitionist candidate, the Bourbon conservatives chose to back the previously unknown Ferguson. He was the one of the two front-running candidates who most closely resembled their conservative platform. The fact was, though, he was not one of the wealthy Texans with a historically established and landed family that this group had long relied on to carry their torch. Ferguson entered politics to make his future and finances, not to conserve what he and others already had. Furthermore, he came to the governor's office without the social training and networks to fit in with either the urban-industrial progressive elites or the landed historically wealthy elites.

The problem was that what got Ferguson elected was his platform of contempt of the existing power structure, but he did not leave that disdain at the door when he became governor. He was not a political team player; he did not know how to be, and he was not interested in learning. One person can get elected to office, but it takes a team of leaders with knowledge, experience, networks, and financial stability to effectively hold that office. None of these factors can replace any of the others and still turn out an effective administration. Ferguson's demagoguery and headline-grabbing antics kept the public entertained and returning for more, but they were a political nightmare. Other than his political knack, Ferguson lacked much of what it takes to govern effectively, and as such, soon after taking office things started falling apart. The book we have established herein highlights the variety of groups involved in calling for and implementing Ferguson's impeachment.

He challenged and provoked the progressive woman suffrage movement, the Texas newspaper editors and publishers, and the educational establishment at the University of Texas. In fact, there was not just one reason for the impeachment of Governor Ferguson; as is one of the major purposes of this anthology, a multitude of personalities, issues, groups, and rivalries coalesced at this point politically and historically, which led to his downfall. He may have been able to weather one or two, but his overzealous pursuit of his opponents in so many directions, his reckless wielding of the bully stick in too many places, and his lack of ardent supporters with social and political power made him vulnerable. His only solid backing came from the brewers, and they, led by Adolphus Busch, had their own agenda. It also turned out not to be enough to obstruct impeachment.

As we know, history is complex. A special session of the Texas House of Representatives in the summer of 1917 was called for the purpose of impeaching Governor Ferguson. The House brought twenty-one impeachment articles against Ferguson; the Texas Senate convicted Ferguson on ten of the charges. Even though he resigned the day before, his impeachment went on legal record as his official removal from office, and Ferguson was replaced with his lieutenant governor, William P. Hobby. It was not a surprise that most of the charges seemed more political in nature than substantial crimes, though he probably appropriated state funds for his own use.

His impeachment both astonished and angered Governor Ferguson. He refused to accept its ramifications even though he was no longer governor. Especially galling to Ferguson was the fact that he could no longer hold political office in Texas. He fought back and unsuccessfully ran against Hobby for governor in 1918. In 1920, he was a candidate for the presidency of the United States from the American Party. In 1922, he ran for the United States Senate by challenging Ku Klux Klan candidate Earle B. Mayfield in the Democratic primary runoff. Ferguson lost. His most successful post-impeachment venture took place in 1924 when his wife, Miriam Amanda Ferguson, won election as governor. Although she lost in Democratic primaries in 1926 and 1930, she successfully challenged the Democratic establishment by winning the governorship again in 1932. It should be noted that she was not only her husband's stand-in, she also governed.[1]

One hundred years ago, not mentioned in the impeachment proceedings, were aspects of Ferguson's gubernatorial behavior that in the twenty-first century would be considered offensive, if not impeachable. They included his failure to provide support for black lives and rights in

1916 after the deplorable Waco lynching of Jesse Washington, and in 1917, as the impeachment proceedings transpired, black soldiers in Houston were faced with extreme racist behavior by whites and retaliated in the "Houston Riot." Virtually Ferguson's last act as governor was to declare a state of emergency in Houston and send in the National Guard. Ferguson also used the Texas Rangers for political purposes; in particular, by adding Ferguson's Special Rangers to the Ranger force. Those Texas Rangers mistreated and murdered Mexican and Mexican American citizens even though their greatest atrocity, the "Porvenir Massacre," occurred in 1918 during Hobby's governorship.[2]

As it turned out, the impeachment of Jim Ferguson was an important event both nationally and locally, and we reexamined its impact in that vein. Moreover, it has been one hundred years since the impeachment proceedings took place; this volume, *Impeached: The Removal of Texas Governor James E. Ferguson, A Centennial Examination*, recognized that vital fact. As will be noted later, in spite of previous investigations, the impeachment of Governor James E. Ferguson, though important, had in reality not garnered substantial and objective analysis. Furthermore, the editors and authors of this project also hope to interest other historians in examining the Ferguson impeachment and to produce additional future works on the subject. Finally, as Norman Brown opined, "the dominant figure in Texas politics from 1914 to 1934 was James E. Ferguson."[3]

What has become apparent is that Governor James E. "Farmer Jim" Ferguson was an enigma. He was exceedingly influential while at the same time disliked by powerful forces. Ferguson upset the progressives. He incurred the wrath of women by opposing their bid for the right to vote. Not content, he challenged the University of Texas, and both its leadership and alumni took offense and resisted his alleged encroachments. His refusal to support prohibition angered that group's supporters. His autocratic and perhaps unlawful behavior offended others, and the press gladly and vociferously reported examples.

Over the past one hundred years, a body of literature concerning the impeachment of Jim Ferguson as well as biographical accounts of the Fergusons has been published. Even though few books have focused solely on either the Fergusons or the impeachment of Governor Jim Ferguson, those few have given us a worthy start toward understanding Ferguson, his supporters, and his enemies, as well as the progressive movement in Texas. To date the sole book dedicated to the impeachment of Ferguson is Bruce Rutherford, *The Impeachment of Jim Ferguson*. Published in 1983, Rutherford's factual account of the impeachment proceedings is helpful; he sought to put the governor's impeachment into legal context by explaining the historical process and precedence of impeachment in larger national aspects. Rutherford's assertion that Jim Ferguson's standing in Texas lore is generally favorable is probably a correct assumption. Ferguson did aid his wife's election to the governorship, they opposed the Ku Klux Klan, they saw that an increased amount of state funds went to education, and they helped make life better for the impoverished rural Texan. In his book, Rutherford goes beyond the Fergusons and describes how their lives and Farmer Jim's impeachment impacted that of Lyndon Johnson and that of Richard Nixon.[4]

The most central and academically thorough work on the impeachment contextually placed in progressive politics is Lewis L. Gould's *Progressives and Prohibitionists: Texas Democrats in the Wilson Era*. Followed by his *Southwestern Historical Quarterly* article, "The University Becomes Politicized: The War with Jim Ferguson," the two pieces are considered classics in the longtime hyperplacement of the political identity of the University of Texas. Together they explain the split that developed between Ferguson and the faculty, alumni, and administrators at the University of Texas and how that split led to and determined the outcome of the impeachment proceedings of Governor Ferguson. *Progressives and Prohibitionists* was first published in 1973. As the field of women's history was forming its foundations academically, women's involvement in Ferguson's impeachment was so central to the story that Gould recognized it and highlighted that fact even though it was not the academic era's norm to do so.[5]

The academics who set the stage for later histories were among those targeted by Ferguson and involved in his impeachment. In the early 1920s, University of Texas College of Arts and Sciences dean and eventual university president Harry Yandell Benedict collected papers in connection with the university's history, especially the conflicts with Ferguson and his gubernatorial impeachment. As part of the process, he accepted the papers regarding the Ferguson controversy remaining in UT professor Mary Gearing's possession and added them to the newly created "UT Memorabilia" Collection at the university. When Benedict died in 1937, he was working on the history of the university; it was never published but exists in manuscript form in Benedict's papers at the Dolph Briscoe Center for American History. Through these efforts and those of others, though, documents and artifacts regarding Jim Ferguson's impeachment and he and Miriam Ferguson's role in politics and history continue to become available and have led to a series of books and articles discussing various aspects of the impeachment and the Ferguson's lives.[6]

Chronologically, the first book published on either of the Fergusons arrived in 1929; it was Clare Ogden Davis's *The Woman of It*, a work of fiction based on the Texas gubernatorial election of 1924. Davis served as press secretary in Miriam's administration and gained considerable insight on the Fergusons. Davis emphasized the difficult role for a female politician/candidate. Should she take advantage of the new opportunities for women as intended by the right to vote, or continue to portray a more conservative woman with older familial, rural values? Miriam used the opportunity and ran for office, but as a more conservative person than suffragists would have liked. Davis's book was followed in 1932 and 1933 with two books, generally muckraking in nature. The first, James DeShields, *The Fergusons, "Jim and Ma": The Stormy Petrels in Texas Politics*, and the second, Don H. Biggers, *Our Sacred Monkeys; or, 20 Years of Jim and Other Jams (Mostly Jim) the Outstanding Goat Gland Specialist of Texas Politics*. Both seemed bent on ridiculing the Fergusons and not with taking them seriously.[7]

A more supportive and understanding but arguably no more objective account written by their daughter, Ouida Ferguson Nalle, *The Fergusons of Texas; or, "Two Governors for the Price of One,"* was published in 1946. A favorable account, the book provides us with interesting insights into the lives and interactions of her parents, both former governors in the Lone Star State. Nalle's book was designed as an attempt at vindicating the author's parents. More recent books, written in the mid-1990s, have focused on the female governor, Miriam Amanda Ferguson. Nelda Patteson published *Miriam Amanda Ferguson: First Woman Governor of Texas* in 1994, and the following year May Nelson Paulissen with Carl McQueary introduced us to *Miriam: The Southern Belle Who Became the First Woman Governor of Texas*. Well-known Texas author and editor Judy Alter wrote *Miriam "Ma" Ferguson: First Woman Governor of Texas*.[8]

The most recent book-length account of the Fergusons is by history enthusiast and first-time author Carol O'Keefe Wilson, *In the Governor's Shadow: The True Story of Ma and Pa Ferguson*. In this easy-to-read work, Wilson vociferously denigrated Jim Ferguson by attacking his corrupt and self-serving political and economic values. Although referred to as "the true story," one should, as always, beware of such lofty pronouncements. Wilson shed important light on Ferguson's sometimes unethical financial and political dealings.[9]

Additionally, a number of published scholarly articles and book chapters provide separate insights and information about the Fergusons and impeachment. A political scientist, Cortez A. M. Ewing, wrote about "The Impeachment of James E. Ferguson" in 1933. Ewing's early article provides invaluable insight into the political process as it unfolded before and during Ferguson's impeachment. A significant element in the impeachment of Governor Ferguson can be attributed to his dislike of the University of Texas; historian Ralph A. Steen emphasized this feature in his 1955 *Southwestern Historical Quarterly* article, "Ferguson's War on the University of Texas." Robert E. Vinson, who became president of the University of Texas over the considerable objections of then governor Jim Ferguson, in 1940 published his analysis of the impeachment process in "The University Crosses the Bar" for the *Southwestern Historical Quarterly*. Two years later, in 1942, one other university participant in the impeachment proceedings, John A. Lomax, published his informative article "Governor Ferguson and the University of Texas." Recently, scholar Patrick Cox contributed an additional view on the struggle between the university and Ferguson in Cox's chapter, "Farmer Jim and 'The Chief': Governor Jim Ferguson and His Battle with Eugene C. Barker and the University of Texas."[10]

Other authors covered various aspects of the Fergusons. Reinhard H. Luthin included "Mr. and Mrs. James E. Ferguson: 'Pa' and 'Ma' of the Lone Star State" in his book on twentieth-century demagogues. Jane Bock Guzman summarized much of what was known about the Fergusons in her overview, "Yet Another Look at the Fergusons of Texas," which was published in the *East Texas Historical Journal*. Two writers concerned themselves with Jim Ferguson's wife, Miriam Amanda Ferguson. Shelley Sallee focused on "'The Woman of It': Governor Miriam Ferguson's 1924 Election." In her article published by the *Southwestern Historical Quarterly*, Sallee noted the relationship between the fictitious version of the campaign as portrayed in the Clare Ogden Davis novel, *The Woman of It*, and the realities Miriam Ferguson faced in her hard-fought battle for election in 1924 against a leading Ku Klux Klan politician. Ralph Steen reviewed Miriam Amanda Fergusons life and actions as governor in "Governor Miriam A. Ferguson."[11]

Our book, *Impeached: The Removal of Texas Governor James E. Ferguson,*

A Centennial Examination, comprises this introduction composed by Jessica Brannon-Wranosky and Bruce A. Glasrud; the first part, "Studies," which includes six original articles that were written for this publication; and "Documents," the part that includes select primary documents connected to different aspects of and the legacy of Governor Jim Ferguson's impeachment. In "Studies," attention is devoted to the impeachment of Governor James E. Ferguson as well as to its ramifications and effects on other people and episodes in Texas and United States history. The existence of the impeachment will not be a surprise to most scholars, and each chapter builds on existing scholarship. Both the inclusion of differed perspectives and new pieces to the individual chapter narratives provide new insights. Furthermore, most of the scholarship on which these chapters, and thus the anthology as a whole, build is scattered across different nooks and corners of the profession's production over the past fifty years. Thus we hope that in addition to new information, the fact that it is all in one place will prove to be a useful tool for readers.

The first chapter, "The Great Texas 'Bear Fight': Progressivism and the Impeachment of James E. Ferguson" by John R. Lundberg, argues that shortly following his election as governor of Texas, Ferguson took umbrage with many faculty members of the University of Texas due to their perceived personal slights against him. This mistrust evolved into a fight against the university community, as Ferguson discovered that many of the faculty members supported political causes he opposed, such as prohibition and woman suffrage. Lundberg maintains that the struggle between Ferguson and the University of Texas did not represent a struggle over higher education per se, but a proxy fight between Texas progressives and the state's conservative political machine over the future of the Texas Democratic Party. The article also serves as a broad overview of the Ferguson impeachment episode, placing it in the context of Texas progressivism and exploring a variety of ancillary episodes and conflicts that contributed to the governor's impeachment and removal. Ultimately, Lundberg's article provides a fresh take on details of the impeachment and allows for larger discussions of important, often eerily similar, contemporary issues such as the fight over factions within political parties, money in politics, academic freedom, and governmental corruption.

The second chapter in *Impeached* is "'Think of the Lives That Might Be Saved': James Ferguson, Women's War Work, and the University of Texas," by Kay Reed Arnold. When the United States entered World War I, existing organizational and institutional infrastructures nationwide had to recalibrate to provide for national war readiness—including the University of Texas. When Ferguson fired beloved faculty members and threatened to close the doors of the University of Texas, he angered university supporters, but he also endangered the university's war work, public education efforts, and those who relied on those services. Loyal to the university they depended upon, Texas women gathered to assist in the campaign to impeach Governor Ferguson. Working independently, yet in concert with the University of Texas Ex-Students' Association, a select group of Texas women leaders formed the Woman's Campaign for Good Government and wrote to leaders of all of the Texas state women's associations and clubs asking for help in the campaign. They were not all woman suffragists or prohibitionists, but the one thing they could agree on was the essential needs of war work. To many, this was about protecting people, and the emotions related to that were raw and they were real. One by one, local women's groups wrote personalized letters, paid visits, sent telegrams, and made phone calls to legislators, lobbying for votes to remove the governor. They were effective.

In the third chapter, "'Without Us, It Is Ferguson with a Plurality': Woman Suffrage and Anti-Ferguson Politics," Rachel M. Gunter discusses the importance of the removal of Texas governor James Ferguson in the votes-for-women fight in Texas and as part of the last stages of the national movement. By January 1917, Texas Equal Suffrage Association president Minnie Fisher Cunningham's initial push for a state suffrage bill to provide Texas women the ability to vote in the state's political primary was defeated. However, when the recently impeached Ferguson sought reelection in 1918, Cunningham struck a deal with recalcitrant male legislative leaders to provide Texas women the primary vote in exchange for women's votes in the primary. As part of her end of the bargain, Cunningham led suffragists and clubwomen from across the state in an effective campaign to reelect William P. Hobby, Ferguson's lieutenant governor who had inherited the gubernatorial office after the impeachment.

The fourth chapter in *Impeached*, "'The News Has Been Condemning Me': The Role of the Texas Press in the Ferguson Impeachment," by Leah LaGrone Ochoa, shows how the Texas press handled the impeachment, how the press played a role in the process for and against Ferguson, including James Ferguson's own press organ, the *Ferguson Forum*, in connection to his gubernatorial presence leading up to and during the impeachment hearings and outcome. As Ochoa notes, the press angle was an important part of the impeachment story and the primary vehicle that Ferguson used in his defense when he made a speaking tour around the state.

The fifth chapter in this part, Mark Stanley's "Fergusonism, Factionalization, and Thirty Years of Texas Politics," persuasively argues that James E. "Pa" Ferguson's administration and subsequent impeachment had long-term effects on gubernatorial politics, and politics in general, in Texas even as late as the 1930s and 1940s. Although the factionalization of Texas Democrats dated to the nineteenth century, Ferguson's impeachment signaled a change in personal and party dynamics between political leaders that lasted for decades. Into the 1930s and 1940s, former governors refused to talk to one another based on their intraparty factional affiliation, and state political conventions turned into violent melees.

The final chapter in this part of the book, "The Texas Governor's Impeachment in History and Memory," written by Jessica Brannon-Wranosky, focuses on a select discussion of the Ferguson impeachment in historical memory and commemoration at different times during the past century. Ferguson's impeachment, Brannon-Wranosky discovered, became a warning to other elected officials, including an Oklahoma governor shortly after Farmer Jim's expulsion as well as to Governor Miriam Ferguson during her first term in office. More recently, governors have been impeached in Arizona in 1988 and Illinois in 2009. Former Texas governor Rick Perry was warned by impeachment efforts. Overall, since some eventually viewed Ferguson somewhat sympathetically, as Brannon-Wranosky phrases it, "it was not necessarily approval of [Ferguson's] actions, but instead, a public understanding that he was likely doing what many in politics did. He just got caught."

The second part of *Impeached* consists of contextualized primary source documents connected with the impeachment or its political aftermath. These include the Farm Tenant Law central to Ferguson's first gubernatorial campaign in 1914, a letter from Minnie Fisher Cunningham to Carrie Chapman Catt, and correspondence between former Texas governors Pat Neff and William Hobby. Each is annotated and commented upon by well-known scholars who are specialists in each area of the field. These valuable components of this volume enable the reader to receive a better idea of the interplay of groups and ideas surrounding the impeachment of James Ferguson; they also provide students and other readers with a glimpse into how historians can and do use primary sources in their research efforts. The book ends with a bibliography of principally secondary sources.

The impeachment and conviction of "Farmer Jim" Ferguson, as he called himself, was a historical first for the state. A sitting governor was charged, tried, and suffered loss of office. The Ferguson impeachment provided important legal precedents. Now one hundred years after those impeachment proceedings, the subject and its impact on the state and nation's political development compels attention and analysis. The editors and authors of *Impeached* offer a variety of approaches and viewpoints to better understand and recognize the resulting effects of that event in history.

NOTES

1. Ralph W. Steen, "Governor Miriam A. Ferguson," *East Texas Historical Journal* 17 (April 1979): 3–17.

2. "The Waco Horror," *Crisis* 3 (July 1916): supplement, 1–8; Patricia Bernstein, *The First Waco Horror: The Lynching of Jesse Washington and the Rise of the NAACP* (College Station: Texas A&M University Press, 2005); Robert V. Haynes, *A Night of Violence: The Houston Riot of 1917* (Baton Rouge: Louisiana State University Press, 1976); C. Calvin Smith, "The Houston Riot of 1917, Revisited," *Houston Review* 13 (1991): 84–102; "Porvenir Massacre," *Handbook of Texas Online*, http://tshaonline.org/handbook.

3. Norman D. Brown, "Progressivism in Texas," in *The Texas Heritage*, ed. Ben Procter and Archie P. McDonald, 3rd ed. (Wheeling, IL: Harlan Davidson, 1998), 96–114, quote on 101.

4. Bruce Rutherford, *The Impeachment of Jim Ferguson* (Austin, TX: Eakin Press, 1983).

5. Lewis L. Gould, *Progressives and Prohibitionists: Texas Democrats in the Wilson Era* (Austin: University of Texas Press, 1973); Lewis L. Gould, "The University Becomes Politicized: The War with Jim Ferguson, 1915–1918," *Southwestern Historical Quarterly* 86 (October 1982): 256–76.

6. Mary Gearing to Harry Benedict, June 2, 1923, University of Texas Memorabilia Collection, folder 1, box 4P162, Dolph Briscoe Center for American History, University of Texas at Austin; *Handbook of Texas Online*, Margaret C. Berry, "Benedict, Harry Yandell," accessed March 26, 2016, http://www.tshaonline.org/handbook/online/articles/fbe48.

7. Clare Ogden Davis, *The Woman of It* (New York: J. H. Sears, 1929); James DeShields, *The Fergusons, "Jim and Ma": The Stormy Petrels in Texas Politics* (Dallas: Clyde C. Cockrell, 1932); Don H. Biggers, *Our Sacred Monkeys; or, 20 Years of Jim and Other Jams (Mostly Jim) the Outstanding Goat Gland Specialist of Texas Politics* (Brownwood, TX: Jones Printing, 1933).

8. Ouida Ferguson Nalle, *The Fergusons of Texas; or, "Two Governors for the Price of One"* (San Antonio, TX: Naylor, 1946); Nelda Patteson, *Miriam Amanda Ferguson: First Woman Governor of Texas* (Smiley, TX: Smiley, 1994); May Nelson Paulissen and Carl McQueary, *Miriam: The Southern Belle Who Became the First Woman Governor of Texas* (Austin, TX: Eakin Press, 1995); Judy Alter, *Miriam "Ma" Ferguson: First Woman Governor of Texas* (Austin, TX: State House Press, 2006).

9. Carol O'Keefe Wilson, *In the Governor's Shadow: The True Story of Ma and Pa Ferguson* (Denton: University of North Texas Press, 2014).

10. Cortez A. M. Ewing, "The Impeachment of James E. Ferguson," *Political Science Quarterly* 48, no. 2 (1933): 184–210; Ralph W. Steen, "Ferguson's War on the University of Texas," *Southwestern Social Science Quarterly* 35 (March 1955): 356–62; Robert E. Vinson, "The University Crosses the Bar," *Southwestern Historical Quarterly* 43, no. 3 (1940): 1–13; John A. Lomax, "Governor Ferguson and the University of Texas," *Southwest Review* 28, no. 1 (1942): 11–29; Patrick Cox, "Farmer Jim and 'The Chief': Governor Jim Ferguson and His Battle with Eugene C. Barker and the University of Texas," in *The Texas Book Two: More Profiles, History, and Reminiscences of the University*, ed. David Dettmer (Austin: University of Texas Press, 2012), 133–40.

11. Reinhard H. Luthin, "Mr. and Mrs. James E. Ferguson: 'Pa' and 'Ma' of the Lone Star State" in *American Demagogues: Twentieth Century* (New York: Beacon Press, 1954); Jane Bock Guzman, "Yet Another Look at the Fergusons of Texas," *East Texas Historical Journal* 44, no. 1 (2006): 40–48; Shelley Sallee, "'The Woman of It': Governor Miriam Ferguson's 1924 Election," *Southwestern Historical Quarterly* 100 (July 1996): 1–16; Ralph W. Steen, "Governor Miriam A. Ferguson," *East Texas Historical Journal* 17 (April 1979): 3–17.

1

The Great Texas "Bear Fight"

*Progressivism and the Impeachment of
James E. Ferguson*

John R. Lundberg

On June 12, 1911, alumni of the University of Texas (eventually renamed the Texas Exes) gathered at the Austin Country Club for the annual barbecue and meeting of the Alumni Association. Although organized in 1885, the Alumni Association had never before functioned as an effective organization, for either serving their members or advocating on behalf of their alma mater. The 1911 meeting began to change that. Edwin B. Parker served as president of the association in 1911, yet other speakers that day included John Avery Lomax, the acting secretary of the organization; Thomas Watt Gregory, UT law professor; president of the university H. Y. Benedict; state senator Alexander W. Terrell (an honorary member); future US senator Tom Connally; and Will C. Hogg, son of the late governor, James Hogg. That day in Austin, Hogg proposed a bold design to increase the funding for the Alumni Association, establish an alumni magazine, provide for a permanent secretary, and most of all to turn the group from "a wishing organization to a working organization." Such a plan, stated Hogg, "necessarily involves a co-ordination of organized thought, which in itself means a liberal education to thousands of sweet-thinking persons in this State. This movement, or any similar movement, undertaken with the right spirit and followed with that persistence which we apply in ordinary affairs to gain any measure of success, will have an educational value that will be felt throughout the civilized world."[1]

The men and women who attended this meeting, in addition to their status as alumni, nearly all shared a similar political outlook that embraced many elements of progressivism. In Texas at the time, this meant most notably a belief in the advancement of civilization through a "liberal education" that included the two main pillars of progressivism during the following decade, prohibition and woman suffrage. By 1913, members of the Alumni Association changed its name to the Texas Ex-Students' Association (commonly known as the Texas Exes) and launched the alumni magazine the *Alcalde*. From this point on the University of Texas, and the Texas Exes in particular, became the locus of progressive politics in Texas, the headquarters of Texas progressivism. This activism placed them and their university squarely in the eye of the storm of Texas politics throughout the rest of the second decade of the twentieth century and beyond.[2]

The impeachment and removal from office of Governor James E. "Pa" Ferguson in 1917 marked a turning point in Texas political history. Although contemporaries feared that the peak of progressivism in Texas had already come and gone during the administration of Governor

Portrait of James Edward Ferguson. N.d. Photo courtesy of William Deming Hornaday Collection, Texas State Library and Archives Commission, Austin.

Thomas Campbell from 1907 to 1911, Texas progressives still had important goals in mind in 1917—namely, to make prohibition and woman suffrage the law of the land. Had Ferguson remained in office, it is doubtful that Texas would have embraced these goals as they did under his successor, Governor William P. Hobby. Historians have traditionally viewed the Ferguson impeachment episode as a battle over higher education, but this interpretation largely misses the point. Ferguson's bear fight with the University of Texas from 1915 to 1917 had less to do with higher education and more to do with the politics of the University of Texas as the center of progressivism in the state.[3]

As a matter of fact, Jim Ferguson was not anti–higher education. Under his influence and leadership, the thirty-fifth legislature founded or purchased for state use seven new colleges with a largesse rarely seen in the Texas legislature. Ferguson, rather than an anti–higher education reactionary, actually campaigned as a rural populist at a time when rural populism in Texas had begun to fade from the political landscape. Ferguson's dispute with the University of Texas and his subsequent impeachment had much more to do with the two warring factions of the Democratic Party in the second decade of the twentieth century: the largely rural old line conservative Democratic political machine that Ferguson led, and the largely urban progressives. Historians should view the Ferguson impeachment episode in a much broader context than a battle over personality, or even the University of Texas, but rather as a turning point in the battle for control of the Texas Democratic Party in the Progressive Era.[4]

The progressive impulse in Texas followed something of an unusual path for a southern state. Many historians date the beginning of Texas's Progressive Era to 1886 with the election of James S. Hogg to the office of state attorney general. After distinguished service as the attorney general, in which he helped pass the nation's first antitrust law in 1889, Hogg ran for the governorship in 1890 and won on a platform promising to create a Texas Railroad Commission to regulate the railroads. Hogg passed a number of reforms during his term as governor, including the creation of the Texas Railroad Commission, but Hogg's tenure as governor ended in 1895, and three decidedly more conservative governors followed him until 1906. That year, Hogg passed away but not before he endorsed his friend Thomas M. Campbell, a progressive reformer in his own right, for governor. Campbell won the governorship that year and helped pass a plethora of reforms covering many areas, including insurance, child labor, ending the convict lease system, and prohibition. Campbell won reelection in 1908, but in his second term, a schism in the Democratic Party began to take hold. A group of legislators came to Austin, campaigning for "fewer and better laws" with a reactionary focus intended to end much of what they perceived as a dangerous path of reform, in particular the push for prohibition.[5]

These new legislators received most of their financial backing from the Texas Brewer's Association, a collection of liquor interests organized in 1901 to fight the growing tide of prohibition sentiment in the state. The Texas brewers also had the backing of Adolphus Busch and access to the almost limitless coffers of the Anheuser-Busch Association of Saint Louis, Missouri. Located primarily in the Hill Country and the southern parts of the state, the Texas brewers intended to throw back the tide of prohibition by any means necessary. Many Texas progressives backed prohibition since the Texas brewers constituted the closest thing to a political machine in Texas; the brewers imitated the large corporations that progressives in other parts of the United States campaigned against. In addition to complaints about the effects of alcohol on the body and the menacing effects of the saloon on society, prohibitionists concentrated primarily on the corrupting influence of liquor money in politics. The battle between conservatives and progressives in Texas became in large measure a proxy fight about the power and the influence of the liquor interests.[6]

In the first decade of the twentieth century, the woman suffrage movement also became a serious force in Texas politics. In 1913, the Texas Woman Suffrage Association (later renamed the Texas Equal Suffrage Association or TESA) reorganized in San Antonio, led by Mary Eleanor Brackenridge. In 1915, the members chose Minnie Fisher Cunningham, a graduate of the University of Texas Medical Branch, as their leader. These suffragists also strongly favored prohibition as a way to weed out corruption in politics. Cunningham and her organization, along with other women's clubs, most notably the Women's Christian Temperance Union, joined the ranks of the progressives in Texas in their fight against the "wets" and the Democratic political machine. In response, the wets strongly opposed woman suffrage because they assumed that votes for women meant votes against liquor. The parallel suffrage and prohibition interests coalesced in a powerful way against Jim Ferguson during the impeachment episode, encouraging the advancement of both.

The year 1910 marked a low point for Texas progressives. Although they succeeded in getting a ballot initiative potentially to ban liquor on the ballot for 1911, "drys" split their vote between two different candidates, allowing a moderately progressive but decidedly wet governor, Oscar B. Colquitt, to win the Democratic primary. Colquitt had the backing of the Texas brewers and won the election with their money and influence.

The ballot initiative, set for July, illustrated the power of the liquor interests in Texas. The Texas brewers poured at least $555,000 into the election statewide, including $100,000 from Adolphus Busch and the Anheuser-Busch Association. San Antonio brewer and Texas House of Representatives member Otto Wahrmund wrote Adolphus Busch that the money "OUGHT to be sufficient for the campaign but when you take into account that everything we have to do has to be paid for . . . and then take into account there are 247 counties in the State, each with it county chairmen and precinct chairman, all requiring money, we will probably have none too much." In July 1911, one month after Will Hogg's rousing speech and organization of the Texas Exes, drys lost the statewide referendum by fewer than six thousand votes. Despite this loss, the battle for prohibition remained unsettled. Colquitt won reelection in 1912, and 1914 became the next battle in the showdown between wets and drys.[7]

The race for the 1914 Democratic primary turned into a free-for-all among a plethora of candidates representing multiple factions of the party. After extensive maneuvering, drys settled on Houston attorney Thomas Ball as their choice for the nomination. Despite his personal vulnerabilities, Ball remained the overwhelming favorite to win the primary. Meanwhile, as the main part of the Democratic machine prepared to choose their candidate, one of the men in contention, James E. Ferguson—a banker from Temple—declared his independence from the process and began taking his case directly to the people. On March 21, Ferguson made his opening speech at Blum, and stated, "If I am elected Governor, and the Legislature puts any liquor legislation in front of me, pro or anti, I will strike it where the chicken got the axe." Avoiding the topic of liquor, Ferguson cut straight to the heart of his program, a bill to help tenant farmers by prohibiting landlords from collecting rent that exceeded one-fourth of the cotton crop or one-third of a grain crop. By bypassing the liquor issue and appealing to Texans on the issue of tenant farming, Ferguson gained an almost cultlike following from "the boys at the forks of the creeks." In an interview with the *Dallas Morning News* on March 22, Ferguson stated his case and began to frame himself as "Pa" Ferguson. Despite the grammatically incorrect speeches and folksy image, James Ferguson remained far from the rural farmer his speeches suggested.[8]

Born in 1871 in Bell County, Ferguson attended Salado College before opening the Temple State Bank in 1907. At Salado College, a preparatory school, Ferguson studied Greek and Latin, among other subjects, and gained an appreciation for the rural school. He began to study law in 1895 and two years later gained admission to the bar. Ten years later Ferguson moved to Temple and opened the bank. He estimated his net worth at $400,000 by the time he entered state-level politics as a candidate in 1914, although his personal finances left much to be desired.[9]

The campaign between Ball and Ferguson gained intensity before Ferguson finally swamped his opponent behind the strength of the rural vote and the backing of the Texas brewers. Ball began losing momentum as soon as Ferguson entered the race, with the latter campaigning at a furious pace. In addition, Ball retained the support of several prominent wets, including Senator Joseph Weldon Bailey, which led to a crisis of confidence among the prohibitionists. Despite the fact that President Wilson belatedly endorsed Ball, Ferguson struck back by pointing out Ball's membership in the Houston Country Club, which served liquor by the drink, a supposedly hypocritical stance for a prohibitionist. Meanwhile, R. L. Autrey, head of the Houston Ice and Brewing Company, coordinated the money and efforts of the Texas brewers to defeat Ball. Between the doubts the drys harbored about Ball, his personal vulnerabilities, and the efforts of the Farmers' Union and Texas brewers on behalf of Ferguson, "Farmer Jim" won the 1914 Democratic primary by a vote of 237,062 to 191,558. Ferguson easily sailed to victory in the regular election—as is usually the case in a one-party state—and entered the governorship in 1915 with an image as a rural populist and a political debt to the Texas brewers to guide his gubernatorial policies.[10]

Ferguson practiced the spoils system of governance, and he quickly went about the business of elevating friends and making new enemies. In January 1915, a dispute arose between Ferguson and Will Hogg, then serving as the chairman of the University of Texas Board of Regents. In addition to his work with the university, Hogg championed education all over the state, and both Hogg and Ferguson favored uniting the University of Texas and Texas Agricultural and Mechanical College under one governing body. However, in the legislative session, Ferguson later maintained that Hogg undercut his idea, and the legislature voted down the proposed constitutional amendment to join the two schools. When Ferguson addressed the legislature he stressed that the rural schools received too little and the University of Texas received too much, and he stated that there "was a real danger of somebody going hog wild over higher education" in what was probably a subtle jab at Will Hogg. Relations between Ferguson and Hogg continued to deteriorate, and by September, matters had grown so acrimonious that Hogg offered an olive branch. Hogg wrote to Ferguson in hopes that they could resolve their differences, but Ferguson ignored the letter.[11]

If Ferguson had no grudge against the University of Texas, he quickly developed one. Ferguson knew his political enemies, and he understood that many of them filled the University of Texas. It became common knowledge among reformers throughout the state during Ferguson's term of office that Adolphus Busch and the Texas brewing interests knew about the many prohibitionists and suffragists who taught at the University of Texas, and that many of them had opposed Ferguson in 1914. Jim Ferguson also understood that his constituents lived in the rural parts of the state and that most of them would receive their education in rural schools, and he therefore determined to control rural education in Texas, from the Texas Agricultural and Mechanical College to the increasing number of normal colleges throughout the state. It followed then that Ferguson wanted to merge the governing boards of the university and the Agricultural and Mechanical College to dilute the influence of men like Will Hogg. Ferguson did not like the University of Texas, but early on in his term in office, he evidently trusted that he could control its influence.[12]

Other skirmishes between the university and Ferguson broke out in the spring of 1915 that deepened the governor's impression of an institution filled with politically active faculty members who opposed him. In August 1906, the Texas State Archives and Historical Commission appointed Ernest W. Winkler, an 1899 graduate of the university, as the state librarian. The first of the skirmishes came over the appointment of a new state librarian. During the 1914 campaign Ferguson indicated his desire to appoint A. F. Cunningham of Temple, a Ferguson supporter and Presbyterian minister, as the Texas state librarian. By the time of Ferguson's election, Professor Eugene C. Barker, chair of the Department of History at the university, held the chairmanship of the commission and evinced alarm in early 1915 when Ferguson went about attempting to replace his old friend and classmate Winkler with Cunningham. Barker sought permission from Ferguson to write to Cunningham, outlining the job qualifications, and the governor consented. Barker penned a strong letter to Cunningham, telling him up front that it was his intent to "dissuade" him from taking the job, and informing him that anyone aspiring to the position should be a "qualified" historian with a thorough knowledge of historiography and bibliography, should be an editor, and must "know Spanish." Ferguson received a carbon copy of the letter the same day.[13]

The next day, Ferguson wrote a letter accusing Barker of attempting to intimidate Cunningham, stating, "I regard your letter as an insult to him and me both. As you have entered into a long discussion of politics in the letter, I hope that you will not hereafter complain if your wishes are not carried out." Barker tried to apologize, but Ferguson ignored him, and when the Library and Historical Commission met in Austin on February 20, 1915, the commission deadlocked between Winkler and Cunningham. After the meeting, Ferguson replaced several members of the commission whose terms were expiring, and at the next meeting, on March 3, the commission voted 3–2 to appoint Cunningham as the new state librarian. Barker then resigned from the commission in protest. The incident with Barker further convinced Ferguson that the "University crowd" intended to wage political war with him.[14]

The next skirmish Ferguson had with the university happened during a stormy meeting in May between Ferguson and acting university president William J. Battle. In the fall of 1914, Sidney Mezes stepped down as president of the university, and the board of regents appointed Battle, a professor of classics, as interim president. Battle, with a PhD from Harvard and a father who had served as president of the University of North Carolina, seemed destined to clash with Ferguson on personality alone. President Mezes prepared a biennial budget for the university before his resignation, and Battle dutifully submitted the budget to the thirty-fourth legislature when they convened in January 1915. The legislature at length passed the budget in the special session in May, and Battle, accompanied by professor of law Charles S. Potts, traveled to the capital to urge Ferguson to sign the appropriation. According to Ferguson's account, with Battle and Potts in his office, he ran his finger over the line-item appropriation bill and asked about $3,250 for a professor of sociology. Ferguson inquired to whom the item referred, only to have Battle inform him that they had not hired such a professor and intended to use the money for other purposes. "Dr. Battle, let me understand you," the governor said, "do you mean to tell me that you have come down to this Legislature and told the Appropriation Committee that you wanted a professor of sociology . . . knowing that you did not have such a man and that you intended to divert the money to some other use which you did not disclose?"

Ferguson found two other such instances in the budget and informed Battle that although he would sign the budget, he was taking notice of what he considered the university's dishonest financial dealings. Although the board of regents and the state comptroller worked out a compromise and the Texas attorney general, Benjamin F. Looney, issued a legal ruling that justified the fiscal practices of the university, this episode killed any chance Battle may have had of becoming the university's permanent president, and increased Ferguson's antipathy toward the University of Texas.[15]

The clash between Ferguson and Battle led to the choice of a new president. Ferguson wrote to Will Hogg, informing him that he felt Battle was "totally unsuited" for the job. When Hogg asked for reasons, Ferguson replied, "I am the Governor of Texas. I don't have to give reasons." Sensing Ferguson's intransigence, Battle withdrew his name from consideration for the post at the meeting of the board of regents in October 1915. A search for a new president began, and even though Ferguson had his own candidate in mind, in April 1916 the regents chose the forty-year-old president of the Austin Presbyterian Theological Seminary, Robert E. Vinson, as the new president of the University of Texas. Although Vinson possessed all of the academic qualifications commensurate with the position, Ferguson became enraged at the choice and with the fact that the regents had not consulted him sufficiently before they appointed Vinson. Ferguson attacked Vinson as a "sectarian preacher," probably because of Vinson's extensive work with the Austin Anti-Vice League, an organization dedicated to fighting prostitution and alcohol near army camps. In Vinson, Ferguson saw yet another political opponent who posed a risk to not only him but also to his political backers, the Texas brewers.[16]

On June 20, 1916, even before his inauguration as president, Vinson called on Ferguson in the company of Major George Littlefield, a member of the board of regents. At this meeting, Ferguson demanded the immediate dismissal of seven members of the faculty. When Vinson asked for charges against these men, Ferguson pounded his fist on the desk and said, "these men had to go." Vinson informed Ferguson that he would act on his own understanding of the facts, and that he was unaccustomed to "acting on any man's dictation." Ferguson then threatened that if Vinson did not fire those men he would face "the biggest bear fight that had ever taken place in the history of the State of Texas."[17]

The men Ferguson demanded fired revealed a great deal about the governor's agenda. Ferguson named Battle, professor of law Charles S. Potts, renowned folklorist and secretary of the Texas Exes John A. Lomax, professor of physics William T. Mather, professor of educational philosophy A. Caswell Ellis, professor of law Robert E. Cofer, and professor of journalism William H. Mayes as those he wanted removed immediately.

Until June 1916 Ferguson's case against the university could be attributed to his desire to have some say in naming the president of the school and genuine worries about the financial practices of the institution, but his conversation with Vinson and Littlefield revealed his actual purpose. The misunderstanding and clash of personalities between Battle and Ferguson probably began with the conversation in Ferguson's office in 1915, but only politics served as a common denominator between the other six professors.

Alexander Caswell Ellis embodied everything that James E. Ferguson loathed. Ellis received his BA in classics from the University of North Carolina in 1894 and his PhD from Clark University in Worcester, Massachusetts, in 1897. That same year he joined the faculty of the university, and beginning in 1908 served as a professor of educational philosophy (educational psychology). He also began directing the University Extension Service in 1911. Ellis offended Ferguson on several different fronts. First, by 1916 Ellis had become the leading voice for prohibition and suffrage throughout the state. Ellis was married to Mary Heard Ellis, a leading suffragist in her own right, and worked closely with Minnie Fisher Cunningham, among others. Ellis also edited the *Texas Democrat*, a prominent suffragist newspaper. In fact, judging from his papers, Ellis served as one of the foremost progressives in the state and was the lynchpin connecting the prohibitionist and suffragist forces. Second came Ellis's work with the extension service; the extension service had the primary mission of reaching out to rural parts of the state to help farmers and rural schools develop better farming techniques. In this capacity, Ellis traveled around the state, lectured on agricultural matters, and coordinated with Texas A&M and other rural colleges and schools. Ferguson publicly stated that he objected to Ellis's work with the rural extension service. He could not tolerate an outspoken prohibitionist and suffragist influencing and preaching to his rural constituents.[18]

Charles S. Potts, professor of law, received his BA and MA from the University of Texas and then worked as a professor of economics at Texas A&M until he graduated from the University of Texas school of law in 1909. He became a member of the political science faculty of the university in 1911 and a professor of law in 1914. Potts helped his fellow professors, Charles W. Ramsdell and Eugene C. Barker, write a 1912 Texas history textbook for the public schools, but apparently Potts ended up on Ferguson's list by virtue of his presence in the room when the spat between Ferguson and Battle took place.[19]

John A. Lomax, by his own admission, steered clear of politics, but he had become a very influential scholar in Texas and far beyond by 1916 and served as not only secretary to the faculty but also secretary of the Texas Exes and assistant to President Vinson. Lomax also worked closely with A. Caswell Ellis and the University Extension Service. With his visibility as a scholar, his close associations with Ellis and Hogg, and his work with the Texas Exes, the faculty, the University Extension Service, and Vinson, it is entirely predictable that Lomax wound up on Ferguson's list.[20]

William T. Mather earned his PhD at Johns Hopkins University in 1897, and in 1907 he joined the faculty of the university as a professor of physics. Mather, in addition to his work in physics, served as an elder in the University Presbyterian Church, worked on the board of directors of the Austin YMCA, and helped organize the Austin Men's Anti-Vice League. The Austin Anti-Vice League organized in response to perceived threats to the virtue of American fighting men in army training camps around the state. The Anti-Vice League worked to create "white zones" around army camps that would ban liquor and prostitution. In this capacity, Mather worked closely with suffragists and prohibitionists like Jane Y. McCallum and Minnie Fisher Cunningham. Ferguson clearly saw Mather as a political threat through his political activities aimed at reining in the liquor industry.[21]

Robert E. Cofer earned a law degree from the University of Virginia in 1892 and joined the faculty of the university as a professor of law in 1911. Before joining the faculty, Cofer practiced law in Gainesville, Texas, and served as a Texas state senator from 1908 to 1911. In the spring of 1916, Cofer attended a ward primary at the Austin YMCA for the Democratic presidential primary aimed at renominating President Wilson. The attendees elected Cofer as a delegate to the Travis County nominating convention, and he served as chair of the convention. Some of the delegates there proposed resolutions criticizing Governor Ferguson, and despite the fact that Cofer helped defeat these resolutions, his political activities evidently aroused Ferguson's suspicion and ire.[22]

William H. Mayes studied at Vanderbilt University and received admission to the Kentucky bar in 1881 and the Texas bar the following year. He practiced law in Brownwood, Texas, from 1882 to 1886, served as county attorney for Brown County from 1882 to 1883, and served as the editor and publisher of the *Brownwood Bulletin* from 1887 to 1914. In 1913, he won the lieutenant governorship of Texas, and in 1914 Daniel Baker College awarded him an honorary doctorate. In 1914, Mayes accepted an appointment to the university as a professor of journalism and founded the Department of Journalism, serving as dean of the school. During the 1914 campaign, the *Brownwood Bulletin* published a series of editorials criticizing Jim Ferguson, and in Ferguson's own words, "skinned me from hell to breakfast." Ferguson readily admitted that he wanted to get rid of Mayes because of this latter episode, although Mayes denied having any editorial control over the paper in 1914.[23]

Therefore, of the seven professors whom Ferguson demanded removed in June 1916, he asserted that two (Battle and Potts) had challenged his personal authority. Additionally, the other five (Ellis, Lomax, Mather, Cofer, and Mayes) directly participated in political activities antithetical to his political career and the liquor industry. Ferguson's grudge did not concern higher education as such, but rather the politics of these professors at the University of Texas.

Despite Ferguson's demand for the removal of these professors, President Vinson did not act immediately, and Ferguson turned his attention to winning reelection in 1916. At the Texas Democratic Party Convention in May 1916 in San Antonio, the delegates expressed their support for the reelection of Woodrow Wilson, but the suffragists and prohibitionists could not make any inroads. Senator Joseph Weldon Bailey and Governor Ferguson dominated the convention and wrote the party platform. Bailey gave a passionate speech against suffrage, alleging that if women gained the right to vote, African American women would also earn the right to vote, threatening the hegemony of white supremacy. This race-baiting worked, and Bailey and Ferguson crushed the drys and suffragists with a platform opposed to any liquor legislation or woman suffrage.[24]

At the Democratic National Convention in Saint Louis in June 1916, Pa Ferguson and his Texas opposition took their fight to the national level. Minnie Fisher Cunningham led a number of her fellow Texas Equal Suffrage Association members to Saint Louis, where the Democrats renominated Wilson and Ferguson gave an impassioned speech against suffrage, a speech that enraged Cunningham and her fellow suffragists. Cunningham remained so disgusted with Ferguson's speech that she and some of her compatriots paraded a Lone Star flag draped in mourning outside the delegates' hotel. Nothing worked, and the official Democratic Party platform failed to endorse either suffrage or prohibition.[25]

In the July 1916 Texas Democratic primary, Jim Ferguson faced a surprisingly strong challenge from rural banker Charles H. Morris. Although Morris began the campaign at somewhat of a disadvantage, he capitalized on Ferguson's growing unpopularity and gained traction by accusing the governor of financial misdeeds from his time at the Temple State Bank. A letter provided by Hosea Poe, Ferguson's successor at the bank, attesting to the irregularities, bolstered Morris's claims. Poe claimed that Ferguson owed the bank $140,000, and this appearance of impropriety followed the governor from that point forward. The governor won the primary, but did so with a weak showing for an incumbent. Despite this reality, Ferguson viewed his reelection as a mandate to continue his policies.[26]

At the outset of the 1916/17 school term, UT President Vinson prepared to submit a budget for the university to the board of regents ahead of their October meeting. In his preparations, Vinson wrote to Ferguson on September 5, informing him of his purpose and relating that sometime in June, in a meeting in Ferguson's office, the governor indicated to Vinson that he wished to make certain "charges" against members of the faculty. Vinson informed Ferguson that he hoped the governor would compile the charges so that he could investigate them and have a report ready for the board of regents. Four days later Ferguson replied by stating, "I emphatically deny that I ever indicated or intimated that I wanted to make any charge against anybody; and I told you then and there the names of the members of the faculty whom I thought objectionable and I have not changed my mind." On September 16, Vinson wrote back, attempting to smooth over Ferguson's feelings, but informing him that the bylaws required charges and an investigation before he could remove any members of the faculty. With Vinson's reply, Ferguson began exploring options to bring formal charges against the offending faculty at the meeting of the board of regents.[27]

Ferguson also began pressuring members of the board of regents to side with him against Vinson and the faculty. On September 11, Ferguson wrote to Rabbi Maurice Faber, whom he had appointed to the board of regents the previous year. Ferguson wanted assurances that Faber would side with him in any dispute he might have with the university president, the faculty, and the other regents, but Faber declined to give any assurances, informing Ferguson that he would remain independent in his judgement. Annoyed, Ferguson railed against Faber, but the rabbi stood firm.[28]

Nine days after his initial letter to Faber, Ferguson wrote W. R. Long, the auditor assigned to the university. The governor asked him for "expense accounts and transactions relative thereto of the various employees of the University." Long began to supply Ferguson with records he required to bring charges of financial irregularity against his political enemies, a supreme irony that no doubt escaped the governor's notice.[29]

On October 10, 1916, the regents, with President Vinson and Governor Ferguson, assembled in the library of the University of Texas to hear the charges against members of the faculty. In the first days of October, just before the meeting, Ferguson finally transmitted to Vinson the charges he held against the various faculty members orally rather than in writing. Regent Dr. Ashley W. Fly served as Ferguson's only firm ally in the stormy hearings that took place over the next two days. Ferguson's complaints of financial misdeeds included allegedly overcharging for mileage, charges made for lectures, drawing pay during leaves of absences, false entries on expense accounts, and profiting off notebooks sold to the students, among others. Over the next two days, the regents and Ferguson cross-examined auditor of the university W. R. Long, secretary of the University Extension Service Samuel Polk, Battle, Ellis, Mather, Lomax, Cofer, Mayes, and Potts. They also questioned Mr. I. P. Lochridge, business manager of the university. None of the questioning involved anything except the minor financial misunderstandings mentioned above, and the overall financial practices of the university—the same complaints Ferguson had raised with Battle the previous year. None of the questioning by the regents yielded any sustainable charges against any of the professors questioned.[30]

On October 11, with eight members of the board of regents present, voting on removal began. In every case, Dr. Fly made the motion for removal, and Fly remained the only consistent vote to remove the parties in question. In the case of Battle, Fly, Major George W. Littlefield, and Dr. George S. McReynolds—an MD and Ferguson appointee from Temple— voted to remove, while Will Hogg, Rabbi Faber, David H. Harrell, Samuel J.

Jones, and Alexander Sanger voted against removal. In the case of Ellis, Fly, Littlefield, and McReynolds voted aye, while again Hogg, Faber, Harrell, Jones, and Sanger voted against removal. The votes against the others fell out in a similar manner. In the end, the board of regents refused to remove any of the men Ferguson had brought charges against. This must have particularly galled Ferguson considering that he had appointed Faber, McReynolds, and Jones. Only McReynolds appeared to support the governor in any meaningful way, while Faber and Jones outright defied him. Before the regents adjourned they formally invited the appropriate committee of the Texas legislature to investigate their actions. This call for an investigation would come back to haunt Jim Ferguson.[31]

Ferguson, dissatisfied with the outcome of the investigation by the regents, intended to continue his attack on his political enemies in the University of Texas in 1917. The next year, the terms of Will Hogg, David Harrell, and Alexander Sanger would expire, allowing Ferguson to appoint three new members to the board of regents. In addition, Rabbi Faber resigned in November 1916, and Ferguson appointed a political ally, William R. Brents of Sherman, in his place. Coupled with McReynolds, Fly, and Brents, the three new appointees would give Ferguson control of the board of regents and control of the university. Once again, Jim Ferguson seemed on the verge of silencing his political enemies.[32]

The thirty-fifth legislature came to order on January 9, 1917, and Ferguson went about the business of filling the three empty seats on the University of Texas Board of Regents. On January 10, Ferguson addressed the legislature, informing the members that he favored liberal appropriations for common schools but not for higher education if that higher education became "autocratic or aristocratic." With this shot across the bow of the University of Texas, the legislators began their work. On January 16, Ferguson was inaugurated for his second term, and ten days later, he sent the names of three proposed regents to fill the slots vacated by Hogg, Sanger, and Harrell. Ferguson proposed W. P. Allen of Austin, J. W. Butler of Clifton, and Dr. D. H. Lawrence of El Paso.[33]

On February 8, Senator Offa Shivers Lattimore of Fort Worth presented a petition from the Central Committee of the Texas Exes (now under the leadership of Will Hogg), requesting that "a sufficient investigation be made to remove from the University any suspicion or mistrust that may have been aroused by the recent controversy." The same day, Lattimore introduced a resolution asking for a committee of five members to investigate Ferguson's three nominees "to determine if any such appointees have committed themselves to or for the retention or dismissal of any members of the faculty." Ferguson now faced powerful opposition in the legislature. Not only had Will Hogg and the Texas Exes thrown their weight behind an investigation, but so also had Lattimore, one of the most prominent advocates of suffrage and an ardent anti-conservative-machine Democrat. The Senate adopted a motion to refer the Lattimore petition to a committee of three senators to determine whether it warranted an investigation. On February 9, the president of the Texas Senate named senators Paul D. Page, George W. Dayton, and Henderson to the committee, and they began their hearings on February 12.[34]

Two days later Senator W. A. Johnson of Hall County introduced a series of resolutions that called for an investigation of Governor Ferguson on six counts. Johnson charged that Ferguson had made illegal expenditures of public funds, sought to dominate the governing boards of the state's educational institutions, and that he had borrowed from the Temple State Bank a sum in excess of $140,000, an amount in excess of that allowed by law. He also charged that special interests paid for his campaigns, that the state had paid excessive commissions to attorneys for the State Penitentiary System, and finally, that Ferguson had withdrawn from the state and deposited in the Temple State Bank a large sum of money intended to rebuild the West Texas Normal School. Ferguson happened to be present in the Senate that day, and Senator Bledsoe invited him to make a rebuttal. Ferguson mounted a spirited defense; although he did not address the first or sixth charges, he vehemently denied that the Texas brewers had contributed to his campaign and admitted that he had borrowed the money from the Temple State Bank, stating that the business he produced entitled him to a line of credit equaling $300,000. Following this harangue, the Senate tabled the resolution on the grounds that the Johnson charges might warrant impeachment, and that process could only originate in the House of Representatives.[35]

On February 16 the committee of three led by Senator George W. Dayton presented their report. The committee decided that they could not offer a recommendation on the proposed regents, although they did reveal that Dr. Fly had recommended Dr. Lawrence to Governor Ferguson for the board of regents. The investigation also showed that Fly and Lawrence conspired to try and get Lawrence appointed to the faculty of the medical school, and that they had already agreed to take away from President Vinson the power to recommend the appointment or dismissal of any faculty members. Instead, Lawrence and Fly planned to vest all such authority in the board of regents. The decision of the committee not to make a recommendation certainly rankled Ferguson's opponents in the legislature.[36]

The day after the Dayton committee presented their report, Representative O'Banion introduced a resolution in the House of Representatives for an investigation of Ferguson on many of the same grounds proposed by Senator Lattimore. Ferguson, now a regular attendee at legislative sessions, rose to defend himself. He readily admitted that he had proposed regents "who are my friends" because as the governor of Texas he felt it his duty to know how money at the University of Texas was being allocated. He also admitted that he had borrowed $150,000 from the Temple State Bank, and asserted, "You ought to be proud of your Governor for being able to borrow $150,000." After some debate, the House tabled the O'Banion resolution by a vote of 104–31 on the grounds that the resolution did not contain any sworn testimony that looked toward impeachment and that at the moment, the House could not take time away from their legislative business to ascertain the truth of the allegations.[37]

On Tuesday, February 20, Senator Lattimore reintroduced his resolution, but Senator Dayton countered with a substitute proposal. Dayton's resolution stipulated that the investigation of the board of regents the previous October "was thorough; that it disclosed some careless practices not amounting to moral turpitude that had grown up in the management of the University during its thirty-three years of existence and that these careless methods have all been rectified." Dayton explained that the effect of his resolution would "place the Senate's stamp of approval on the decision of the former Board of Regents, will relieve the University of any blame, and is expected to have the effect of removing forever any cause for criticism or suspicion that the former investigation may not have removed." In this proposal, Dayton sought to end the controversy surrounding the university and the board of regents, and allow Ferguson to appoint his nominees to the board.[38]

The Senate continued to debate the Dayton resolution until March 3, when Representative Davis of Van Zandt County rose in the House and offered a series of charges against Ferguson, which if sustained, would result in impeachment. Davis charged that Ferguson had (1) illegally applied public funds to his own personal use, (2) had violated state banking laws by borrowing too much money from the Temple State Bank,

(3) that he assisted in aiding and abetting the president of the Temple State Bank in violating the law, (4) that he had gained money on property already secretly mortgaged, and finally, that (5) he had convinced the Texas State Commissioner of Insurance to go along with his illegal loan from the Temple State Bank.

Ferguson remained silent during the reading of the Davis resolution, but some members of the House invited him to address the body. Ferguson finally lost his cool and launched into a tirade against the House and Davis in particular. He accused President Vinson and the "University crowd" of being behind the resolution, and said, "Well, the bridle is off. We are going to see whether the State University can maintain a lobby around this legislature and come down here and ruin a public official who has tried to do his duty to the people." Ferguson continued in his rant, this time aiming his anger at Senator W. A. Johnson, who was also present in the House.

Ferguson called Johnson "a Nigger lover from the North," and concluded by saying "You look like a Nigger and you are a Nigger." Outraged by this tirade, several members of the House jumped to their feet to demand an apology from the governor. Ferguson refused to take back a single word.[39]

On Monday, March 5, the House voted 102–26 to order an investigation of Ferguson on numerous charges. Speaker of the House Frank Fuller appointed a committee of seven members to begin hearings on the charges on Wednesday, March 7. Jim Ferguson had finally pushed the war with his political enemies in the University of Texas and the legislature so far that he brought an investigation of his personal finances, which did not bode well for the governor.[40]

The committee had to determine the validity of ten allegations against the governor. The allegations were that (1) Ferguson had misappropriated public funds in 1915–16 in violation of the Constitution and court decisions, (2) that he had misapplied and misused funds appropriated for the governor's mansion and grounds, (3) that he had embezzled public funds for his own personal expenses in the governor's mansion, (4) that he had misapplied and misused funds appropriated for "Rewards and other expenses for enforcement of the law," (5) that he approved accounts against public expenses for use by his own family, (6) that he had violated the civil and criminal banking statutes of the State of Texas, (7) that he was indebted to the Temple State Bank in the amount of $170,000, (8) that he had "executed certain mortgages to the Temple State Bank and requested that they be withheld from the record," (9) that he was aware of a plan to change the Temple State Bank from a "bond bank" to a "guarantee bank" to save the bondholders in case of a bank failure, and finally that (10) Commissioner of Insurance Charles O. Austin became aware of the violation of banking laws by the Temple State Bank and made no effort to enforce the law. The House appointed attorney Martin M. Crane, former lieutenant governor, state attorney general, and member of the Texas House from Johnson County, as the state prosecutor. Ferguson retained the services of William A. Hanger, an attorney in private practice in Fort Worth, to defend him.[41]

The committee began their work at 10:00 a.m. on Wednesday, March 7, 1917, in the Railroad Commission Hearing Room of the capitol. "Exhibit A" in the investigation became the letter, written by Hosea Poe, outlining Ferguson's dealings with Temple State Bank. Poe circulated the letter during the 1916 campaign, and Charles Morris took full advantage of the allegations to discredit Ferguson. Many of the charges contained in the letter made their way into the charges of the Davis resolution. This virtually guaranteed that at some point in the hearings, Crane would call Poe as a witness.[42]

On the first day of hearings, Crane and Hanger argued back and forth about procedure, and Ferguson requested permission to address the committee with a brief statement. Instead, he offered another tirade, complaining about a lack of fairness, delays, and persecution. The governor's rant took so much time that the committee, after some further business, decided to adjourn until the next day. The committee called as their first witness H. B. Terrell, the Texas state comptroller. Texas state law provided for only a meager appropriation for entertaining at the governor's mansion. Terrell detailed his advice to Ferguson not to incur certain expenses, including the $4,600 in groceries Ferguson charged to the state, some of which violated state law. Complicating matters for Ferguson, the Texas courts had already ruled against expenditures of this type under Governor Colquitt in the case of *Middleton v. Terrell* (1915), otherwise known as the "chicken salad case." However, Ferguson went further than Colquitt and actually attempted to contract with an Austin grocer for future expenses, against the advice of the comptroller. Just to drive home the point, Crane called former governor Joseph Sayers to testify to how he had adhered to the law in paying for many of his own expenses while in office.[43]

On March 9, Crane called Hosea Poe to the stand. Poe succeeded Ferguson as president of the Temple State Bank, and had resigned amid a cloud of controversy, some of it as a result of Poe's attempts to straighten out the bank accounts of Jim Ferguson. Evidently, Ferguson used the names of some of his friends to take out lines of credit from the bank, and Poe did not discover the practice until he tried to call in the loans, and the individuals involved swore they did not owe the debt. He also detailed his meeting with Ferguson at the Democratic state convention in Houston in 1916, where Ferguson expected to receive a large amount of cash that never materialized. Ferguson then offered to sell his stock in Temple State Bank to Poe, but the latter backed out when Ferguson raised his asking price. Poe also alleged that Ferguson waited until he was out of town on business to travel to the Temple State Bank to intimidate the bank clerk into giving him two additional loans of $25,000 each. The former bank president also alleged that Ferguson took out additional mortgages against land he used for collateral at the bank and used that same land as collateral at other banks. Poe insisted that Ferguson asked him not to put any of it down on paper because he did not want his political enemies to learn of his finances. All told, it appeared that Ferguson owed the Temple State Bank $170,000. After further testimony on March 10, the committee dismissed Poe.[44]

Following the testimony of Hosea Poe, the investigating committee called Governor Ferguson to the stand. When questioned about the expenditures for the governor's mansion, Ferguson replied that he believed that the Texas Supreme Court had not ruled on the rehearing on *Middleton v. Terrell*, and that he would abide by their ruling when it came down. He admitted to taking out liens on the same properties through multiple banks, but swore that he had not asked Poe to keep the transactions off the books. The governor's testimony regarding the loans taken out in the names of his friends proved contradictory at best as he attempted to explain each transaction. In all, Ferguson admitted his total indebtedness at $425,000, but claimed that he owned $260,000 in bank stock that he could liquidate at any time. Ferguson's personal financial disclosure in December 1916 revealed that he owned less than $51,000 in bank stock. The governor concluded the statement about his debt to the Temple State Bank by claiming ignorance of the law. Ferguson stated, "I think Mr. Poe said something about violating the Criminal Statutes, and I said to Mr. Poe, I have got little knowledge about the law, I don't pretend to know and understand a great deal about it; but I said there is no penalty attached to it, and there is no bank in this town but what has violated that law time and again under some circumstances, it might be a technical violation but there was no penalty attached." On cross-examination, Ferguson essentially admitted that he did not think he should have to follow the law because there was no penalty attached. Ferguson's testimony certainly did nothing to help his position, and it put even his staunchest allies on the House investigation committee in an awkward position.[45]

The House investigating committee next called Charles Austin, the head of the Texas Insurance and Banking Commission and a Ferguson appointee, to testify. Austin admitted that he knew about the irregularities at the Temple State Bank and refused to do anything, merely telling Poe that he should clean up the mess left by Ferguson. By admitting these facts, Austin confirmed the charges leveled against himself and Ferguson. The committee concluded the testimony and cross-examination of all the witnesses on March 11.[46]

For four days, the House investigating committee debated the charges before reaching a conclusion. On March 15, the committee presented their conclusions to the entire House. The committee found Ferguson guilty of the first charge, misappropriation of public funds in contravention of the constitution and court decisions; guilty of the second charge, misapplication and misappropriation of funds for the governor's mansion and grounds; guilty of the third charge of misappropriating public funds for expenses for which he was liable; guilty of the fourth charge of misapplying and misusing funds for "rewards and other expenses for enforcement of the law," guilty of the fifth charge of approving accounts against the public funds for the personal use of himself and his family; guilty of the sixth charge that he had violated the banking laws of Texas; guilty of the seventh charge, that he owed $170,000 to the Temple State Bank; guilty of the eighth charge of taking out multiple mortgages on the same property, but not guilty of conspiring to keep it off the books. They found no evidence on the ninth charge, his alleged plan to change the nature of the Temple State Bank, and found him innocent of the tenth charge—any collusion between him and Charles Austin, although they found Austin guilty of ignoring the banking laws.[47]

Despite the findings of the committee, they refused to recommend impeachment, instead condemning Ferguson in the strongest language; they concluded,

> Relative to the transactions between the Governor and the Temple State Bank, we beg to say in our judgement they are deserving of the severest criticism and condemnation. As Governor of the state he was and is charged with the enforcement of all laws. The large sum of money borrowed by him from said bank, and far in excess of its capital and surplus, was a plain violation of at least the letter of the law. All laws, regardless of what any man may think about them, should be fairly and impartially enforced. He knowingly encouraged the officers of the bank to violate the banking law, and we neither excuse nor condone the same.

With the refusal of the committee to recommend impeachment, Ferguson had weathered a serious storm and challenge to his authority.[48]

Even while the House worked on their investigation of Ferguson, the legislature remained busy with the blessing of Ferguson, passing bills to establish no fewer than seven land grant normal colleges in rural Texas. With the support of Senator Claude Hudspeth of El Paso, the citizens of West Texas pushed for the establishment of a university of their own, and the legislature created West Texas A&M University with House Bill 46. The legislation specified that a three-man commission headed by the governor would establish the location of the new university. House Bill 72 established Stephen F. Austin Normal College in Nacogdoches (now Stephen F. Austin State University), and Senate Bill 397 established Sul Ross Normal College at Alpine (now Sul Ross State University). The legislature also purchased Grubb's Vocational College in Arlington with Senate Bill 449 (now the University of Texas at Arlington), and purchased Mayo's College in Commerce, renaming it East Texas Normal College (now Texas A&M University–Commerce.) The legislature also purchased John Tarleton Agricultural College in Stephenville (now Tarleton State University), and finally established South Texas Normal College at Kingsville (now Texas A&M University–Kingsville.) The legislature also voted out generous appropriations for the Texas College of Mines (now the University of Texas at El Paso), and Prairie View State Normal College (now Prairie View A&M University). His signature on this flurry of legislation marks Governor James Ferguson as one of the friendliest governors toward higher education in the history of Texas. Clearly, if Jim Ferguson hated higher education, as his critics at the University of Texas claimed, his actions did not show it. Ferguson's problem with the University of Texas lay not with the idea of higher education, but with the governor's political enemies in the university.[49]

Before adjourning the regular session, the legislature finally settled the question of Ferguson's appointments to the University of Texas Board of Regents. The Texas Senate outright rejected the nomination of Dr. D. H. Lawrence with only five dissenting votes because of the revelations about his relationship to Fly. On March 17, the Dayton Resolution, originally offered as a compromise, passed the Senate unanimously, confirming the sense of the legislature that the investigation by the board of regents in the spring had settled the charges against the faculty in question at the University of Texas. On March 20, the Senate confirmed the nominations of J. W. Butler, W. P. Allen, and Charles Edgar Kelly, former mayor of El Paso, to the board of regents to fill the three vacancies. The next day, the regular session of the thirty-fifth legislature adjourned. Ferguson called for a special session of the legislature to begin meeting on April 18, 1917, to consider, among other things, budgets for the institutions of higher learning in the state.[50]

Even as the first called session of the thirty-fifth legislature came to order, Governor James Ferguson began taking steps to rectify his personal financial situation. Ferguson turned to his most reliable source of campaign money, the Texas brewers, and they welcomed the chance to aid

Portrait of Otto Wahrmund, a Texas House of Representatives member (1909–19) and a powerful San Antonio brewer. 1913. Individual Portrait from "Thirty-Third Legislature 1913." Composite photo of House members, House Chamber 3W.2 Gallery, Third Floor, Texas State Capitol Building, Austin, Texas, under stewardship of Texas Preservation Board. Photo of individual portrait in composite by Jessica Brannon-Wranosky.

their chief ally in the state. Ferguson approached Otto Wahrmund, and Wahrmund approached the brewers about getting Ferguson $25,000 in cash. In short order, B. Adoue and other Texas brewers pitched in to give Ferguson a total of $156,500 in unsecured loans at 5 percent interest. With this windfall, Ferguson could put his finances in order and place himself above suspicion. At this point, Ferguson had weathered the storm. He could easily have left well enough alone, but apparently, the receipt of the illicit money emboldened the governor to finish destroying his political enemies. The Texas brewers never loaned money without the expectation of a return, and they knew as well as Jim Ferguson that as long as their enemies in the University of Texas spread prohibitionist sentiment, these professors would continue to undermine their efforts to keep Texas wet.[51]

The first called session of the thirty-fifth Texas legislature finished its work and adjourned on May 17, 1917, having voted out an annual budget of $710,698.50 for the University of Texas, and an additional $98,755 for the University of Texas Medical Branch at Galveston. Ferguson decided at this junction to call a meeting of the board of regents and demand removal of President Vinson and several of the faculty members investigated the previous October. On May 25, Ferguson wired Chairman Wilbur Allen and asked the board of regents to hold a meeting in the governor's office on May 28, and Allen acquiesced. Word got around to Vinson about the meeting, and he accurately predicted the purpose of the gathering. On Saturday, May 26, the entire university faculty planned their annual picnic on Lake McDonald, and while at the boat landing, Vinson took aside John A. Lomax and said, "Well, Lomax, after next Monday I will no longer be president of the University of Texas. Governor Ferguson has called the Board of Regents to meet that day in his office. He has now a majority on the Board. His purpose is to remove me from the presidency." Lomax, by then in no mood for a picnic, jumped ashore as the boat pushed off from the landing and drove back into Austin to relay the story to three different Texas newspapers. By 10:00 p.m. on Saturday, Lomax reached the editor of the *Dallas Morning News* and later the editors of the *Houston Post* and *San Antonio Express*. Lomax conveyed the urgency of running headlines the next morning informing their readers that Ferguson had called a secret meeting of the board of regents for the purpose of ousting President Vinson from his position.[52]

Many copies of these three papers with the recommended headline made their appearance in Austin by daylight, and according to Lomax,

"A dozen giant bombs, dropped without warning, would have caused no more intense excitement." Dan Williams, editor of the *Daily Texan*, announced an early-morning mass protest to gather at the capitol to protest Ferguson's action. At 10:00 a.m. nearly two thousand students gathered around the capitol, awaiting the beginning of the meeting of the board of regents scheduled for 11:00 a.m. The students paraded around the capitol with signs like "Down with Kaiser Jim" and "No Autocracy in the University."[53]

Six of the nine regents arrived in Ferguson's office by 11:00 a.m. and listened to his list of complaints against the university that justified his threatened veto of the appropriations. Ferguson also attacked Vinson as a "sectarian preacher" and declared, "If the University cannot be maintained as a democratic University, then we ought to have no University." At that point, the noise from the student rally drifted in through the open window of the governor's office, and Ferguson stuck his head out the window to address the crowd. The students managed to get George Peddy, president of the Students' Association, as their keynote speaker, despite the fact that he was at that time in military officer's training camp at Leon Springs. Peddy, dressed in his officer's uniform, made a speech to the

Protesters with signs describing their views of Governor James Ferguson gather at a May 28, 1917, rally outside the Old Main Building at the University of Texas before marching through Austin to the Texas state capitol grounds. 1917. Photograph courtesy of Prints and Photographs Collection, di_06861, Dolph Briscoe Center for American History, University of Texas at Austin.

students and then exchanged insults with Ferguson when the governor stuck his head out the window and verbally assaulted him. Ferguson also shouted insults at the students, including some of the young women, and denounced the protestors as hoodlums in quotes run in the newspapers. Ferguson also stated that Peddy should be stood up against a wall and shot for treason.[54]

The parade abruptly ended the meeting of the board of regents and hardened Ferguson's resolve to veto the appropriation bill. On the morning of May 31 the board of regents again met, this time in Galveston, and there Regent J. W. Butler resigned because he would not vote to remove Vinson as president. At the same time, Ferguson removed Dr. S. J. Jones from the board because "of a lack of harmony with the administration." Ferguson proposed to replace Butler and Jones with Mr. J. M. Mathis and Dr. J. P. Tucker.[55]

On May 31, Travis County attorney J. W. Hornsby and John A. Lomax both filed injunctions against Ferguson and the board of regents respectively in the Twenty-Sixth District Court in Austin. Hornsby's injunction, granted by the court, prevented Ferguson from placing Tucker on the board because of the restraint against the governor of removing a member of the board of regents without cause. In his injunction, also granted, Lomax prevented the board from removing either himself or President Vinson on the grounds that Ferguson had conspired to get rid of certain members of the faculty.[56]

On the evening of Saturday, June 2, at about 7:30 p.m., news began to circulate that Ferguson had carried out his threats and vetoed the appropriations for the University of Texas. At the same time, Regent Mathis urged the faculty to assist him in finding a suitable replacement for Vinson, in which case Mathis would do everything he could to secure a reversal of the veto. On June 5, two of the regents contacted Vinson and Lomax and stated that if they resigned Ferguson would withdraw the veto. Both Lomax and Vinson refused, and just hours later the governor filed his veto with the secretary of state's office. With the stroke of a pen, Ferguson denied almost all funding for the University of Texas.[57]

Ferguson's veto message amounted to little more than a rehashing of the complaints the governor had held against the university from the beginning of his term in office, although it ignored the underlying issues. Ferguson maintained that the University of Texas took too much money to educate each student, that President Vinson lacked the qualifications to run the university, that the university mismanaged its funds badly, and finally that the university opposed Ferguson because of his support for rural schools. Even though Ferguson appealed to his rural populist constituents with this veto message, he ignored the very real issue: his problems with the University of Texas stemmed from his political opposition to many of the university faculty.[58]

On June 9, a large mass gathering met in Austin even as Attorney General Benjamin F. Looney reviewed Ferguson's veto. Former Governor Joseph Sayers presided over the mass meeting in Austin with several hundred in attendance, lamenting the fact that the university would have to close its doors. They soon adjourned, but called for another mass meeting on June 16 in Dallas to discuss ways to keep the university open. Meanwhile, Attorney General Looney ruled Ferguson's veto invalid, because the governor had marked through all but one of the line-item appropriations, but left the total sum intact, to be spent at the discretion of the board of regents.[59]

On June 11, Judge Ireland Graves of the Twenty-Sixth District Court in Austin held hearings on the two injunctions filed against the board of regents. Graves heard the testimony of Vinson, Harrell, Hogg, Mathis, Fly, Love, Kelley, Littlefield, Cook, Brents, and Allen, among others. These men testified that Ferguson intended to control the board of the regents and through it the University of Texas. Graves took their testimony under advisement and delayed until July 3 before making his decision.[60]

Five days later a mass meeting assembled in Dallas, led by Will Hogg and other members of the Texas Exes, with over 1,600 people in attendance. Chester W. Terrell offered a resolution to recommend the impeachment of Governor Ferguson, but the delegates voted it down. However, they did adopt a resolution denouncing the governor's veto as unconstitutional because it had the effect of destroying the university. The delegates also made a provision to provide for a permanent campaign of public education regarding the actions of Governor Ferguson. Will Hogg agreed to bankroll the campaign.[61]

Will Hogg remained busy in Galveston on June 23 when the executive council of the Texas Exes met and issued an address "to the people of Texas." The council denounced the actions of Governor Ferguson. Furthermore, the Texas Exes announced their intention to use "every honorable means" to keep the University of Texas open and to remove the university from any further political influence.[62]

Even as the Texas Exes worked against him, Jim Ferguson did not remain idle. He toured the western part of Texas, searching for a suitable site to place the new West Texas A&M University, and used his tour to give speech after speech against the University of Texas. He delivered speeches at Kerrville, Abilene, Sweetwater, Hamlin, Snyder, Lubbock, and Plainview between June 10 and June 18. Near the end of his tour, Ferguson told the *Dallas Morning News*, "I do not care a damn what becomes of the University of Texas. The bats and owls can roost in it for all I care." Ferguson did not yet realize that his involvement with West Texas A&M University would be the central catalyst for the final phase of his political downfall.[63]

On June 29, 1917, the five-man committee tasked with locating West Texas A&M University met in Governor Ferguson's office and decided to cast secret ballots to determine the location of the new university. The committee consisted of Governor Ferguson, Lieutenant Governor William P. Hobby, Speaker of the House Frank Fuller, Superintendent of Public Education W. F. Doughty, and Commissioner of Agriculture Fred Davis. After two ballots, Ferguson announced that the committee had chosen Abilene. Ferguson and Doughty had voted for Abilene, but Lieutenant Governor Hobby announced that he had voted for Snyder, then Amarillo on the second ballot, and Davis voted for Snyder twice. This meant that Speaker Fuller must have voted for Abilene, but Fuller swore he had not. As a result of the confusion, the legislature eventually repealed the bill to create West Texas A&M, but more importantly, Frank Fuller came to think that Ferguson had betrayed him and lied about it.[64]

In July, Will Hogg, the Texas Exes, and the rest of the university community began coordinating with the TESA to campaign against Jim Ferguson. TESA president Minnie Fisher Cunningham wrote to an associate, "This is the chance of a life time to get rid of Ferguson and break the power of the liquor ring and straighten out some of the awful things that have been going on in our state." Professor Mary Gearing, chair of the Department of Home Economics at the University of Texas, sought the help of George Brackenridge, wealthy brother of TESA honorary lifetime president Eleanor Brackenridge. He agreed to fund a "women's" campaign against Ferguson with $2,000. Gearing and Cunningham formed the Woman's Campaign for Good Government (WCGG). Working for sixteen hours a day in the hot month of July, the WCGG began a whisper campaign against Ferguson and worked to raise public opinion against the governor. Cunningham held that Ferguson

Portrait of Mary Edna Gearing, the first woman to achieve the rank of full professor and department chair at the University of Texas. She was chair of the Department of Domestic Economy and one of the key leaders of the Woman's Campaign for Good Government, the latter who campaigned for the impeachment of James Ferguson. N.d. Photograph courtesy of Prints and Photographs Collection, di_06020, Dolph Briscoe Center for American History, University of Texas at Austin.

had only escaped unscathed after the investigation in March because she and the other suffragists had not raised the moral conscience of the people of Texas enough. She was determined not to let that happen again, and as July wore on, public indignation grew, fueled by the WCGG and their covert campaign.[65]

Meanwhile, the injunction suits made their way through the courts. On July 3, the circuit court set aside the temporary injunction granted to John Lomax, stating that constitutionally, the board of regents had the right to run the university any way they saw fit. The other court injunction banned Tucker from taking his place on the board, and Ferguson instead appointed John Ward, one of his attorneys, to replace Tucker. The same court then banned Ward from taking his place on the board of regents. At the same time, another court barred Fly from performing his duty as a member of the board because he had accepted a federal appointment as a physician to a military draft board.[66]

On July 12, 1917, the board of regents assembled in the Galvez Hotel in Galveston. Although now rejected as a member of the board, Ashley Fly showed up anyway, brandishing a pistol in his coat pocket, and declared, "Well, I may not be a legal member, but I guess I'm still a *de facto* member of this board." That day Fly resigned his federal appointment, and the next day the board seated him as a member after Ferguson reappointed him in place of John Ward. The board of regents voted to dismiss L. M. Keasbey, professor of institutional history, because of his antiwar activities, and also voted that day to dismiss W. T. Mather, A. Caswell Ellis, R. E. Cofer, G. C. Butte, W. H. Mayes, and John A. Lomax. The board tied on whether or not to dismiss professor of English R. H. Griffith because of a report that he had led a song in the student parade at the capitol in May. The board of regents also voted to retain President Vinson that day, but in all at that point it appeared, Jim Ferguson removed many of his political enemies in the university.[67]

Ferguson took a brief respite at his ranch in Bosque County, and many began calling for a special session of the legislature to consider impeachment. In the meantime, a Travis County grand jury assembled to consider indicting Ferguson on several counts of misuse of public funds and embezzlement based on his personal finances. Protected by Texas Rangers, Ferguson unexpectedly turned up in Austin on July 21 to testify before the grand jury in his own defense.[68]

Two days later, Frank Fuller, still smarting from the West Texas A&M debacle, issued a call to assemble the legislature starting August 1 to consider impeachment. Constitutionally, only the governor can call the legislature into special session, and so from the beginning the legality of Fuller's call came into doubt. Ferguson immediately denounced the call to convene the legislature as unconstitutional. Addressing a large gathering of farmers in Austin on July 26, Ferguson outlined his legal objections to Fuller's call to assemble the legislature.[69]

By this time, Texas Rangers accompanied Ferguson everywhere he went to protect his safety. That summer, Will Hogg set up offices in the Driskill Hotel on Sixth Street in Austin to direct the anti-Ferguson campaign. According to a contemporary account of the impeachment episode, both Hogg and Ferguson had quite a few spies running around in the summer heat reporting on the actions of the other side.[70]

In late July, Hogg came up with a plan to trick Ferguson into calling a special session of the legislature in order to guarantee the constitutionality of the impeachment proceedings. Hogg sent out an invitation to selected, prominent members of the legislature to meet with him in a secret gathering on July 30 in Austin to discuss matters. Furthermore, Hogg asked that the legislators keep the contents of his letter a secret. On the appointed day, the prominent legislators began arriving in Austin, and the first reports of this gathering came to Hogg in the Driskill by way of one of his own messengers, whom he knew to be a Ferguson spy. The messenger asked Hogg what he thought it meant, and Hogg replied that it must mean that a quorum of the legislature would assemble in accordance with Fuller's call. The Ferguson man then left the hotel and raced all the way to the capitol to inform the governor that the legislature would assemble with or without him. That afternoon, all the newspapers began reporting that Ferguson would call a special session of the legislature to convene on August 1. With this chicanery, Will Hogg tricked Jim Ferguson into legitimizing the call for a special session of the legislature to consider impeachment.[71]

On July 27, the Travis County Grand Jury indicted Ferguson and four of his appointees on nine counts, seven for misapplication of public funds, one for embezzlement, and one for diversion of public funds. Most of these charges derived from the findings of the legislative committee in March. Ferguson issued a bond of $13,000, declared himself the victim of politically based persecution, and announced his intention to run for a third term as governor.[72]

On July 30, the House of Representatives assembled to consider impeachment. The governor's friends in the House attempted to block the investigation, but pro-impeachment forces had a 70-vote majority. By August 6, the House secured Martin M. Crane as prosecutor in the case and organized the entire House into a grand court of inquiry. After discussing Ferguson's financial dealings, the legislators came to the subject of the University of Texas. At this point, President Vinson rose and gave a stirring defense of the actions of both the larger university community and himself, pointing to the difference between an appropriation and a budget, an idea he claimed the governor never quite understood. After Vinson stepped down, Speaker Fuller explored the controversy over the location of West Texas A&M University. Fuller, though, proved a poor witness whose memory often failed him, and the House rested their case on August 15. Once again, it appeared that Jim Ferguson would escape unscathed.[73]

Two days later, against the advice of his attorneys, Ferguson took the stand on his own behalf. While discussing his relationship with Temple State Bank, Ferguson bragged that he had borrowed $156,500 from "friends" to pay off his debts. Crane jumped on this statement and asked Ferguson from whom he had borrowed the money. Ferguson declined to answer, stating that he would under no circumstances reveal the sources of the loan. Crane dropped the subject for the moment, but returned to it the next day. Finally, Crane requested that the chair of the committee compel Ferguson to answer, which he did, but the governor remained silent. By a vote of 70–56 the House of Representatives commanded Ferguson to answer, but still the chief executive refused to say anything. By refusing to answer the question, Ferguson convinced the legislature and the people of Texas that he had something to hide, and in effect sealed his own fate.[74]

On August 23, the House prosecutors concluded their case, and the next day, the full House approved twenty-one articles of impeachment against Governor Ferguson, concerning his private financial dealings, especially the $156,500; the University of Texas; and his controversies with the courts and Speaker Fuller over West Texas A&M. On August 25, the House formally submitted the charges. That same day, Ferguson left the governor's office, making Lieutenant Governor William P. Hobby acting governor of Texas. Ferguson, though, remained confident that the Senate would vindicate him.[75]

The trial in the Senate went forward almost exactly as in the House. Again, Ferguson's attorney warned him not to testify, and again Ferguson ignored his advice and took the stand for five days in his own defense. On September 20, Crane again brought up the subject of the loan, and Ferguson still refused to disclose the source. Even after the Senate voted 23–7 to require Ferguson to disclose the source of the $156,500, the governor ignored the vote. On September 22, Ferguson rose to give the closing argument in his defense and simply rehashed the same rhetoric he had used throughout the controversy. Finally, the Senate voted to uphold ten articles of impeachment, six dealing with the governor's financial dealings and four dealing with his relationship with the University of Texas Board of Regents.[76]

In one final attempt to avoid penalties, Ferguson formally resigned the governorship on September 24, while the upper house had adjourned for the weekend. On Monday, September 25, the Senate reconvened. A motion simply to remove Ferguson from office failed by a vote of 17–9, and the Senate passed a substitute resolution, barring Ferguson from holding any political office in the state of Texas ever again by a vote of 25–3. The Court of Impeachment then adjourned.[77]

The removal of Jim Ferguson from office marked a major watershed moment in Texas politics during the Progressive Era. Although Ferguson continued to run for office in a variety of campaigns in following years, and eventually helped get his wife Miriam elected to the governorship, the removal of Ferguson allowed both woman suffrage and prohibition to pass at the state and national levels in 1918–19. In the next legislative session, Governor Hobby recommended and the legislature passed a bill to prohibit alcohol sales within ten miles of an army base. The Texas legislature also endorsed the proposed Eighteenth Amendment to the Constitution in 1918, but Texas prohibitionists would not wait long enough for the amendment to go into effect and pushed for a referendum on both woman suffrage and prohibition set for May 24, 1919. Prohibition won out in this election, preempting national Prohibition, but despite the endorsement of Governor Hobby, woman suffrage failed in the same referendum, and Texas women would have to wait until 1920 with the ratification of the Nineteenth Amendment to gain full enfranchisement. These goals at the state level would have probably been nearly impossible to achieve had Pa Ferguson remained in office at the behest of the Texas liquor interests.

The Ferguson impeachment episode also marked a turning point in the control of the Texas Democratic Party. The impeachment helped to break the back of the old rural Democratic machine that controlled Texas politics for much of the first two decades of the twentieth century, and for a time provided an opening for a group of younger, more progressive, largely college-educated Democrats to have a voice in the party. Democrats like Will Hogg and Minnie Fisher Cunningham increasingly gained ascendance, adding their voices to various reform causes.

Traditionally, historians have framed Jim Ferguson's impeachment and removal as a battle over higher education, because that is how Ferguson himself framed it in his rhetoric, and how his political opponents in the University of Texas community framed it in their own defense. The rhetoric, though, was deceptive because at the heart of the controversy lay the politics of prohibition and to a lesser extent woman suffrage. The faculty of the University of Texas in question could not cloak themselves in a mantle of academic freedom without admitting that they actively, politically, opposed Jim Ferguson and his proliquor, antisuffrage agenda outside their normal teaching duties. At the same time, Ferguson could not really claim it was about anything other than higher education without revealing his actual political motives.

However, had Ferguson not pushed the dispute with the university past the breaking point, his own questionable financial dealings and alienation of other Texas Democrats may never have amounted to impeachment. In reality, Jim Ferguson's hubris contributed as much to his own demise as the efforts of his political enemies. In this bear fight for the future of the Texas Democratic Party, young Texas progressives led by suffragists, prohibitionists, and the Texas Exes took full advantage of the governor's mistakes and engineered the campaign to oust him from office, overcoming one of the last hurdles to prohibition and suffrage in Texas.

NOTES

1. The *University Record* (Austin: University of Texas, 1911), 11: 79–103. Because the legislature of Texas founded the University of Texas in 1883 as a coeducational institution, many women also attended this 1911 meeting and cheered loudly when Terrell, in his remarks, announced his support for woman suffrage. The sheer number of Texas progressives who attended and spoke at this meeting, from John Lomax to Will Hogg, was staggering.

2. It was John A. Lomax who engineered the name change to the Texas Exes as a way to attract more members, beyond those who had graduated from the university to those who may only have been enrolled at one time, and it was Lomax who founded and edited the *Alcalde*, named for former Governor Oran Roberts, the "Old Alcalde," who served as governor at the time of the founding of the university in 1881 and taught there as an influential professor of law in the first decade of the school's existence. Nolan Porterfield, *Last Cavalier: The Life and Times of John A. Lomax* (Urbana: University of Illinois Press, 1996), 163–64.

3. For the view that an anti–higher education agenda dominated Ferguson's dealings with the University of Texas, see Lewis L. Gould, *Progressives and Prohibitionists: Texas Democrats in the Wilson Era* (Austin: University of Texas Press, 1973), 185–200; Lewis L. Gould, "The University Becomes Politicized," *Southwestern Historical Quarterly* 86, no. 2 (1982): 255–76; John A. Lomax, "Governor Ferguson and the University of Texas," *Southwest Review* 28, no. 1 (1942): 11–29; Robert E. Vinson, "The University Crosses the Bar," *Southwestern Histor-*

ical Quarterly 43, no. 3 (1940): 1–13; Cortez A. M. Ewing "The Impeachment of James E. Ferguson," *Political Science Quarterly* 48, no. 2 (1933): 184–210.

4. The thirty-fifth legislature provided appropriations for West Texas A&M University (forerunner to Texas Tech), Stephen F. Austin Normal College at Nacogdoches (now Stephen F. Austin State University), South Texas Normal College (now Texas A&M Kingsville), Sul Ross Normal College in Alpine (now Sul Ross State University), purchased John Tarleton Agricultural College in Stephenville (now Tarleton State University), purchased Mayo's College in Commerce and renamed it East Texas State Normal College (now Texas A&M Commerce), purchased Grubb's Vocational College in Arlington (now the University of Texas at Arlington), and voted out generous appropriations for the Texas College of Mines (now the University of Texas El Paso), and Prairie View State Normal College (now Prairie View A&M University). See HB 46 (West Texas A&M), HB 72 (Stephen F. Austin and South Texas Normal), HB 40 (construction at Prairie View), HB 103 (construction at the Texas College of Mines), SB 397 (Sul Ross Normal College), SB 449 (Grubb's Vocational School), and SB 231 (purchase of land for East Texas Normal). *Journals of the House and Senate, Regular Session Thirty-Fifth Legislature of the State of Texas* (Austin: Von Boeckmann-Jones, 1917).

5. For an excellent overview of progressive Texas politics from 1886 to 1906, see Alwyn Barr, *Reconstruction to Reform: Texas Politics, 1876–1906* (Dallas: Southern Methodist University Press, 1971). For the administration of Governor Thomas Campbell, see Janet Schmelzer, *Our Fighting Governor: The Life of Thomas M. Campbell and the Politics of Progressive Reform in Texas* (College Station: Texas A&M University Press, 2014). Schmelzer argues convincingly that Campbell represented an extension of Hogg style reform.

6. For the activities of the Texas Brewer's Association, see Anti-Saloon League, *The Brewers in Texas Politics*, 2 vols. (San Antonio: Passing Show Printing, 1916). These two volumes come from the case files of the lawsuit filed by the state of Texas and Attorney General B. F. Looney against seven Texas breweries. The prosecution ended up with almost a thousand pages, principally of correspondence between the breweries and their strategies in Texas politics from 1901 to 1915. As such, these primary documents are an invaluable resource for examining Texas liquor interests in the Progressive Era. "It would seem we may look for a hard scrap in the next Legislature as no doubt the pros will try and rush matters while Campbell is governor." S. T. Morgan to Otto Wahrmund, November 11, 1907, in *Brewers in Texas Politics*, 1: 440. Morgan was head of the Dallas Brewery, Wahrmund of the San Antonio Brewer's Association. For the direct connection to Adolphus Busch, see Arthur Koenig to Otto Wahrmund, February 18, 1908, in *Brewers in Texas Politics*, 1: 447–48.

7. See Adolphus Busch to B. Adoue, February 1, 1911, and Wahrmund to Busch, February 1, 1911, in *Brewers in Texas Politics*, 1: 150–52. The Texas brewers

also had a way of taking financial care of their allies. See the discussions of loaning Colquitt money to begin a business after he left the governor's office in 1915: *Brewers in Texas Politics*, 1: 181–82.

8. Gould, *Progressive and Prohibitionists*, 120–24; *Dallas Morning News*, March 22, 1914.

9. Gould, *Progressives and Prohibitionists*, 130.

10. Ibid., 120–49.

11. Gould, "University Becomes Politicized," 262; Hogg to Ferguson, September 22, 1915, box 2J314, Hogg Papers, Dolph Briscoe Center for American History, University of Texas at Austin.

12. For the influence of the liquor interests in Texas, see "A Beer Fight, not a Bear Fight," *Houston Chronicle*, May 29, 1918.

13. Eugene C. Barker to A. F. Cunningham, February 19, 1915; Ferguson to Barker February 20, 1915; Barker to Ferguson, February 22, 1915; and Barker to Thomas M. Marshall, March 4, 1915; Eugene C. Barker Papers, Dolph Briscoe Center for American History, University of Texas at Austin. For more on Barker, see William C. Pool, *Eugene C. Barker: Historian* (Austin: Texas State Historical Association, 1971); and Patrick Cox, "'Farmer Jim and the Chief': Governor Jim Ferguson and His Battle with Eugene C. Barker and the University of Texas," in *The Texas Book Two: More Profiles, History, and Reminiscences of the University*, ed. David Dettmer (Austin: University of Texas Press, 2012), 133–40.

14. Cox, "Farmer Jim and the Chief," 133–40.

15. "Investigation by the Board of Regents of the University of Texas of Certain Members of the Faculty," *Bulletin of the University of Texas*, 1916, no. 59 (Austin: University of Texas Press, 1916), 20–22; Ferguson to Hogg, August 18, 1915, Hogg Papers, Dolph Briscoe Center for American History, University of Texas at Austin.

16. [Eugene C. Barker], *Ferguson's War on the University of Texas, a Chronological Outline January 12, 1915–July 31, 1917*, inclusive (Austin: Ex Students Association of the University of Texas, 1917), 7. Although this pamphlet has no stated author, Professor Eugene C. Barker compiled it on behalf of the Texas Exes. Pool, *Eugene C. Barker*, 70. For Vinson's work with the Anti-Vice League, see *Austin Statesman*, February 23, 1915.

17. Gould, *Progressives and Prohibitionists*, 194.

18. "Ellis, Alexander Caswell," *Handbook of Texas Online*, http://www.tshaonline.org/handbook/online/articles/fe114, accessed July 31, 2015; Larry D. Hill and Robert A. Calvert, "The University of Texas Extension Services and Progressivism," *Southwestern Historical Quarterly* 86, no. 2 (1982): 231–54. See also Alexander Caswell Ellis Papers, Dolph Briscoe Center for American History, University of Texas at Austin.

19. Patrick Cox and Kenneth E. Hendrickson Jr., *Writing the Story of Texas* (Austin: University of Texas Press, 2013), 19; Joseph W. McKnight, "Potts, Charles

Shirley," *Handbook of Texas Online*, http://www.tshaonline.org/handbook/online/articles/fp032, accessed July 31, 2015.

20. Nolan Porterfield, *Last Cavalier: The Life and Times of John A. Lomax* (Urbana: University of Illinois Press, 1996), 202.

21. Vivian Elizabeth Smyrl, "Mather, William Tyler," *Handbook of Texas Online*, http://www.tshaonline.org/handbook/online/articles/fma73, accessed August 3, 2015; Janet G. Humphrey, *A Texas Suffragist: Diaries and Writings of Jane Y. McCallum* (Austin: Ellen C. Temple, 1988), 79, 83.

22. Documents of the General Faculty, "In Memoriam Robert Emmett Cofer," 1944, http://www.utexas.edu/faculty/council/2000–2001/memorials/AMR/Cofer/cofer.pdf, accessed August 3, 2015; "Investigation by the Board of Regents," 119.

23. "Mayes, William Harding," *Handbook of Texas Online*, http://www.tshaonline.org/handbook/online/articles/fma89, accessed August 3, 2015; *Journal of the House of Representatives of the Second Called Session of the Thirty-Fifth Legislature of Texas August 1, 1917–August 30, 1917* (Austin: Von Boeckmann-Jones, 1917), 751; "Investigation by the Board of Regents," 121–23.

24. Judith N. McArthur and Harold L. Smith, *Minnie Fisher Cunningham: A Suffragist's Life in Politics* (New York: Oxford University Press, 2003), 50.

25. Ibid.

26. *Dallas Morning News*, February 15, February 18, and March 6, 1917.

27. See Vinson to Ferguson, September 5, 1916; Ferguson to Vinson, September 9, 1916; Vinson to Ferguson, September 16, 1916, all in "Investigation by the Board of Regents," 6–9; and testimony of President Vinson, "Investigation by the Board of Regents," 11–12.

28. See correspondence between Ferguson and Faber, in "Investigation by the Board of Regents," 131–33.

29. See Ferguson to W. R. Long, September 20, 1916, in "Investigation by the Board of Regents," 57.

30. For Ferguson's charges, see "Investigation by the Board of Regents," 144–54.

31. For the votes and the appeal to the legislature, see "Investigation by the Board of Regents," 139–40.

32. See the records of the former regents of the University of Texas at http://www.utsystem.edu/bor/former_regents/decade.htm. Ferguson began appointing fellow bankers to the board of regents. Brents organized and served as president of the Commercial National Bank of Sherman from 1898 to 1917. *Alcalde* 5, no. 1 (1917): 199.

33. [Eugene C. Barker], *Ferguson's War on the University of Texas: A Chronological Outline; January 12, 1915, to July 31, 1917*, inclusive (Austin: Ex-Students' Association of the University of Texas, 1917), 10–11. Allen graduated from the University of Texas School of Law in 1899 and was, at the time of his nomination,

the American National Bank director. James W. Butler was the president of the Texas State Bankers' Association, Former Regents of the University of Texas System.

34. [Barker], *Ferguson's War*, 11–12. For more on Lattimore, see Jessica Brannon-Wranosky "Southern Promise and Necessity: Texas, Regional Identity, and the National Woman Suffrage Movement, 1868–1920," unpublished manuscript, 200.

35. [Barker], *Ferguson's War*, 11–12.

36. Ibid., 14–15.

37. Ibid., 16–17.

38. Ibid., 17–18.

39. Ibid., 19; *Fort Worth Star Telegram*, March 4, 1917. Ferguson did retract his statement a few days later, but the damage was done.

40. *Proceedings of Investigation Committee, House of Representatives Thirty-Fifth Legislature: Charges against Governor James E. Ferguson Together with Findings of Committee and Action of House with Prefatory Statement and Index to Proceedings* (Austin, TX: A. C. Baldwin and Sons, 1917), 3–5. Fuller named W. E. Bledsoe of Lubbock, R. L. Carlock of Tarrant, W. M. Fly of Gonzales, R. E. Thomason of El Paso, E. R. Bryan of Midland, W. E. Pope of Midland, Bruce W. Bryant of Haskell, D. S. McMillan of Grayson, and Barry Miller of Dallas to the committee. *Proceedings of Investigation Committee*, 3.

41. *Proceedings of Investigation Committee*, 3–5. Crane certainly had reason to dislike Ferguson. He was a member of the Farmers' Alliance in the 1880s, closely aligned himself with Governor Hogg as a reformer, and remained a known political enemy of Senator Joseph W. Bailey. David Minor, "Crane, Martin McNulty," *Handbook of Texas Online*, http://www.tshaonline.org/handbook/online/articles/fcr04, accessed August 14, 2015.

42. *Proceedings of Investigation Committee*, 7–11. Poe's letter in its entirety is included in the committee report.

43. *Proceedings of Investigation Committee*, 38–54; Carol O'Keefe Wilson, *In the Governor's Shadow: The True Story of Ma and Pa Ferguson* (Denton: University of North Texas Press, 2014), 87–90. Interestingly enough, one of the witnesses the committee chose not to call was Charles Maedgen, former vice president of the Temple State Bank, who had accused Ferguson of taking money from the Texas brewers for his campaigns. In a full-page ad Maedgen took out in the *Temple Telegram* on July 20, 1916, he accused Ferguson of taking three donations of $10,000 each, two consisting of cash stuffed into suitcases and one in the form of a check from the Houston Ice and Brewing Company. Maedgen took the unusual step of asking to be recused as a witness, before either attorney in the Ferguson investigation called him. When Hanger brought up the subject, Crane replied that he did not want Maedgen as a witness, perhaps because of his previous, well-publicized

bad blood with Ferguson. The veracity of Maedgen's newspaper attack is almost impossible to determine, although it would fit with a long pattern of Fergusonian behavior. *Proceedings of Investigation Committee*, 53; *Temple Telegram*, July 20, 1916.

44. Wilson, *In the Governor's Shadow*, 91–98; *Proceedings of Investigation Committee*, 80–169.

45. Ferguson's testimony is contained in *Proceedings of Investigation Committee*, 187–288, 342–44. For the quotation, see 236. For Ferguson's bank stock valuation, see 246.

46. Commissioner Austin's testimony is contained in *Proceedings of Investigation Committee*, 295–307.

47. *Proceedings of Investigation Committee*, 1–4.

48. Ibid., 5.

49. See note 4.

50. Charles E. Kelly headed up an influential Democratic Party machine in El Paso known as "the Ring." He was accused of "bossism" during his administration and was a Catholic, a religion that tended toward antiprohibition during this period of time. Clinton P. Hartmann, "Kelly, Charles Edgar," *Handbook of Texas Online*, http://www.tshaonline.org/handbook/online/articles/fke76, accessed August 26, 2015; [Barker], *Ferguson's War*, 20–21.

51. *Dallas Morning News*, August 2, 1918, August 3, 1918; *Houston Chronicle*, May 29, 1918. In 1918, federal prosecutors indicted several of the Texas brewers for income tax evasion over the loans to Jim Ferguson.

52. Lomax, "Governor Ferguson and the University of Texas," 18–19.

53. Ibid., 20.

54. Gould, *Progressives and Prohibitionists*, 203; Lomax, "Governor Ferguson and the University of Texas," 20–21. It is a mystery how Peddy escaped from Officer's Training Camp long enough to take part in the protest. Some of the more imaginative proponents of the University of Texas claimed that two alumni, Albert Burleson and Watt Gregory, then serving in Woodrow Wilson's cabinet, convinced the POTUS to allow Peddy to return briefly to Austin. Lomax, "Governor Ferguson and the University of Texas," 20.

55. [Barker], *Ferguson's War*, 23.

56. Ibid.

57. Ibid., 24. Ferguson left one line item intact, the salary of Dr. H. Y. Benedict, the dean of the College of Arts, a sum of $3,500. It is impossible to say why Ferguson left this one item alone.

58. [Barker], *Ferguson's War*, 24–25.

59. Ibid., 32–33. Ferguson even went so far as to veto the appropriation for the Texas State Historical Association.

60. [Barker], *Ferguson's War*, 33.

61. Ibid., 33.

62. Ibid., 34.

63. Ibid., 34–38; *Dallas Morning News*, June 17, 1917.

64. Homer Dale Wade, *Establishment of Texas Technological College, 1916–1923* (Lubbock: Texas Tech University Press, 1956), 25–26. Even though the legislature repealed the bill for West Texas A&M, the citizens of West Texas persisted and finally got their own university with the establishment of Texas Technological College in 1923.

65. McArthur and Smith, *Minnie Fisher Cunningham*, 53–55.

66. Ewing, "Impeachment of James E. Ferguson," 194.

67. J. Evetts Haley, *George W. Littlefield: Texan* (Norman: University of Oklahoma Press, 1943), 247–48.

68. Ewing, "Impeachment of James E. Ferguson," 196.

69. Ibid., 196.

70. Ibid.

71. Lomax, "Governor Ferguson and the University of Texas," 24–25.

72. [Barker], *Ferguson's War*, 46.

73. Fuller evidently said many different things to different people in the days after the disputed vote on the location of West Texas A&M, and he contradicted himself as a witness several times, destroying any chance he had at credibility. For Fuller's testimony, see *Journal of the Texas House of Representatives, Thirty-Fifth Legislature, Second Called Session August 1–30, 1917* (Austin: Von-Boeckmann-Jones, 1917), 390–459.

74. *Journal of the Texas House of Representatives, Thirty-Fifth Legislature, Second Called Session August 1–30, 1917*, 676–80, 716–17.

75. *Dallas Morning News*, August 26, 1917. See *Journal of the Texas House of Representatives, Thirty-Fifth Legislature, Second Called Session*, 78–103, for the list of impeachment charges.

76. *Record of Proceedings of the High Court of Impeachment on the Trial of Hon. James E. Ferguson, Governor before the Senate of the State of Texas, Pursuant to the State Constitution and Rules Provided by the Senate during the Second and Third Called Sessions of the 35th Legislature August 1–September 29, 1917* (Austin: A. C. Baldwin and Sons, 1917). See 11–16 for the articles of impeachment, and 732–51 for Ferguson's testimony. The ten articles of impeachment and the votes appear on pages 767–95.

77. *Record of Proceedings of the High Court of Impeachment*, 844–54.

2

"Think of the Lives That Might Be Saved"

James Ferguson, Women's War Work, and the University of Texas

Kay Reed Arnold

As the United States prepared to enter into World War I in 1917, Texas governor James Ferguson was gearing up for a different kind of war, a war with the University of Texas. Because these two historical narratives centrally focus on two different series of events thousands of miles apart, they appear to be separate stories. Yet they were not. As Texans, like Americans nationwide, prepared themselves to support the United States war effort in a variety of ways, they knew the effectiveness of their efforts would regularly be the difference between life and death for US soldiers and allies. During the previous decade, the University of Texas (UT) established itself as a provider of services and training for its student body but also for the general population of Texas. The university offered food preservation courses and access to technology, public education resources, and agricultural information, and many communities across the Lone Star State had come to rely on the university as a lifeline in their daily lives. World War I enormously increased the need and the immediacy of these continued services, and by 1917 Ferguson was a threat to UT and its continued operations.[1]

As soon as the United States went to war in April 1917, women quietly feared that their sons, brothers, husbands, or other loved ones would be killed in battle. Poor and rich, rural and urban, American women unwittingly became a sisterhood, as no one was exempt from the perils of war. Determined to do their part in the war effort, in Texas and across the nation, women scrimped and saved food, substituting and doing without so that excess food and fuel could go to US soldiers and allied countries. To ensure the moral and physical health of the soldiers, Texas women vowed to clean up military camps, learning about venereal diseases, the ravages of alcohol, and the lifelong effects of both.

Previous studies regularly discussed women's roles in anti-Ferguson rhetoric and the campaigning for his impeachment and its aftermath. Thus readers may already be aware that Ferguson was anti–woman suffrage and that female leaders worked toward his impeachment to further the votes-for-women movement. This chapter does not discount the significance of suffrage in the impeachment rhetoric or in the role pro-suffrage sentiments played in women's activism in the Ferguson impeachment and subsequent pro-Hobby campaign. The reason woman suffrage has been a central theme of the discussion in studies about Texas progressivism and Ferguson's impeachment is because it was important. Such focus on suffrage has led to a master narrative about Texas women's involvement in Ferguson's impeachment that is incomplete.

Not all women were assertively pro-suffrage, and not all efforts by Texas women—even suffragists—to remove James Ferguson were solely about advancing women's right to vote. Ferguson threatened their established reliance on UT as an educational source both academic and public, and as a result, he endangered the services many Texas women and their families needed. Furthermore, he refused to support war work-related prohibitionist and antivice efforts aimed at protecting servicemen and others associated with Texas military bases. Because of his position as Texas's head of state, his inaction was perceived as an active obstruction. By examining the activities of the Extension and Domestic Economy departments at the University of Texas, the messages and efforts of Texas women's campaigning for Ferguson's impeachment—including the Woman's Campaign for Good Government, and the war work efforts by Texas women and the University of Texas, a new narrative emerges showing the diverse reasons why many Texas women saw the benefits of removing the Ferguson obstacle.

Years before the start of World War I, the Extension and Domestic Economy departments (the latter popularly referred to as home economics) at the University of Texas, located in Austin, laid the groundwork for much of what became, by 1917, the core of Texas women's war work. University of Texas president Sidney Mezes cited the "Wisconsin Plan," as a model approach to education that allowed universities to reach out to the rural community to provide education about home, farm, and community life. In June 1909, Mezes proposed to the board of regents the creation of three university initiatives: Teaching through Correspondence, Public Discussion lectures by members of the faculty, and the preparation of School Libraries.[2]

In 1911, UT professor Alexander Caswell Ellis became acting director of Extension for the university. Known for his focus on psychology, education, and child development, and his farming interests, Ellis was active and accessible to his students, and his interests extended beyond the classroom. Extension enrollment surpassed projections during the first years and contemporary reports suggest they eclipsed any other program of its type anywhere else. To help with unforeseen growth, university administration hired John A. Lomax as assistant director of Extension. An alumnus, Lomax held the rank of faculty member and was charged with publicity and with the tasks of secretary to the faculty.[3]

"Special training for women" was another progressive measure Mezes brought to the attention of the regents. Apparently, it was not the first time the idea of catering to the educational needs of women was proposed, as Mezes needled the regents with barbs of "again" and "two years ago it was suggested." Recommended among the topics were sciences, many of them directly related to the household through chemistry of foods, dietetics, and sanitation. Other universities around the nation offered domestic economy, household economics, household management, legal rights of women, architecture, and fine arts.[4]

Also urging the advancement of studies for women and the advancement of women as instructors was university regent George W. Brackenridge. No stranger to advocating for women's rights, he was brother and advisor to clubwoman leader and suffragist Mary Eleanor Brackenridge, who in 1913 became president and subsequently honorary lifetime president of the Texas Equal Suffrage Association (TESA). Mezes announced to the board of regents in October 1910 the creation and private funding of the Department of Domestic Science. He reported, "I am authorized by Regent Brackenridge to tender to the Board $6000 annually for this and the two sessions succeeding it for the employment of a competent woman as Professor of Domestic Economy and for such other expenditures in that department."[5]

Enthusiastic letters between Mezes and Brackenridge in 1910 and 1911 indicate finding that "competent woman" in this relatively new discipline was not as easy as they had hoped. In March 1912, the regents were informed that Mary "Mamie" E. Gearing had been hired as associate professor of Domestic Economy at an annual salary of $2000, effective January 1912. Gearing previously started a similar program in the Houston school districts and came highly recommended by professors at Columbia University. In 1913, Mezes reported to the board of regents the progress made by both the popular Extension and Domestic Economy departments as having "convinced the people of the desire of the University to serve them in directions in which they need to be served."[6]

Under Mary Gearing, the Domestic Economy department worked to improve child welfare, safety, and efficiency in the home. Besides giving instruction in practical skills, topics of interest for women delivered through the Public Discussion division included legal issues for women, child labor laws, alcoholism and prohibition, and suffrage. Courses in practical work in the home, including food preservation and hygiene, helped homemakers economize in tough financial times as well as helping to keep their families safe from food-borne illnesses. These topics were also discussed in the Women's Division of the Farmers Institute. Initially led by university-trained students, "canning clubs" were formed as a means to teach the classes but also served as social opportunities for isolated rural women. So popular for their mothers, "girls' canning clubs," in both rural and urban settings, were designed for school-age girls; these grew to memberships of over 6,000 by 1917.[7]

The Progressive Era's combination of the dissemination and application of scientific information in daily life through associationalism created a natural foundation for domestic war work. As the head of the US Food Administration, Herbert Hoover called upon the nation's women to conserve food. By conserving food, they eliminated waste in their home, enabling extra grain to be used to feed the soldiers and US allies. Also by using what was on hand, fuel normally used in transporting goods went to fighting the war. The work of the Extension and Domestic Economy departments laid the foundation for the food conservation campaign five years earlier.[8]

Gearing and fellow UT professor Jessie Rich were so well respected that they were called to Washington, DC, to advise the federal government on plans for food conservation. "The most disloyal thing a woman can do today is to hoard food," said Mary Gearing addressing a women's club. She lectured on the rising prices of grain and the bread riots in larger cities of

Food conservation was essential to home front efforts in the United States during World War I. The above US Food Administration poster was one of many used to campaign for these measures. Ca. 1917–19. Courtesy of Record Group 4, Records of the US Food Administration, National Archives and Records Administration, College Park, Maryland.

the North. The home economics team was in the foreground of research for alternative grains to be used in making bread, including the use of cottonseed meal. Urging women to cooperate, she said, "Never was the need for cooperation so great as in this, America's darkest hour. We are going to win the war and we will do it by food conservation."[9]

Despite her well-known expertise in food conservation strategy, Gearing, and her colleagues, were overlooked by Ferguson when he formed the statutory State Defense Council in May 1917. Reports of the council showed in-fighting, disorganization, lack of understanding of established organizational entities, and little progress. Ferguson called the measure of war work a very serious matter, yet by June his council had little to show for three months of work.[10]

In contrast, less than a week after the United States declared war on Germany on April 6, 1917, UT faculty voted by a large margin to provide and require military and/or war work training curriculum to every student at the university, women and men, to prepare them for the realities of war. Almost overnight, Americans were stuck with the reality that an entire generation of soon-to-be soldiers had little to no military or combat training. US general George Pershing, after meeting with UT President Vinson, agreed to assign a military commander to the campus to head the military drills ordered to begin immediately. UT officials planned for women students, in lieu of military training designed for the men students, to train in nursing, first aid, food conservation, and chemistry. The plan was to frontload preparation for potential military and civilian assignments, respectively, while the nation geared up for full military deployment.[11]

Furthermore, entry into the war brought hardship for everyone served by UT's Extension Department; as such, fieldwork was enhanced to meet their needs. Farmers in Texas struggled against falling cotton prices, rotating crops, and growing food to help the cause coupled with concerns over loss of laborers who either fled the country or were called into service. Progressives urged legislators to outlaw growing grains for making liquor. While Ferguson cut state agriculture budgets, the Extension Department continued to work along with the Farmers Institute and the Texas Department of Agriculture to help the farmers adapt to the shifting landscape of agriculture.[12]

As part of the national war efforts toward food conservation and protectioning troops from alcoholism, prohibitionists launched their most successful campaigns. Many working for the regulation of alcohol did so with the idea that limiting its sale and distribution would significantly reduce the financial lobbying power of those in the industry and their conservative allies. There were additional reasons; prohibitionists emphasized that the amount of agricultural raw materials that went into the production of beer and liquor were a waste and in contradiction to the need to conserve food for the war effort. Additionally, new war-related antivice arguments increased as reformers and government and military leaders pressed the vital need to separate soldiers from factors that could reduce their health and ability to serve in the war.[13]

University faculty included a number of vocal prohibitionists, including education and extension professor Alexander Caswell Ellis and physics professor William Tyler Mather. Widely known to citizens as a devout Christian, Mather served as an elder in the University Presbyterian Church. As president of the Austin Anti-Vice League, Mather challenged county officials as they looked the other way while wealthy male clients enabled prostitution and liquor sales to flourish. County officials, Mather concluded, were as guilty as those directly involved in committing the crimes. *Missionary Review of the World* boasted that the Austin Anti-Vice League had cleaned up Austin and now served as a model for other Texas cities.[14]

Jane Y. McCallum served as vice president of the Austin Anti-Vice League. The mother of five, McCallum was active in several clubs. She filled her diary with discussion of her family and thoughts surrounding the university troubles and the war effort waged by women. She and her husband, Arthur Newell McCallum, came to Austin in 1906 when he was appointed superintendent of schools. At that time, those welcoming them to Austin included university president William Prather and members of the education faculty, including A. Caswell Ellis. Ellis and Superintendent McCallum were formidable allies in improving Austin schools. Ellis is credited for founding the first Mother's Club in Austin, the precursor to today's Parent-Teacher Association. Ellis and his wife, Mary Heard Ellis, became members of the Austin Equal Suffrage Association just as Jane McCallum became president of the chapter in 1915.[15]

Also joining in the war effort was Anna Pennybacker. Arriving in Austin in 1900, a widow with three children, Pennybacker was an established teacher, public administrator, and writer, and was quickly associated with fellow progressive educators at the university, often joining them in Public Discussion lectures. Like many other women of the time, Pennybacker was associated with many clubs and served as president of the Texas Federation of Women's Clubs from 1901 to 1903. She raised funds for community libraries statewide, preceding the work of the Extension department. She also solicited funds for women's scholarships at the university and pressed the legislature for building appropriations for a women's dormitory on the campus. Pennybacker went on to preside over the federal Greater Federation of Women's Clubs from 1912 to 1916, giving her unparalleled access to an immense network of women.[16]

Although women were prepared for food conservation, they were newly alerted by antivice watchdogs to problems encountered in new military training camps in Texas. Not surprisingly, when the camps were established, vice followed. On June 5, 1917, Minnie Fisher Cunningham, president of TESA, and Pennybacker hosted a luncheon for women from across the state to discuss the serious issue. Over tea sandwiches, Texas clubwomen and suffragists learned about the indelicate subjects of venereal disease and alcoholism plaguing the camps. Mothers from around the nation had sent their sons to Texas, and the women of Texas were going to do their best to protect them.[17]

The agreed-upon strategy was to create a "white zone" around the military camps, providing a moral buffer for the young soldiers. Cunningham, in addition to her suffrage work, agreed to serve as president of the Texas Women's Anti-Vice Association. The National American Woman Suffrage Association (NAWSA) asserted that war work now would translate later into suffrage. While local and state affiliated suffragists were supposed to put it aside, many Texas suffragists continued to work on both simultaneously. With Cunningham in the lead, the suffrage machinery was used in the campaign to clean up the camps. The "girls" from the Present Day Club at the University of Texas, under the guidance of Gearing, raised and contributed $400 for efforts to start immediately. Women were "trying to save the boys of the Nation before the bullets begin their deadly work," claimed Zoe Rodman Aubrey of the City Federation of Women's Missionary Societies.[18]

Being at the helm of the suffrage campaign, Cunningham learned that it was of foremost importance to mobilize local leaders. Military camps were in San Antonio, El Paso, Waco, and Fort Worth, and she recruited county and city chairwomen to put pressure on local officials to enforce the mandate made by the federal government to keep vice away from camps. As in the suffrage campaign, in areas more remote in South Texas, field workers collected information and solicited help from local leaders and officials. Waco was an especially big camp, requiring the attention of many. Arrest reports of prostitutes were examined, pictures taken, inspections made, and letters circulated. Antivice women reformers did not want the offending women institutionalized or put onto poor farms. Instead, they circulated ideas about the possibilities of helping these women escape this type of life, including employment in factories, mills, and agriculture and trades.[19]

Secretary of War Newton Baker ordered the establishment of white zones around military camps. Despite the declaration and despite the outcry by women publicized in the newspaper accounts, records fail to show a response by Governor Ferguson. There is no way to know whether this lack of response indicated that his attention was focused on the trouble brewing with the university or if it was to keep from mobilizing in a way that opened doors to further prohibition activity. The latter was a move that would undoubtedly anger and alienate his key support base by that point—brewers.[20]

Corporate brewer and political powerhouse Adolphus Busch aimed at winning over the people of America to his side, to make them all lovers of beer and to gain respect for the master brewer and the brewing industry. Less than a year after Ferguson's eventual impeachment in August 1917, a *Houston Post* writer referred back to events in the recent past putting the role of Busch and other connected Texas brewers into context. "That was at a time when temperance advocates in Texas were beginning to make their efforts felt. The effects of liquor on the human organism were being taught in the public schools. . . . There were certain professors in the University of the State who made it their practice to preach prohibition whenever they could do so," reported the *Houston Post*. Busch gave orders to his Texas lieutenants to "get control of the Texas University and forever hush the voices of the men who were teaching and preaching prohibition. . . . The master brewer knew that the University was moulding [sic] more public opinion in a day than he could unmould [sic] in a week." Busch attributed the woes that had come upon his business in Texas directly to that institution, and he wanted that influence to stop. In cahoots with the master brewer, Ferguson pressed the board of regents to fire the prohibitionist faculty. It turned out, though, that gaining control over the university was not as quick nor as easy as either man had hoped it would be.[21]

Those Ferguson started to call the "University crowd" were in full swing of cleaning up and advancing programs around the state when Ferguson arrived on the scene in 1915, and the only thing they seemed to agree with Ferguson about was much-needed improvement in rural education. Ferguson's perception of the "University crowd," or clique, was recalled later by his daughter, Ouida. She wrote, "There is the University group, who bask in their intellectual superiority, but who, for the sake of the University appropriations, tolerate, and at times are very sweet to, the political group on Capitol Hill." In a sense, Ferguson was right about it being a clique, and by 1916, the two sides were at odds. By 1917, they were at war—both figuratively and literally. The "University crowd" included A. N. and Jane Yelvington McCallum, Anna Pennybacker, William Mather, Elizabeth Speer, Mary Gearing, and A. Caswell Ellis and Mary Heard Ellis. Neither the brewery-backed governor nor the "University crowd" backed down on the work they saw as necessary.[22]

When the regents chose Robert E. Vinson as the university president, the governor was irate. As former president of the Austin Presbyterian Seminary, Vinson previously worked with Mather in the Austin Anti-Vice League, and many of the university crowd knew him through University Presbyterian Church. Meeting with the governor in the summer 1916, Vinson was surprised to find that there was a list of faculty members that the governor wanted fired. Vinson spent the first few months of the academic year asking the governor about specific charges for what he assumed was an investigation. Although the governor said he did not need to have reasons, those few he gave were negligible; Ellis was accused of cheating in financial accounting of expenditures and Mather was accused of making great profits off the students by having his notes sold at the newly formed University Co-op.[23]

Vinson corrected those issues, yet the governor insisted that the professors, whom he considered offensive, be dismissed. Ferguson's list of offenders changed often, but ever-present were Lomax, Ellis, and Mather, and often accompanying them was the entire Domestic Economy department. Although he would not formally say that prohibition, suffrage, and antivice work were his real charges against the professors, most everyone knew better. John Lomax had a hand in extension work and was well positioned with alumni and faculty to be a thorn in Ferguson's side. As early as October 1916, Jane McCallum recorded in her diary, "Went by the recep[tion] to Vinsons at the University Club rooms. Every body [sic] was agog over Governor Ferguson's outrageous behavior. We suffragists concluded that, had we the vote, we'd impeach him—or rather force the legislature to do so. . . . It takes such an ignorant, common personage to let an illy gained honor turn his head. He seems to fancy himself a Kaiser." She went on to record the effect the harassment and looming dismissal had on the faculty and their spouses: "it will go hardest with the Mathers."[24]

Regents charged with dismissing faculty wrangled with Ferguson for the rest of 1916. When they did not bend to his will, Ferguson either removed or failed to reappoint regents, including the post of Regent Will C. Hogg, son of a former governor and law school alumnus, and by now a heated opponent of the governor. Trying to stack the deck in his favor, Ferguson chose new men he thought would "stand hitched." By early 1917, he was getting closer to his and Busch's dream of a board full of members who would follow the plan to rid the university of "objectionable" administrators and faculty. He did not get this board without a fight.

By May 1917, Ferguson made a bold move. He demanded that Regents remove faculty members Ferguson found objectionable and that Vinson resign or he would veto appropriations that funded the university for the next two years. In protest, angry university students marched on the capitol while the governor was meeting with the regents. Vinson refused to resign, saying the regents would have to fire him and the objectionable faculty. On June 3, Ferguson made good on his threat of eliminating funding for the university with the exception of the $3,500 salary of Harry Yandell Benedict, dean of the College of Arts. The *Austin Statesman* speculated that Ferguson was advised to maintain one professor, Benedict, and appoint him as new president of the university. When word of this got out, the *Austin Statesman* reported, faculty members chided Benedict for his newfound friend and great fortune.[25]

While there was still some question as to the legality of the veto, the possibility was enough to rally alumni and supporters to find a solution. Whether or not the university was closed was still debatable, and the board of regents was scheduled to meet on July 12 to settle many issues. It was rumored that not only would faculty be fired, despite the incredible war efforts being led, but also that the entire Domestic Economy department was slated for elimination. Knowing the value of the department to the citizens of the state, Pennybacker asked Cunningham to use her influence as the leader of TESA to write to the board of regents to tell them of the important work of the department and to ask them to spare it.[26]

Reacting to the governor's action, the Ex-Students' Association, led by Will C. Hogg, law school alumnus, moved off campus and went into full-scale assault on the governor. Telephone records show calls by Hogg, John Lomax, John Brady, McClendon, Vinson, and Helen Knox—Pennybacker's secretary. On June 6 and 8, Knox made several phone calls to influential women, including to Minnie Fisher Cunningham. Knox's call presumably paralleled a telegram, inviting her on behalf of the Ex-Students' Association to be an honored guest at their annual alumni luncheon. Although Pennybacker was not an alumna of the university, her calls and telegrams to the women of Texas at this time may have been to garner support for the beleaguered university.[27]

A large rally was held in Austin on the evening of June 13 to educate the crowd about the university issues and to encourage participation in a mass meeting to be held in Dallas the following Saturday. Impassioned speakers asserted their reasons for wanting to keep the university open. Longtime Austin mayor A. P. Wooldridge was largely responsible for the university being placed in the city and knew that it could be relocated in any number of cities eager to give the university a new home. School superintendent A. N. McCallum reminded the crowd that the university was a powerful ally in developing and improving Austin schools. Others spoke who saw the loss of the university as a loss for all businesses. Jane McCallum reflected upon the night in her diary: "Ah, if only Ferguson can and will be impeached. He deserves to be hung for treason. Think of the lives that might be saved by money we are compelled to spend to try to save our loved University from him—but not having the vocabulary of a sea captain and being partly responsible for the respectability of my family, I can't express what I think of Jim Ferguson."[28]

Faculty members were not permitted to attend the Dallas mass meeting, lest Ferguson think it was a faculty uprising. However, they did lend their contacts and skills behind the scenes. Between June 10 and 12, Ellis was in Dallas to consult with organizers of the event and was asked to contact leading women across the state to form a women's division to garner support, presumably because of his involvement in education, extension work, and suffrage.[29]

At the urging of Pennybacker and Ellis, Cunningham called on suffragists to support the university by issuing a statement to the press. She then sent a circular letter to presidents of the suffrage associations encouraging them to "consider the welfare of the University of Texas." The form letter refuted allegations made by Ferguson that it was a rich man's school. She reminded suffragists that the university should be free from politics, that the charges made by the governor against faculty had been dismissed by the board of regents, and that he had denied the suffrage plank at the Democratic convention in Saint Louis, but made no mention of war measures.[30]

Reflecting upon the breadth of his reach afforded him by years of working in the state, Ellis thanked the "womanhood of Texas" for their magnificent response to his pleas for help. He added,

> When they asked me Sunday to get every prominent club president to telegraph every club to take action, I think they had a vague idea that there were fifty or a hundred clubs in Texas and that I might reach about half of them—or less. When I notified them that over 500 Federated Clubs, 200 Mother's Clubs, 150 Suffrage Clubs, 125 WCTU Clubs, and about a hundred chapters of the Daughters of the Republic, Daughters of the Confederacy, Daughters of the Revolution, and Daughters of 1812, and Colonial Dames would be called by lettergram at once by their presidents, the Committee was lifted off its feet! They were as delighted at the splendid support as they were paralyzed to see what a telegraph bill they had got themselves into. I am so glad of it! It is time the men were learning what a power the organized women of Texas are.[31]

Thousands of women from across the state with varying reasons to support UT, many of whom had relied upon its public and higher educational services, were called to action to save the university.

Over five hundred alumni and friends gathered at the Dallas mass meeting on June 16, 1917. Former Texas governor Joseph D. Sayers agreed to chair a permanent committee to ensure survival of the university. In her enthusiastic speech at the rally, Pennybacker cast the support of tens of thousands of clubwomen. The plan called for educating the masses rather than attacking the governor personally. Their first request was to ask the legislature to investigate publicly the allegations against university faculty and administrators, and, if guilty, they were to be removed from the university. They also called on the legislature to remove any possibility for politics to interfere in the operations of any institution. Not surprisingly, George Brackenridge agreed to head up the Finance Committee of the newly formed University Citizens Committee (UCC) and had already agreed privately with Vinson to help fund the university should the legislative appropriations fail.[32]

McCallum recorded her thoughts of the Dallas trip in her diary: "How can I ever remember even half of the things I should like to record. The meeting at Dallas was what a Texan reporter would call a 'humdinger.' Can just jot notes to make me remember. For instance the service car man charging Mrs. Will Hart and me only half fare to show sympathy with what we were there for (we had on badges)." The combination of entering the war with the rest of the nation and the increasingly public knowledge of their own governor of Texas' refusal to facilitate war efforts must have been overwhelming and confusing for many Texans. The number of supporters and critics Ferguson had during this time is impossible to ascertain. With the lack of public polling, which was not fully established until decades later, accurate quantification does not exist. The show of support of the taxi driver in Dallas, though, suggests a widespread public knowledge of the issues.[33]

Not all progressive reform leaders in the state were physically present for the Dallas meeting, but instead, showed their solidarity in other ways. In response to a letter of gratitude from Ellis regarding Cunningham's support of the activities, Cunningham provided information about her own support efforts by explaining that the telegram bill associated with organizing advocates would have been too high. Thus she sent out night letters that were more detailed, yet less costly, and she was glad to donate the cost for the good of the university. Noting that the university was fighting the same "gang," as Cunningham called the brewers, that Texas suffragists had been battling for years, she thanked him and others who were leading the fight for the university. She sent her regrets for missing the Dallas mass meeting but congratulated Ellis for the success. Busy with the Texas Women's Anti-Vice campaign, she was still on the fringes of the university's fight with the governor.[34]

The anticipated but dreaded news came on July 12, 1917, that the board of regents had dismissed Ellis, Mather, William H. Mayes, Charles S. Potts, and Robert E. Cofer. Although initially spared, warning was given to Vinson and others that their services would be determined at the next meeting in October. Reviewing the budget for the Domestic Economy department, two regents voted to close the department. Although he thought the $3,000 salary too high for a woman, Regent Littlefield argued to keep the department but agreed to reduce the salaries of all Domestic Economy faculty by 20 percent. Despite sparse comments recorded in the Regents' Minutes, news of the conversation was carried outside the boardroom, fanning the flames of women who worked in the department and their supporters.[35]

Word of the firings traveled fast, and spirits were down. After a going-away party hosted by the Ellises, Jane McCallum, in her diary, emotionally expressed the sentiments of many regarding a departing faculty member and his family, "who are leaving before being muzzled or fired and most of the guests were fine, brainy men—University men—who are in the most humiliating positions. It may be wicked, but how delighted, and supremely happy we'd all be if Ferguson, [Regents] Littlefield, Allen, Fly and McReynolds were to be killed."[36]

Once the new board of regents fired the faculty and vetoed the majority of the university appropriation, the Dallas plan was a moot point, and the campaign to impeach went into full force. Although the impeachment campaign started as a coordinated effort between the Ex-Students' Association (ESA) led by Hogg, Woodward, and Brady and the UCC led by Sayers, the shift from sustaining the university to impeachment caused Sayers to question the continuing role of the UCC. The leadership recognized the success of Ellis's call to the many women's organizations for mobilization, so they saw value in creating a women's division for this campaign.[37]

The UCC called Cunningham to come to Austin to "swing the women's end of it." She saw this as "the chance of a lifetime to break the power of corrupt politics. . . . We came into the campaign just at the time when everybody was worn to a frazzle and feeling discouraged and beaten; our interest and enthusiasm and immediate success of our first bits of work seemed to put new life and vigor into the men who were working." Knowing that if Texas women proved themselves in this campaign, perhaps suffrage could be won, she added, "The men are tremendously grateful as well as not a little surprised at the effectiveness of our work, and I believe we can get most anything we ask of them if we do win."[38]

Campaigns such as the one these women leaders planned require financial backing. The funds became available and coyly were attributed to the generosity of "someone not particularly interested in the affairs of the University." Although he refused to participate visibly, George Brackenridge placed $2,000 in the trust of Mary E. Gearing to wage a women's uprising against the governor.[39]

The initial idea was for this to be a two-week statewide campaign "to put before the people the full facts, many of which have not been published because of the state libel law." The appeal was signed by the leaders of all of the women's organizations, with two curious points. First, Nannie Webb Curtis, president of the WCTU, was not listed. Curtis wrote to Ellis to say that she was away for the summer and, though she supported the efforts as much as anyone, she would have to support from afar. It can be speculated that listing the leader of the WCTU would alienate antiprohibitionists and distract from the issue of impeachment. Second, Minnie Fisher Cunningham, as president of TESA, was slipped in close to the end of the list, as though she was merely joining in with the others. At the time of the campaign, it was decided to act in somewhat secrecy as to the involvement of Cunningham and TESA.[40]

The first action of this new Woman's Campaign for Good Government (WCGG) was to send out a questionnaire formulated to collect data from the responders about how they might help, asking if she was an alumna, did she have children at the university, did she have a car, and can she give public speeches. Further, they also asked about other organizations with which she may have been affiliated. Over two thousand volunteers responded.[41]

Pennybacker spoke at the Dallas meeting and encouraged Cunningham's involvement, but as the president of the Chautauqua literary society, Pennybacker annually spent her summers at the society's seasonal literary institute held in Chautauqua, New York. Records indicate that her involvement fell to that of occasional letter writing, but because she was such an icon to the clubwomen of the state, she still had enormous influence over their actions. Thus, by urging them to support the WCGG, Pennybacker delivered the invaluable network of Federated Women's Clubs of Texas.

Early disagreements set about when the men of the UCC chose Clara Driscoll Sevier as the representative of the women on legislative matters. Gearing and Cunningham expressed their disapproval of working with Sevier, whose husband had just formed a newspaper in Austin, the *American*, which was not found to be favorable with anyone in the anti-Ferguson crowd. Woodward and Brady relented in allowing Cunningham to manage the lobbying efforts, presumably when Cunningham showed them the depth of her knowledge of the voting records of every Texas legislator that had been accumulated over the years of the suffrage campaign.[42]

Cunningham joined Brady at the University Methodist Church in Austin on the evening of July 23. Speaking to summer school students, Brady "castigated the governor" and many of the regents. Despite the rumors of the Littlefield attack on the Domestic Economy department, Brady came to Littlefield's defense, arguing that Littlefield may have thought that perhaps the appropriations could be saved if the offending faculty members were sacrificed. Brady added that the governor was hostile toward the university because he alleged that the Ex-Students had raised money to investigate and charge the governor with impropriety in his finances earlier in the year. Brady reminded his listeners that the hostilities were justifiably aimed at Governor Ferguson for the false charges made against the faculty the previous year.[43]

Cunningham spoke briefly, adding that the university had been an invaluable tool for Texas women in their war work. She praised the Domestic Economy department as being an example to women of the North despite the fact that a regent had disparaged the worth of the work. Concluding with, "They speak of disloyalty. I ask you, is it loyalty to close a department of the University that is doing so important a work to help win the war?" she asked. "We women want to do our share to make effective the sacrifices which our boys are called upon to make on the other side of the water." Perhaps she was thinking of her brother who would soon serve in France, or, like many women, she knew she was surrounded by young men with uncertain futures.[44]

For this campaign, the WCGG was able to reach out to all women in all organizations and in all communities, urban and rural. Armed with "dodgers" (campaign flyers), women drove cars with girls jumping out on both sides of the road to put them in mailboxes and hand them to those they passed. Despite all the work performed by the university in rural communities, there were still solid pockets of Ferguson supporters, and it was uncertain if farmers would stand with the governor.[45]

The state's Farmers Institute held their 1917 annual meeting in Austin in July. Thousands of farmers gathered to hear lectures about agriculture and livestock while their wives met to discuss issues unique to the home. In years past, Ferguson was at the front of the House chamber where the Speaker presided with Agriculture Commissioner Davis, as well as Ellis and Gearing, welcoming the participants. In 1917, though, the program did not include the governor. Instead, he insisted that he speak at one thirty in the afternoon, when the Institute was technically in recess. Knowing "Farmer Jim" would address the Institute in the afternoon, the women conspired to get a jump on the governor in the morning to ensure that the facts were known. Under secrecy, a twenty-four-hour rally was planned on the grounds of the capitol. A stage was fashioned out of a dray (flatbed truck) with eight-foot-long banners, painted in orange, "Women of Texas Protest."[46]

Surprised attendees saw that there was no break in speakers, and the list of participants ranged from the president of the Colonial Dames of America to the son of a tenant farmer who had worked his way through "State," meaning UT. The size of the crowd—made up of farmers, townspeople, and legislators arriving for the special session—blocked traffic. Thus the rally was moved to a nearby park later in the day. Although event organizers originally planned for twenty-four hours, shortly before midnight it came to a rousing close with a speech by "fighting Bob Shuler," a well-known Methodist minister and prohibitionist.[47]

Inside the capitol at the opening ceremony of the Institute, Commissioner of Agriculture Fred W. Davis addressed his farming constituents first. Reminding them that the job they did was of the utmost importance in the war effort, he lamented that his department was unable to meet their needs because of the governor's veto of much of his legislative appropriations. These vetoes, he asserted, left the department significantly understaffed and underfunded.[48]

By afternoon, Ferguson addressed a divided crowd. Some were loyal followers while others now had their doubts, particularly those who had heard speakers outside and Davis's claims of inability to help them. Reports claimed that nearly five thousand people crowded into the House of Representatives Hall to hear the governor. McCallum recalled that cheers rose from the floor while hisses and boos fell from the gallery above. Ferguson claimed that his intents were not to close the university, but to save it from those from those who sought to destroy it.[49]

At the Women's Division, much of the discussion was about food conservation. Called to give a talk about the Austin Canning Club, Mrs. R. L. Penn said what was on the minds of many attendees. She stated,

> I cannot resist diverging from my subject a little just here in order to try to tell you in my feeble way what this great University has meant to me, a widowed mother of nine children, especially in the bringing up of my five sons who have gone out from its doors to do their part in the world's work. First, I want to brand as absolutely untrue the slanders against this splendid institution now being circulated by

Governor James Ferguson. From one to three of my sons have gone in and out the doors of the University as students for eleven years. Two of my sons, seniors have gone into the training camps, and a son and daughter will be among the happy students, I trust, this fall. I've mothered hundreds besides my own—not rich men's sons and daughters—for I've tried to help those who, like my own were struggling along on small allowances and some of them on no allowance at all,—boys and girls making their own way but filling positions of honor in the University, beloved and honored by their fellow students, assisted and encouraged in every way by their teachers. I've known these boys and girls almost as a mother knows her children and they will testify as I do, that no institution in their State today is doing so much for rich and poor alike by developing men and women of perfect poise, high ideals and worthy accomplishments. Poor men's sons and widows' sons carry off most of the honors, not because the University discriminates against the rich, but because wealth lavished upon the undeveloped boy or girl except in exceptional instances, is a handicap to effort.

The other report I wish to brand as a falsehood is the one circulated by one high in authority that the farmers, the bend at the forks of the creek, wish to destroy this great University. I can look in your faces and feel my kinship to you, for while I am not a farmer's wife, I've worked with my hands, and have lived so close to Mother Nature that I feel you recognize me as a sister. I know that the greatest longing in your heart and mine is to bring our children the best that life offers. No University offers opportunities too great or culture too broad for the sons and daughters of the workers of Texas. We want the best for our State and our children, and we will stand by this University, rejoice in its growth, protect it against slander and envy, for all of us feel that the greatest University in the world would not be too good for the sons and daughters of Texas.

Penn summarized what so many saw in the University of Texas: a bridge to the future well-being of her own children and the rest of the state. Further, with this future threatened by war, UT became even more dear to her as a partner in the preparation for the survival of Texas's youth. She and others poised like mother lions ready to protect "our children"—even from the state's own governor. Like prohibition's many political purposes, Texas women's roles in Ferguson's impeachment held the promise of advancing a number of their reform measures and personal priorities.[50]

Also speaking that day before the Women's Division on the topic of war work were Jane McCallum, Elizabeth Speer, and Minnie Fisher Cunningham. McCallum spoke of the challenges she and others faced in Austin in trying to keep safe the children (university students) they entrusted to them. Mather, she reminded them, was fired from the university because of his antivice efforts and, because she was the vice president of the antivice group, she warned that they could be subject to harassment simply by hearing her speak.[51]

Speer enlightened attendees about the troubles in the Texas training camps to which American mothers had sent their sons. She said that the camps were assembled hastily and the sons were recruited hastily—neither being ready for the other. The sons, innocent about the ways of the world, found themselves at the mercy of liquor, prostitutes, and venereal disease. Cunningham claimed that they would put aside suffrage for the time to work for the safety of the boys. She encouraged women to rise up and help with the efforts by educating themselves and their communities. Commissioner Davis closed the Farmers Institute in 1917 by denouncing the political speeches given, but he still asserted that the gathering had been a success.[52]

Back at WCGG headquarters, Cunningham dispatched a committee to see Regents Allen and Littlefield, likely to ascertain if they still held the position stated at the July 12 regents meeting. Cunningham attended a meeting with the UCC, which illustrated that the women were operating collaboratively, yet separately. Cunningham conferred with Mayes (another ousted faculty member from the journalism department) about posters that were being prepared, and Hogg agreed to pay the printing costs.[53]

The resulting "Campaign Material: Issued by the Headquarters Committee of the Woman's Campaign for Good Government" was considered to be the answer to every accusation against the university made by Ferguson. Because of the level of detail regarding each offense, this was clearly a collaboration. Thousands of copies were printed at the expense of Will Hogg and sympathetic Austin printer A. C. Baldwin. According to archival resources detailing the production process of the "Campaign Material," during the gathering of the different pieces as new materials were prepared, "Dr. Ellis revised to such an extent that it could not be completed until this morning, July 31st. Hence Mr. Woodward did not get until about 10:00 o'clock. Holding carbon copy to check against printed copy when it comes out."[54]

The first page of the "Campaign Material" made it clear that the Texas women called for impeachment of the governor. Cunningham's contribution included clear campaign instructions to recipients to write letters to their legislator insisting upon clean government. The strong language and detail of steps left no question of what efforts were needed.[55]

The women leaders' voices and concerns are reflected again in the passages describing Ferguson's interruption of the war effort. The document's authors wrote, "He has through attempting to close the University given the greatest aid he could possibly give to Germany. The greatest and most pressing needs of America in this war are aviators, engineers, doctors and nurses, experts on food and feeding, experts in chemistry, electricity and physics, and educated officers to lead the men." They go on to exclaim that his closing of the aviation school leaves one hundred aviators going to France in a month without training. "We do not say that Governor Ferguson is in the employ of the Kaiser, but if he were we do not see how he could give him any better service than he is giving."[56]

The authors of the "Campaign Material" claimed that the abuse of power by the governor was the real issue and refuted his claims against the university. They state that the university was audited and that it was not a rich man's school as Ferguson has proposed, citing several students who worked their way through school. The cost per student and faculty-to-student ratio was listed and compared to other universities around the country. Facts regarding the university costs, student-teacher ratio, and anecdotal stories about students who worked their way through school are found in Hogg's and Ellis's records, indicating they helped frame this portion of the "Campaign Material."[57]

The final page of the document packet provided readers with information about the assault on the Domestic Economy department. It asserted the importance of the department by citing that the faculty educated more than 50,000 individuals around the state on food conservation, participated in consulting with the national plans on food conservation, and contributed research in food advancements. Finally, the campaign packet's authors forcefully closed with a counterattack to Ferguson's efforts to sink the home economics department, its faculty, and their efforts.[58]

As forms and requests came into WCGG headquarters, the new "Campaign Material" was sent out under strict instructions that it not be

CAMPAIGN MATERIAL.

Issued by the Headquarters Committee of the Woman's Campaign for Good Government.

Object of the Campaign:

To bring to the attention of the people of Texas the facts that have convinced the Committee that James E. Ferguson is unfit to conduct the affairs of our state. These facts are set out in the inclosed outline.

Results to be obtained:

1. A stream of letters, telegrams and resolutions to Speaker Fuller assuring him of the support of the people of Texas in his fight for a clean administration of our state in these times of national stress and expressing our appreciation of his courage and loyalty.
2. A stream of letters, telegrams and resolutions to your representatives in the state legislature stating in unmistakable terms that you, his constituents, are backing every effort for clean government in Texas, and demand a thorough investigation of the serious charges against Governor Ferguson. Make it clear that should these charges be established the people will be satisfied with nothing less than his impeachment and the establishment of the reins of government in the hands of men able and willing to give us a clean administration and uphold our National government in its fight for a graft-free, thoroughly efficient government in all states during the period of the war.

Method of conducting a campaign:

1. How to campaign a city or town,—
    A. Secure a list of all organizations in your town,—social, religious, fraternal, education, etc.
    B. Secure a hearing before each of these organizations for one of your speakers.
    C. Lay before them our appeal for an investigation of the Governor by the legislature. Acquaint them with the true facts of his administration.
    D. Ask them to pass resolutions addressed to Speaker Fuller and your representative covering the points in "Results."
    E. After covering the organizations, call a mass meeting to discuss the same facts and pass similar resolutions.
    F. AT ALL MEETINGS ASK INDIVIDUAL FRIENDS OF CLEAN GOVERNMENT TO WRITE PERSONAL LETTERS TO SPEAKER FULLER AND YOUR REPRESENTATIVES COVERING THE SAME GROUNDS.
    G. Call on all the business men, professional men, clergymen and leading citizens, and ask them to write similar letters.

2. To Campaign a County,—
    A. Appear before all organizations as in a city campaign.
    B. Call on all the leading men in the county and ask them to write Speaker Fuller and your representatives.
    C. Arrange public meetings at points all over the country in the school houses, churches, etc. Pass resolutions and ask for personal letters at these meetings.

3. To arrange a Mass Meeting:
    A. Secure the most popular meeting places,—court house, school, church, or court house lawn.
    B. Have your posters announcing the meeting put up over the town and county. Distribute dodgers.
    C. Ask the ministers to announce the meeting in church and at prayer meeting.
    D. Run slides at the picture shows.
    E. Run announcements in the county papers.
    F. If possible, get a band to play thirty minutes before the meeting.

The Woman's Campaign for Good Government issued information to aid local supporters in lobbying members of the Texas legislature and the public for their support in impeaching Governor James Ferguson. Above is the first page in a four-page broadsheet, which they referred to as "Campaign Material," containing information from the WCGG headquarters on how to organize events to spread information. 1917. Image courtesy of Woman's Campaign for Good Government Campaign Material, from the Jane Y. McCallum Papers (AR.E.004), Austin History Center, Austin Public Libraries, Austin, Texas.

OUTLINE OF INFORMATION.

When George the Third and Santa Anna repeatedly violated the natural rights and overran the constitutional protection of our fathers, they refused to endure such tyrrany and, even at the cost of revolution and bloodshed, asserted their constitutional rights like free men. We are in Texas today, again in the presence of tyranny, denying us the rights guaranteed by our constitution. Revolution and bloodshed are not necessary, but it is imperative that the honest, thinking people of Texas rise in their might and through their legislature dethrone the man who has abused the confidence of the people, violated his oath of office, and ignored the constitution and the laws of the state. The following acts of Governor James E. Ferguson are not only just ground for his impeachment and removal from office, but make such impeachment necessary for the honor and welfare of the state.

1. He has violated his oath of office, set aside the Constitution, disobeyed the ruling of the courts, and defied the laws which he has sworn to uphold, to such an extent that the Grand Jury of Travis County has indicted him on account of embezzlement of public funds, and on eight other charges of law breaking.

2. He has been found guilty by the Committee of the House of Representatives of repeated violations of the laws of the state and severely reprimanded by almost unanimous vote of the House. The fact that he was not ordered tried for impeachment then was not due to any lack of evidence of his guilt but to the difficulties of carrying out such proceedings at the very end of a session of the legislature.

3. He has failed to refund a sum of money belonging to the State of Texas which he was found guilty of misapplying to his private use, by the Legislative Committee, in March, and which he promised to refund should the Court so rule. The Court did so rule finally on March 28, 1917, but no part of the money has as yet been paid into the treasury.

4. He has, contrary to the plain mandate of the constitution, laid a ruthless hand upon one after another of our public institutions, including the state library, the asylum at San Antonio, the asylum at Austin, the Gatesville reformatory, the Prairie View Normal School, and the University of Texas, and forced the constitutional boards to do his bidding in removing men whose characters and records for splendid service performed bear no blemish. In their stead, in many cases, were placed men whose chief recommendation was their personal friendship for or political services to the Governor.

5. In spite of the requirement of the Constitution that the state shall have a University of the first class, and the Governor's oath to support the Constitution, and in spite of the provision made by the people's representatives to maintain the University, he has without just cause, vetoed, or attempted to veto, practically the entire appropriation made for the University, and is still doing all the additional damage he can to the State's University by repeating all over the state outrageous charges and statements that have been proven to be utterly false.

In addition to the above unquestionable grounds for impeachment, there are other facts, while perhaps not technical, legal grounds for impeachment, are a no less serious menace to the welfare of the state and make it all the more necessary that Governor Ferguson be impeached and the state relieved of his evil influence:

1. He has delivered in the Capitol at Austin and throughout the state, speeches of such coarseness and vulgarity that decent men and modest women have felt humiliated and outraged that such an example should be set before their children and should appear to the world as a representative leader of Texas civilization.

2. He has not only rendered himself ridiculous by having himself surrounded day and night by a body guard of rangers, but he has seriously injured the reputation of the state in the Nation. Only in recent years have people in the older states begun to get rid of the idea that Texas is a wild frontier state, full of gunmen and dangerous characters. Governor Ferguson's action in going always guarded will result in reviving the old notion that Texas is only half civilized.

3. He has through attempting to close the University given the greatest aid he could possibly give to Germany. The greatest and most pressing needs of America in this war are aviators, engineers, doctors and nurses, experts on food and feeding, experts in chemistry, electricity and physics, and educated officers to lead the men. Yet Governor Ferguson's veto would close the University Aviation School that is sending over 100 aviators a month to France, would shut up the University Engineering Department, the Medical Department, the Departments of Nursing and Domestic Science, close the School of Chemistry, Physics and Electricity and prevent the course in Military Science which last year prepared over 300 University boys for the officers' training school at Leon Springs. We do not say that Governor Ferguson is in the employ of the Kaiser, but if he were we do not see how he could give him any better service than he is giving.

4. He has, in locating the West Texas A. and M. College, so conducted the whole affair as to leave grave doubts in the minds of the citizens of the state as to the legality and fairness of the final decision, and those doubts have been confirmed by affidavits which have been made by other members of the locating board. There is no excuse for conducting important business of the state in such manner.

The above facts make it painfully plain that for the good of Texas, Governor Ferguson should be deprived of the power that he has so shamelessly abused, and should be retired to private life where his bad influence will not be so potent in corrupting the ideals of youth or lowering the political life of the state.

His impeachment is not demanded because of his fight on the University, as he is trying to make the people believe. His abuse of power with regard to the University is only one of a dozen or more violations of his oath of office, of the demands of the Constitution and of the laws of the state, which he is especially obligated to uphold.

While the University is really only incidental, still, because of the fact that Governor Ferguson is trying to becloud the real issue of his moral turpitude and hide behind the University, we wish to correct some of the

The second page of the broadsheet.

numerous false statements that he is circulating concerning the University. It is entirely unnecessary to even bring in the University in order to find sufficient ground for the impeachment of Governor Ferguson, but if any one should bring it in, the following facts will show how shameless are Governor Ferguson's statements:

1. Governor Ferguson states that the University had no auditor until he forced one upon them. As a matter of fact, the University has had an Auditor since 1904, and before that time the President of the Board of Regents acted as Auditor as required by law.

2. Governor Ferguson says that the University finances have been dishonestly managed. The fact is that every cent of money has been expended only by order of the Board of Regents, approved by the University Auditor, by the State Comptroller, and by the State Treasurer, as required by law, so that there was not a possibility of peculation or loss. The books have yearly been audited by a reliable firm of accountants, and publicity given to their itemized report. These reports are right now, and always have been, available to the Governor and all others for reference in the printed report of the Board of Regents. Notwithstanding which fact his slanders continue to this hour.

3. Governor Ferguson says that "dead men" have been carried on the University pay roll. The fact is that no "dead man" has ever been carried on the University pay roll and could not be so carried without collusion between the Board of Regents, the President, the Auditor, and the Comptroller, all of whom have to approve every salary paid. This shameless charge is based upon the fact that the legislature granted and the Regents set aside two salaries to employ two professors. These two professors were never employed because no one could be found competent to fill the places who could be induced to come to Texas. As the men could not be secured, the salaries were not used for them but were reappropriated by the Regents for other important needs as they were authorized to do by the act of the legislature and the ruling of the Attorney General.

4. Governor Ferguson says the University is a rich man's school. The fact is that it is the poor boy's school. Fifty-four per cent of the student body, or more than 1500 boys and girls, worked their way through the University this past year. In previous years many thousands have put themselves through by honorable labor and achieved not only good standing in the student body while there, but places of distinction in the world. The following instances are typical:

S. F. Acree:	Waiter at B. Hall. Now Professor of Organic Chemistry in the University of Wisconsin and Director of Research in the United States Forestry Service.
Lamar Crosby:	Chore and yard boy. Mule-car driver at Austin. Now Professor of Greek in University of Missouri.
Thomas Fletcher:	Chore and yard boy in the home of a University professor. Now State Visitor of Schools of University of Texas.
Nancy Lee Swann:	Office clerk in Woman's Building. Now Baptist Missionary in China.
Annie Gabriel:	General assistant in a private home in Austin. Now Superintendent of the County Hospital in Little Rock, Arkansas.
John H. Keen:	Carpenter; later Psychologist, Dean of Southern Methodist University, Dallas. Now in Federal service at Washington.

These are only a few out of hundreds who have achieved greatly solely through their own efforts at the University.

The poor boy or girl who works his or her way while in the University is just as much respected there as the son of the rich man with his automobile. Only a year or two ago, a boy working his way through the University by serving as sexton of a church, was elected President of the Students' Council, the most honored position within the gift of the student body. At the present time, the President of the Students' Council is a non-fraternity man.

5. Governor Ferguson has repeatedly stated that the University spends $545.00 per year per student. The fact is that the University spent only $276.00 per student. This is, of course, more than elementary education costs, but actually much less than first class university education usually costs. The average cost of university education in the United States is $335.00 per pupil per year; at the University of Virginia it is $592.00; University of Mississippi $502.00; University of Michigan $394.00; University of Iowa $354.00. The Governor made no objection to the appropriation for our A. and M. College and yet the cost there is $449.00 per student, as against $276.00 for the University. We do not make this comparison to criticise the A. and M. College expenditure. We believe they need all they get and wish they could be given more. The figure is given to show the injustice and inconsistency of Governor Ferguson's criticism of the University.

6. Governor Ferguson says the research work of the University consists in attempts to "grow wool on the back of an armadillo." So absurd a misrepresentation indicates such an estimate by him of the gullability and stupidity of his audience, as to be an insult to the intelligence of the people of Texas. If Governor Ferguson had desired to tell the truth, he could have found out about the important and successful investigations that the University is carrying on in the prevention of disease; the use of cottonseed flour, nuts, peanuts and grain sorghum for human food; the use of cotton stalks for paper making; the use of Texas lignites for coal tar, and other fuel and chemical products; the use of various road-building materials, and so on.

7. Governor Ferguson states that in the University each professor has only six students and works only fifteen hours a week. To say that professors work only fifteen hours per week because they teach only fifteen hours per week of class work is as dishonest as it would be to state that a farm wife or housekeeper works only three half hours a day because she serves only three meals a day. Furthermore, instead of having only six students per professor, the University actually has over thirteen per professor. The professors at the College of In-

The third page of the broadsheet.

dustrial Arts have only 12.5 students each; at the A. and M. they have only 10.2 each; and at the Prairie View Negro Normal there are only 8.4 students for each teacher. Why does the Governor object to one teacher for each thirteen white students in the University and not object to one for each 8.4 negro students in Prairie View?

8. The Governor and his henchmen on the Board of Regents have seen fit to attack the Department of Home Economics in the University. Three of his regents voted to abolish the department entirely, and a majority finally did cut the salaries of all the teachers in this department 20% without any excuse and against the recommendation of President Vinson. One member of the Board even stated that "no woman in the world is worth $3000.00 a year," and compared the work of the distinguished women in this department with that of his cook. This inexcusable attack upon woman and upon her work is no more than can be expected from Governor Ferguson and the kind of men he is putting in charge of our state institutions.

This Department of Home Economics was established by the former Board of Regents, six years ago, at the repeated requests of the women of the state in order to furnish for the more than a thousand girls who attend the University each year a course of training to fit them as directly for the important work of womanhood as the various courses fit the men for their work. The extension work, and the teaching, and the investigations of this department have already placed it in the very front rank of such University Departments. Over fifty thousand of its bulletins pertaining to the betterment of home life are sent out on special request each year to eager housewives of Texas. Its speakers and demonstrators have held short courses in all parts of the state, and the scientific investigations of cotton seed flour have been accepted as the standard of the world on this subject. The head of the department was called to Washington by Mr. Hubert C. Hoover to advise with him on the plans for national food conservation. Another professor has been called by the United States Department of Agriculture to carry out scientific investigations in the chemistry of food for the national government, and another to direct conservation work in a Northwestern state. This will indicate that the professors in this department are among the few leaders of the nation in their lines, and yet they have been insulted and are to be driven from the state.

In this unpardonable attack upon the women of the faculty and upon the work of woman, Governor Ferguson and his henchmen upon the Board of Regents have not only shown their low opinion of the value of women and of her work, but have crippled out state in its efforts to meet the demands of the war by depriving the women of the state of their ablest, best educated, and most experienced leaders in the great work of conserving our food resources and building up our manhood resources for the life and death struggle that is before our nation.

Surely it is high time for the men and women of Texas to wake up and to leave no stone unturned until Texas is freed of the man who has so shamelessly abused the power of his office and is bringing such injury and disgrace upon our state.

The fourth page of the broadsheet.

copied. Local workers were only to use it as a guideline for articles or letters. Throughout the latter part of July and through mid-August, Cunningham and League worked sixteen- to eighteen-hour days on the WCGG, antivice, and suffrage campaigns, often keeping those with whom they corresponded in the dark about alliances and activities.[59]

Cunningham sharply reminded an antivice worker, Marion Fisher, who may have been critical of Cunningham's presence in Austin: "We beg to advise you that it is in no sense on account of the University that Mrs. Speer and myself are here working, except incidentally. The real issue is much bigger than that and goes back to the antivice situation, otherwise we would not be here but in the field doing the work, which as you now so pertinently say, we planned to do." Cunningham reminded Fisher that Ferguson had not answered the secretary of war's call for law enforcement regarding moral conditions around the military camps, adding, "If the present effort to impeach Governor Ferguson fails and he is permitted to go Scott free, his example and our negligence will corrupt the morals and lower the standards of generations yet unborn in this state; and, undoubtedly, in the eyes of the Nation, Texas will revert to its former condition of unsafe frontier state."[60]

While Cunningham was careful in her correspondence to separate topics with certain individuals, intermingling occurred with others. Helen Moore, a suffrage worker in Galveston, knew about the dual campaigns and was encouraged to keep the Suffrage Headquarters running and to separately get word out about Ferguson and antivice work. Showing that women's moral influence was vital, Cunningham instructed, "Write as many letters throughout the state, to your personal and Suffrage acquaintances, as possible, urging them to do just as you are doing. They must have letters every day, each one of them, constantly expressing our faith in them and our desire for a better government in Texas." The women were relentless in their campaign.[61]

When the special session of the legislature convened on August 1, the House agreed to conduct a hearing to determine whether impeachment was warranted. The hearing lasted weeks, with Texas women representing large numbers among those crowding the gallery above to hear testimony. While the legislature carried out its duties, late August found Cunningham back in Galveston carrying out antivice work. When the House voted to impeach and declared a trial to be held by the Senate, Gearing wrote to Cunningham, "Half of the fun of the victory is lost however in not having you to gloat over it to me." The fast pace and number of parallel reform activities often meant that in lieu of celebration upon successes, the need to move on to the next thing prevailed.[62]

With the impeachment trial underway in the Senate, Gearing, looking for support, invited Eleanor Brackenridge to come to Austin with her brother, George Brackenridge, to attend the hearings. In his testimony, Ferguson foolishly dismissed the importance of the work by the women in the field of home economics and their contributions toward the war. Likely in an effort to further divide the university community from his rural constituency, the governor doubled his insults by asserting that if one sorority girl could preserve peaches that last six months that he would pay the tuition of two poor girls. It did not help.[63]

By the end of September, the Texas Senate found Ferguson guilty of ten of twenty-one charges against him, ordered removal of Ferguson from the office of governor, and barred him from holding office ever again. Texans resumed their war work. Cunningham and League returned to Galveston to resume antivice and suffrage work. Having been reinstated by the new board of regents that included returning regent George Brackenridge, faculty members Ellis, Mather, Mayes, Cofer, and Gearing returned to teaching at the university. Further, their salaries in the Domestic Economy department were returned to previous levels.[64]

At the end of the 1917 fall semester, Gearing made a final accounting of expenses of the WCGG. The original accounting was sent to Mary Ellis with a copy sent to Cunningham. Because of the generosity of Will Hogg and A. C. Baldwin, the WCGG efforts cost only half of what had been budgeted. Gearing contacted Brackenridge to return the balance, but he instructed her to award it "where it could do the most good." Given that Cunningham had made such a sacrifice in laying aside her antivice and suffrage work, the sum of $947.54 was conveyed to her. An examination of the final accounting prepared by Gearing reveals that the salaries of NAWSA suffrage field workers were paid by WCGG funds. Thus, even NAWSA-sent campaigners even paused their own work to aid in the campaign to oust Ferguson.[65]

Following Ferguson's removal from office in September 1917, Texans worked further to support World War I efforts. University leaders at whom Ferguson had aimed his vitriol so vehemently, by January 1918, worked with federal office holders, military leaders, and college and university administrators across the nation to provide space at the institutions of higher education to train specialists for military work. UT president Vinson offered for UT "to take here 1200 of those vocational students at a time. . . . The engineering department of the university is able to train men along the various lines of engineering, chemistry and particularly in radio work." Also, a UT Reserve Officers' Training Corps was planned. The space, equipment, and instructional ability colleges and universities had readily available meant faster preparation and a significantly reduced cost for the federal government.[66]

In spring 1918, Jim Ferguson attempted to retake the governorship, and again, Cunningham and the Texas woman suffrage network sprang into action. By March 1918, Cunningham and other state suffragists successfully lobbied for Texas women's right to vote in the state's Democratic primary to ensure Ferguson's defeat. Texas subsequently became the first southern state to ratify the federal amendment for full suffrage in June 1919. While the most lasting and measurable way in which Texas women reformers benefited from their efforts in Ferguson's impeachment and continued direct removal from elected office was the furthering of woman suffrage initiatives by state legislators, it was not the only reason women participated. For many, he was a threat to everything they stood for—their children's safety from lack of preparation from war, from lack of pure food, the strength of the state university as a bridge to and bastion of the future, and even a woman's own right to a voice in government.

NOTES

1. For this article's title quotation, see Jane Y. McCallum, *A Texas Suffragist: Diaries and Writings of Jane Y. McCallum*, ed. Janet G. Humphrey (Austin, TX: Ellen C. Temple Press, 1988), 81.

2. Larry D. Hill and Robert A. Calvert, "The University of Texas Extension Services and Progressivism," *Southwestern Historical Quarterly* 86, no. 2 (1982): 233; Minutes of the Board of Regents, June 7, 1909, University of Texas Systems, 462–63, www.utsystem.edu/sites/utsfiles/offices/board-of-regents/board-meetings/board-minutes/1909minutes.pdf.

3. Minutes of the Board of Regents, May 31, 1910, University of Texas Systems (hereafter cited as Minutes of the Board of Regents), 30, http://www.utsystem.edu/sites/utsfiles/offices/board-of-regents/board-meetings/board-minutes/1910minutes.pdf.

4. Minutes of the Board of Regents, June 11, 1910, 39, www.utsystem.edu/sites/utsfiles/offices/board-of-regents/board-meetings/board-minutes/1910minutes.pdf.

5. Minutes of the Board of Regents, October 22, 1910, 77, www.utsystem.edu/sites/utsfiles/offices/board-of-regents/board-meetings/board-minutes/1910minutes.pdf.

6. Minutes of the Board of Regents, March 29, 1912 www.utsystem.edu/sites/utsfiles/offices/board-of-regents/board-meetings/board-minutes/1912minutes.pdf; Minutes of the Board of Regents, April 12, 1913, 289, www.utsystem.edu/sites/utsfiles/offices/board-of-regents/board-meetings/board-minutes/1913minutes.pdf.

7. Farmers Institute, July 1917, Bulletins 53–63, 137, Texas Department of Agriculture, digitized by Cornell University, retrieved by GoogleBooks; Girls Canning Club Report, Farmer's Institute Bulletin, July 1917, Bulletins 53–63, 129, Texas Department of Agriculture, digitized by Cornell University, retrieved by GoogleBooks.

8. George H. Nash, *The Life of Herbert Hoover: Master of Emergencies, 1917–1918* (New York: W. W. Norton, 1996).

9. "Tells Women They Must Conserve Food," *Statesman*, May 3, 1917.

10. "Defense Council Closes Meeting," *Statesman*, June 2, 1917.

11. "Editorial," *Austin Statesman*, April 13, 1917; McCallum, *Texas Suffragist*, 81.

12. "Mexicans Leave Texas for Fear of Conscription," *Statesman*, May 24, 1917.

13. Nash, *Life of Herbert Hoover*.

14. *Alcalde*, 744, UT Memorabilia Collection, folder 1, box 4P162, Dolph Briscoe Center for American History, University of Texas at Austin; "Court of Inquiry Fails to Reveal Any Vice in Austin," *Statesman*, February 23, 1915; *Missionary Review of the World*, January–December, 1914, Funk and Wagnalls, New York. Accessed through GoogleBooks.

15. Farmers Institute, Women's Division, July 1917, Bulletins 53–63, 153, Texas Department of Agriculture, digitized by Cornell University, retrieved by GoogleBooks; Austin Woman Suffrage Association 1915–1916 Membership Ledger, folder 12, box 31, Jane Y. McCallum Papers, Austin History Center, Austin Public Library (hereafter cited as McCallum Papers). Jane McCallum became president of the Austin Woman Suffrage Association in fall 1915. McCallum, *Texas Suffragist*, 37.

16. "Women Pledge Aid," *Statesman*, April 24, 1917; Stacy A. Cordery, "Pennybacker, Anna J. Hardwick," *Handbook of Texas Online*, https://www.tshaonline.org/handbook/about-handbook.

17. Cunningham to Carrie Chapman Catt, June 20, 1917, folder 8, box 1, Minnie Fisher Cunningham Papers, University of Houston Library Archives, Houston, Texas (hereafter cited as Cunningham Papers); Zoe Aubrey to Cunningham, June 15, 2017, folder 7, box 6, Cunningham Papers.

18. Farmers Institute, Women's Division, July 1917, Bulletins 53–63, 155, Texas Department of Agriculture, digitized by Cornell University, retrieved by Google-

Books; Cunningham to Carrie Chapman Catt, June 20, 1917, folder 8, box 1, Cunningham Papers; Zoe Aubrey to Cunningham, June 15, 2017, folder 7, box 6, Cunningham Papers.

19. Laura Hart to Minnie Fisher Cunningham, Report from Resolution Committee, Texas Women's Anti-Vice Association, June 8, 1917, folder 10, box 6, Cunningham Papers.

20. Judith N. McArthur and Harold L. Smith, *Minnie Fisher Cunningham: A Suffragist's Life in Politics* (New York: Oxford University Press, 2003), 55–59.

21. "Beer Fight," *Houston Daily Post*, May 29, 1918.

22. Ouida F. Nalle, *The Fergusons of Texas* (San Antonio, TX: Naylor, 1946), 83.

23. Testimony of Robert. E. Vinson, Impeachment Hearing, House Journal, 33, digitized by New York Public Library, retrieved through GoogleBooks online.

24. McCallum, *Texas Suffragist*, 63–64.

25. "Final Veto Raises New Question," *Statesman*, June 7, 1917.

26. Pennybacker to Cunningham, June 8, 1917, folder 5, box 5, Cunningham Papers.

27. Telephone Records of the Ex-Students' Association, box VF2/B.a., UT President's Office Records 1907–1968, Dolph Briscoe Center for American History, University of Texas at Austin; Pennybacker to Cunningham, telegram, June 8, 1917, folder 5, box 5, Cunningham Papers.

28. "300 Will Attend Varsity Meeting from This City," *Statesman*, June 14, 1917; McCallum, *Texas Suffragist*, 81.

29. Telephone records of A. Caswell Ellis, folder 1, box 2P30, Alexander Caswell Ellis Papers, Dolph Briscoe Center for American History, University of Texas at Austin (hereafter cited as Ellis Papers).

30. Cunningham to Dear Madame President, June 11, 1917, folder 25, box 7, Cunningham Papers.

31. Ellis to McAllister, June 11, 1917, folder 2, box 2P374, Ellis Papers.

32. "Sayers Calls on Texans to Rescue Their University," *Statesman* June 9, 1917; "Ask Legislature to Save University," *Statesman* June 17, 1917; "Second Meet Is Called," *Statesman*, June 10, 1917; Marilyn McAdams Sibley, *George W. Brackenridge: Maverick Philanthropist* (Austin: University of Texas Press, 1973), 234.

33. McCallum, *Texas Suffragist*, 81.

34. Cunningham to Ellis, June 18, 1917, folder 25, box 7, Cunningham Papers.

35. Minutes of the Board of Regents, July 12, 1917, www.utsystem.edu/sites/utsfiles/offices/board-of-regents/board-meetings/board-minutes/1917minutes.pdf; Minutes of the Board of Regents, July 12, 1917, www.utsystem.edu/sites/utsfiles/offices/board-of-regents/board-meetings/board-minutes/1917minutes.pdf; David Gracy II, Historian of Alice and George W. Littlefield, e-mail to Kay Arnold, July 7, 2015.

36. McCallum, *Texas Suffragist*, 86.

37. Sayers to Pennybacker, July 24, 1917, folder 3, box 2m14, Anna J. Penny-

backer Papers, Dolph Briscoe Center for American History, University of Texas at Austin, Austin, Texas (hereafter cited as Pennybacker Papers).

38. Cunningham to Catt, July 31, 1917, folder 8, box 1, Cunningham Papers.

39. Knox to Pennybacker, July 24, 1917, folder 3, box 2M14, Pennybacker Papers; Brackenridge to Gearing, August 22, 1917, folder 1, box 4P162, UT Memorabilia Collection, Briscoe Center for American History, University of Texas at Austin, Austin, Texas (hereafter cited as UT Memorabilia Collection).

40. "An Appeal to the Friends of the University of Texas by the Women of Texas," folder 1, box 4P162, UT Memorabilia Collection; Curtis to Ellis, June 14, 1917, folder 1, box 2P30 Ellis Papers; Cunningham to Dear Suffragist, July 21, 1917, folder 1, box 4P162, UT Memorabilia Collection; Cunningham to Aubrey, July 9, 1917, folder 7, box 6, Cunningham Papers. This is an example of the discord between the two suffrage organizations.

41. Form, folder 1, box 4P162, UT Memorabilia Collection; McArthur and Smith, *Minnie Fisher Cunningham*, 54.

42. Knox to Pennybacker, August 5, 1917, folder 3, box 2M14, Pennybacker Papers; List of Legislators and Notes throughout box 5 and box 6, Cunningham Papers.

43. "Summer Students Hear John Brady," *Statesman*, July 24, 1917.

44. Ibid.

45. Edith Hinkle League to Lavinia Engle, August 7, 1917, folder 8, box 63, McCallum Papers.

46. Jane Y. McCallum, "Activities of Women in Texas Politics," in *Texas Democracy: A Centennial History of Politics and Personalities of the Democratic Party 1836—1936*, 2 vols., ed. Frank Carter Adams (Austin, TX: Democratic Historical Association, 1937), 1: 475, 476.

47. McCallum, "Activities of Women in Texas Politics," 476.

48. "Farmers of Texas in Session," *Statesman*, July 25, 1917.

49. "Ferguson Addresses Farmers," *Statesman*, July 26, 1917.

50. Farmer's Institute, Women's Division, July 1917, Bulletins 53–63, Texas Department of Agriculture, digitized by Cornell University, retrieved by GoogleBooks.

51. Ibid.

52. Ibid.; "Davis Declares Political Speeches No Part of Institute," *Statesman*, July 28, 1917.

53. "List of things accomplished, July 25, 1917," folder 1, box 4P162, UT Memorabilia Collection, box 4P162.

54. Campaign Material, folder 1, box 4P162, UT Memorabilia Collection.

55. Ibid.

56. Ibid.

57. For examples of correspondence and reports reflecting the socioeconomic diversity of the contemporary UT student body, see folder 1, box 2P30, Ellis Pa-

pers, and box 2J314 and box 2J315, William Clifford Hogg Papers, Dolph Briscoe Center for American History, University of Texas at Austin.

58. Campaign Material, folder 1, box 4P162, UT Memorabilia Collection.

59. Correspondence, folder 9, box 6, Cunningham Papers; Campaign Material, folder 1, box 4P162, UT Memorabilia Collection.

60. Cunningham to Fisher, August 2, 1917, folder 9, box 6, Cunningham Papers.

61. Cunningham to Moore, (undated), folder 1, box 20, McCallum Papers.

62. Gearing to Cunningham, August 28, 1917, folder 7, box 6, Cunningham Papers; Edith Hinkle League to Lillian Batjer, August 13, 1917, folder 7, box 6, Cunningham Papers.

63. Gearing to Brackenridge, September 7, 1917, folder 1, box 4P162, UT Memorabilia Collection; "Governor Called on to Reveal the Source of Loan," *Statesman,* August 21, 1917.

64. Minutes of the Board of Regents, September 1917, www.utsystem.edu/sites/utsfiles/offices/board-of-regents/board-meetings/board-minutes/1917minutes.pdf.

65. Gearing to Mary Ellis, December 21, 1917, box 2P30, folder 1, Ellis Papers; Gearing to Cunningham, December 21, 1917, folder 7, box 6, Cunningham Papers; Catt to Cunningham, September 26, 1917, folder 8, box 1, Cunningham Papers.

66. "Editorial," *Austin Statesman*, January 20, 1918; "Editorial," *Austin Statesman*, May 15, 1918; "Editorial," *Austin Statesman*, September 8, 1918.

3

"Without Us, It Is Ferguson with a Plurality"

Woman Suffrage and Anti-Ferguson Politics

Rachel M. Gunter

James Edward Ferguson had a complicated history with woman suffrage from the beginning of his political career. In 1914, Texas Woman Suffrage Association (TWSA) president Annette Finnigan wrote the candidates for governor asking, "if elected, [will you] favor a submission to the voters of the question of woman suffrage as a constitutional amendment?" Ferguson evaded the question. His campaign manager replied with the opening speech of the campaign, which failed to mention votes for women. Ferguson won election with William Pettus Hobby as lieutenant governor. This gave Finnigan some reason for hope, because unlike Ferguson, Hobby replied to Finnigan's inquiry in the affirmative. However, Finnigan remained displeased with the avoidance from Ferguson. She heard rumors that Ferguson at least supported putting the issue to a vote. In 1915, she wrote an acquaintance asking if hearsay about Ferguson being pro-suffrage was true. No response was forthcoming. Again, Finnigan wrote the new governor, and Ferguson ignored the request.[1]

Ferguson was a populist, conservative, and "wet" (antiprohibition) Democrat. He was supported by a coalition of struggling farmers and powerful conservatives, including former US senator Joseph Weldon Bailey. The political bosses of the Rio Grande Valley also supported Ferguson, and they effectively controlled the Mexican American and Mexican immigrant voters in their area. Citizenship was not a requirement to vote in Texas. Immigrants, or "legal resident aliens," obtained the right to vote by filing their intention to become citizens. In South Texas, the political machine bosses controlled these voters. Historian Evan Anders describes "boss rule" as a "semifeudalistic system" in which Mexican Americans or Mexican immigrants were given some care in exchange for control of their social and political lives. These voters were economically dependent, and many did not understand the English language, democratic elections, or the workings of the Texas or American governments. Anders maintains, "All of the bosses systematically violated the election laws of the state by paying the poll taxes of their Mexican American followers, recruiting ineligible aliens to vote, marking the ballots of illiterate voters, and tampering with the results when necessary." The violation of these laws concerned progressives, who sought to purify elections in part by eliminating corruption. Additionally, immigrant workers typically voted against prohibition and woman suffrage. This further irritated the woman suffragists who were already displeased that noncitizens had the right they were fighting for.[2] When the Texas Democratic party divided over these issues, party leaders shifted the balance of power by further enfranchising the most ideologically attractive groups to break the tie and by further disenfranchising those who disagreed.

The Texas Woman Suffrage Association changed its name to the Texas Equal Suffrage Association (TESA) in 1916, the same year its president, and Finnigan political protégé, Minnie Fisher Cunningham first battled Governor Ferguson. Elected the year prior as TESA's president, Cunningham led the state suffrage association in asking for a woman suffrage plank in the Texas Democratic Party's platform. That plank was defeated when Bailey denounced woman suffrage "as an open invitation to the federal government to force black voting rights on the South." Conservative politicians routinely used the specter of black voting to argue against woman suffrage, but black voting had been severely restricted at the turn of the century by the rise of the all-white primary and the poll tax. As black women would be subject to the same restrictions that kept black men from voting, black voter participation after woman suffrage was not a threat to the political establishment. Ferguson finally made his stance on the suffrage issue publicly known. He and Bailey wrote the platform, taking a states' rights stand on suffrage and prohibition and declaring their "unalterable opposition" to a federal amendment for either cause. One supporter consoled Cunningham, arguing that Bailey and Ferguson's highhanded tactics would only bring about votes for women and prohibition sooner.[3]

That June, the National Democratic Convention met in Saint Louis

Texas suffragists participated in the "Golden Lane" demonstration as part of the lobby efforts pressing for a woman suffrage plank in the Democratic Party platform. The National American Woman Suffrage Association organized the demonstration on the steps of the old City Art Museum (Wayman Crow Museum) and running down the street in Saint Louis, Missouri, during the Democratic National Convention in June 1916. Photo courtesy of Swekosky-Notre Dame College Collection, Missouri History Museum, Saint Louis, Missouri.

and the National American Woman Suffrage Association (NAWSA) demonstrated for a plank advocating votes for women. Suffragists lined the street in a parade wearing white dresses with yellow sashes and parasols. While the convention did not accept the plank NAWSA advocated, they did endorse a weaker plank encouraging states to act for suffrage. Ferguson supported a version that would have left suffrage to the states without endorsing votes for women in any way. He expressed his disdain for the successful plank in a thundering antisuffrage speech. One Dallas newspaper reported:

Suffragists in the galleries hissed Ferguson roundly when he was outspoken in denouncing the ballot for women. Governor Ferguson declared it was not because the minority loves women less, but that they loved her more, that they made the dissenting report. He declared their desire was to protect women from the corruption of politics and politicians. Senator Stone replied on behalf of the majority, declaring that the Texan "made a man of straw and demolished him." He insisted that the Governor misconstrued the whole situation.

Cunningham responded to Ferguson by organizing an impromptu protest. She led a parade in front of the convention hotel with a Texas flag in mourning draped with strips of black cloth that she had cut from one of her black dresses shortly before the demonstration.[4]

A fellow clubwoman wrote Cunningham that Ferguson's fight only confirmed how hopeless the cause was in Texas. She further decried the fact the Ferguson would likely sail to reelection. With this in mind, Cunningham embarked on an automobile tour with NAWSA suffrage organizer Lavinia Engle through "wet" counties in South Texas. They stumped for woman suffrage and encouraged voters to oust Ferguson in the primary. Cunningham wrote to one supporter, "You will have my earnest and prayerful assistance in the neck wringing that you propose Bailey, Ferguson, and Henry and Culberson. Mercy, let me at them!"[5]

Texas suffragists were livid after Ferguson's speech at the DNC, and their indignation made great headlines for the news. "Suffragists say Ferguson Stand 'Cheap Politics,'" said one article, which quoted Dallas suffrage leader Tex Armstrong, saying that the governor made "a laughing stock of himself" in Saint Louis. A Dallas headline announced, "We Will Nail Ferguson to the Cross Declares Advocate of Suffrage." A Galveston paper's article titled "[Suffrage speaker] Declares Ferguson Starts His Funeral," quoted Engle, "We raised a monument for Bailey, and now that Ferguson has started his own funeral, we will get a monument for him. And we shall not shed any crocodile tears, either." Even with the fight from TESA, both Ferguson and Hobby were reelected in 1916 as expected. Cunningham wrote that TESA "had done all we humanly could to punish Mr. Ferguson for his unwarranted behavior in St. Louis." Texas suffragists never forgot nor forgave Ferguson's performance at the 1916 convention as they continued to advocate for votes for women.[6]

At the post-primary state Democratic convention in August 1916, Cunningham secured a hearing before the platform committee. A supporter wrote Cunningham that the Ferguson crowd would dominate the convention and offered her this advice: "when you inlist [*sic*] in a war of this kind it should not be for one battle or for two battles, but for the full term of the war." Cunningham proved to be a worthy adversary in Ferguson's war. Knowing the likelihood of defeat at this juncture, she pushed forward anyway. Her plan was to get a politician friendly to suffrage to write a minority report. "Find a hero who [would] head a minority report," she noted, "we aren't beaten yet." She reported a few days later, "It was a very courteous and *apparently* successful hearing. BUT the business was then turned over to a small sub-committee, who failed to report Suffrage. I suppose there must always be a 'first' times before success is ours, but they had just as well give it first as last, because we are going to *have* Suffrage in Texas. That is settled!" For Cunningham, the convention only emboldened her desire to "organize, educate and besiege, as patiently as in us lies." It turned out that she did not have to be as patient as she anticipated.[7]

In 1917, Ferguson embroiled himself in controversy over his attempts to remove the University of Texas president, Robert L. Vinson, and faculty members he viewed as political enemies, to stack the board of regents with men loyal to Ferguson, and the governor's veto of university appropriations. Texas suffragists watched Ferguson's battle with the university unfold, and they sought ways to limit his power while protecting or even furthering their own interests. Suffragist Elizabeth Herndon Potter even suggested to Will Hogg—Texas progressive Democrat and leader of the UT Ex-Students' Association—the idea of allowing women to serve on the board of regents to counter Ferguson appointees. Hogg replied that it "might be well to back up a bill asking for eligibility of women on all public boards."[8]

In June, Ferguson offered to allow the university funding on the condition that Vinson and another employee resign. Embattled UT professor Alexander Caswell Ellis, married to Austin suffrage leader Mary Heard Ellis, was a suffrage supporter himself. Upon hearing of Ferguson's offer, Ellis concluded, "We must have got his Titanic Majesty considerably uneasy . . . he and his henchmen have offered us two compromises, both of which were such that no gentleman could accept, or would offer." Cunningham heard rumor of the deal, but she immediately wrote Ellis advising against it:

> Just for a minute [your letter] gave me the "cold shivers," that remark of yours about the opposition forces trying to set the University out of danger and getting the dogs called off of Ferguson. Indeed it would be a crime against civilization, and I am strong for not letting it happen; however, I do not think there is any danger of anybody on our side being willing to stop anywhere short of impeachment.⁹

With Ellis's help, Cunningham and clubwomen throughout the state organized the Woman's Campaign for Good Government (WCGG) to educate Texans about the university situation and to lobby the state legislature to go forward with impeachment proceedings. Only some of these clubwomen were suffragists, but all were opposed to Ferguson's war on the university. When Ellis wrote thanking her, she replied, "You see it is the same 'gang' fighting the University that the Texas Suffragists have been going down in defeat before for a number of years. . . . We take pleasure in doing this for the just cause and against our common foe." Ellis later noted his colleagues' pleasant surprise at the response of Texas women: "It is time the men were learning what a power the organized women of Texas are."¹⁰

In July, Vinson sent Ellis a letter of termination, noting the board of regents was ending the employment of multiple faculty members contrary to his recommendations. University supporters were furious. One wrote in response to Ellis, "Doubtless, they think to drive Dr. Vinson to resign, I do pray he will hold out and at least save the University from such a president as they and their dictator would select. Dr. Vinson's greatest service to the State, just now is to hold on."¹¹

State suffrage leaders sprang into action. Cunningham sent out a circular on TESA letterhead to her membership, arguing that "the only hope left for the University is to get the Legislature in called session within the next three or four weeks." She asked suffragists to work to get as many letters as possible sent to Texas Speaker of the House Franklin Oliver Fuller, urging him to call a special session of the legislature to investigate Ferguson. She advised women to write to university regents, asking if the Department of Home Economics was singled out as part of a "German plot" in the midst of World War I. TESA also focused on reaching rural voters with circulars, challenging Ferguson among the struggling farmers who were some of his most ardent supporters.¹²

On July 23, Speaker Fuller called a special session of the legislature to convene August 1, although only the governor had the legal authority to call a session. With legislators gathering in Austin, Ferguson issued his own call, which made the session legal. Cunningham wrote Speaker Fuller thanking him and offering the support of TESA. When newspapers reported which local legislators did not plan to attend the called session, Cunningham wrote them personally to beg that they get to Austin and help in the fight against Ferguson. Cunningham also urged local suffragists to convince their representatives to attend. She asked one woman to gather as many other Methodist women as possible and go to ask their representative as a fellow Christian to get himself to Austin. She asked the women not to use Cunningham's name, but to appear as individuals representing their own interests. She also urged them to act quickly as TESA was concerned that not enough legislators would attend the session to meet quorum. Cunningham's tactics depended on the representative. Sometimes she appealed to a legislator's religious piety. Sometimes she advised women to present the session as a war measure, arguing that a corrupt governor would contribute to an ineffective war effort.[13]

After some confusion over whether they were responding to the Speaker's or the governor's call for a special session, the legislature convened and on August 6, 1918, began investigating the thirteen charges against Ferguson presented by Speaker Fuller. The House hired M. M. Crane as its counsel. Cunningham issued circulars during the investigation urging continued letter-writing campaigns. She instructed women around the state to "systemize your work for the impeachment of the Governor by arranging that *no* day shall pass without [your representative] getting ten letters from home on this subject, expressing the sincere belief of the women in his integrity, and beseeching him to stand fact for ridding Texas of the menace of this man." She again cautioned the women not to publicize the campaign. The letters would prove more persuasive if they appeared to be spontaneous.[14]

Ferguson eventually took the stand and testified that he had paid his debt to the Temple State Bank after appealing to friends who helped raise the necessary $156,000. On cross-examination, Crane asked Ferguson who had given the governor the money. Ferguson refused to answer. Crane returned to the issue on August 21, and Ferguson again refused to comment. Crane appealed to representative E. R. Bryan to force Ferguson. Bryan sided with Crane, and the legislature upheld the ruling 70–56. Still, Ferguson refused. Cunningham became concerned that fifty-six votes against the ruling would be fifty-six votes against impeachment. She urged supporters in those representatives' counties to lobby their districts' legislators, "Is there [no] way in which you can bring pressure to bear upon this man to make him see the error of his ways. . . . It is most essential that we should have the vote of every man possible, as the larger it is in the House the greater the moral effect upon the Senate; and if the state does not get rid of this man now, no telling what vengeance he may be able to reek [sic] upon it."[15]

TESA continued lobbying representatives to impeach Ferguson, while keeping a watchful eye on which way each representative appeared to be leaning. Hopeful suffragists anxiously followed the trial, and TESA secretary Edith League kept them informed. By relaying the details of the process, she emphatically urged Texas suffragists to keep pressure on the elected officials from their districts.[16]

The House met in an evening session for final arguments and returned a bill of impeachment on August 22, 1917. A board of managers drew up the articles of impeachment, which then were presented to the Senate, and Ferguson was automatically suspended from office. With Ferguson at least temporarily out, some of his damage to the university was remedied. The Senate declined to confirm two of his appointees to the board of regents and instead confirmed Hobby-appointee George Brackenridge. Acting Governor Hobby also called a second special session of the legislature to move forward with Ferguson's trial. Shortly thereafter, Vinson wrote Ellis that the board rescinded the action ending his and his colleagues' employment.[17]

The House again hired Crane to serve as prosecutor for the trial before the Senate, which began August 30. A university supporter concluded to Ellis, "It now looks like they have 'Him' where the 'wool is short.'" In the Senate, Ferguson again testified on his own behalf, even calling upon God to strike him dead if he were lying. He refused to provide information about the $156,000 loan, even when the Senate voted 23–7 to force his response. After frustrating efforts to make him name his financial backers, Ferguson delivered his defense's closing remarks, "There isn't a thing in the articles that can impeach me." On September 22, 1917, the Senate convicted Ferguson on ten articles of impeachment. However, they still had to deliver a judgment. They could remove Ferguson from office or go further and bar him from ever holding public office in Texas. Fearing the harsher judgment, and although he swore he would rather face impeachment a thousand times than resign, Ferguson submitted a letter of resignation before the Senate took its final vote. The Senate announced its judgment, removing Ferguson and disqualifying him from holding any "office of honor, trust or profit under the state of Texas." Ferguson maintained the judgment did not apply to him as he had resigned instead of being convicted.[18]

Either way, Ferguson was out of office, making the fight for woman suffrage a little easier. The new governor previously expressed some vague support for a referendum for the cause. Suffragists had reason to be hopeful. Cunningham wrote to Potter in DC, "Isn't it a great day for Texas? Some time when I see you, I will give you the story of this summer's work!" In an earlier correspondence, Cunningham summed up the summer's work against Ferguson:

> The women of Texas are maintaining a headquarters here [in Austin], very quietly, and conducting an education campaign designed to react upon the Legislature in great many counties in the state.... We distributed about one hundred thousand of the dodgers, and close to one to two thousand of the folders. These have been placed in the hands of interested individuals with a personal letter asking them to follow instructions. You may imagine the amount of work this has meant but we feel fully repaid by some of the results. Please understand this is confidential information.[19]

TESA and its membership had also spent the summer supporting the war effort by selling war bonds, working for food preservation, and establishing white zones around military camps. Cunningham even left Austin to visit Waco on antivice work in the middle of the impeachment proceedings, because she felt both the WCGG work to impeach Ferguson and the war work were necessary for suffrage success. When the WCGG ran a positive balance at the end of their campaign, they donated the $947.54 to one of Cunningham's causes in order to thank her for her efforts and to make up for the time she spent away from those causes.[20]

Despite being pulled in so many directions, Cunningham never stopped fighting for woman suffrage. That winter, Ellis wrote NAWSA that he and Cunningham planned to blanket the state with pro-suffrage editorials in every newspaper to encourage Senator Charles A. Culberson to support the federal suffrage amendment when it went before Congress. As suffragists continued to lobby the president of the United States, Woodrow Wilson, the political landscape took a surprising turn back in Texas. Ferguson ignored the impeachment and verdict and announced his candidacy for governor; he ran against Hobby. This kind of split was dangerous for Texas Democrats. With the party split so evenly, a small faction could decide the victor. The party enacted voter restrictions in the 1890s and early 1900s to prevent threats from third-party groups like Populists and limit the voting rights of black Texans, but this time the threat came from within the party. As Texas was a one-party state, the Democratic primary was the election that mattered. Ferguson was now solidly anti–woman suffrage. Hobby's views were less clear and certainly less public. The split between the two governors reflected the larger split within the Texas Democratic Party between progressive, dry Democrats who supported prohibition and conservative, wet Democrats who were against it. A splinter group would cast the deciding vote between the two factions.[21]

Watching from Washington, DC, Potter expressed her faith in Cunningham: "Thank God you belong to Texas—that benighted land of Ferguson." Cunningham and TESA watched the campaign closely, even secretly subscribing to the *Ferguson Forum*, the weekly populist newspaper published by Ferguson. League informed Potter, "We subscribe in the office boy's name, but this is CONFIDENTIAL. Gives us a clew [*sic*] of what he is up to. Of course you know he is declaring for a third as Governor!! Do not grow alarmed."[22]

Amid the wet-dry split within the party, Carrie Chapman Catt's "Winning Plan" worked its magic in Texas, as Cunningham brilliantly exploited the rift between Ferguson and Hobby. Catt instructed suffragists to exploit the weaknesses of one-party states to achieve partial suffrage measures. In Texas, that meant primary suffrage, the ability to vote in party primaries, which the legislature had the power to grant.[23] The Texas Democratic Party had disenfranchised groups that threatened its political power in the past, but Cunningham urged party leaders instead to enfranchise women to counter the threat of pro-Ferguson voters in the Democratic primary.

Shortly after Ferguson announced his candidacy, Cunningham wrote dry representative Charles B. Metcalfe. She promised to deliver the women's vote for Hobby's reelection if Metcalfe would get a primary suffrage bill enacted. She informed him that TESA's board had resolved to put all their power behind Hobby, should he submit the bill, as a special session of the congress could only address matters brought before it by the governor. She also noted that all of the candidates, except Ferguson, were pro-suffrage, and if Hobby would not support the bill, the women would not support him. This was a quid pro quo agreement, primary suffrage in exchange for votes. Cunningham warned Metcalfe, "Without us, it is Ferguson with a plurality." A hesitant Metcalfe wrote Cunningham that he would be able to call on the governor but asked if she was sure she had the votes to reelect Hobby.[24]

TESA did not simply rely on Metcalfe to seal the deal. Cunningham personally visited Hobby as well. She also wrote to one of his close advisors asking for him to help sway the governor. Additionally, to further pressure the governor, Potter was tasked with getting a letter from President Wilson to Hobby endorsing the bill. The usually unabashedly racist Potter wrote Cunningham, "See that no emphasis is laid on 'white supremacy' or that white Democratic women *only* will get a vote. It seems *that* two or three Repub senators are very touchy over the way the South disfranchises the colored man through its primary system." NAWSA feared a suffrage campaign on the state level could hurt the chances of the federal amendment. Undue attention to the all-white primary in Texas could sway Republican congressmen representing other states to vote against the federal suffrage amendment.[25]

Potter got the endorsement from President Wilson, but there was something amiss. The letter contained the phrase "to the states," which could have raised a states' rights debate instead of helping the bill. Potter returned the letter to the president and anxiously awaited the weekend for his reply. With the new letter in hand, she wrote Cunningham,

> I have *furnished* the little special Texas job of getting the "favorable expression from the President." It made me very nervous to give back the first letter! And ask Mr. President to please revise it so it didn't sound so states-rightsey—but this *is* a secret you must keep. I nearly died for fear the press or other great affairs of the president which must take precedence would make the letter come too late to do you any good.

The letter from Wilson to Hobby was read into the record of the Texas legislature. The bill passed and Hobby signed it on March 26, 1918. Texas women could participate in all primary elections and nominating conventions.[26]

The primary suffrage bill appealed to progressive Texas Democrats for many reasons. By enfranchising women in primary elections, Democrats took advantage of the restrictions to black voting presented by the all-white primary. White women were enfranchised partially by a law that did not mention race and yet stood very little chance of meaningfully enlarging the black vote. Cunningham noted that because of the all-white primary, primary suffrage "'call[ed] the bluff' of those who resent the negro vote"; politicians who claimed that woman suffrage would only enhance black voting.[27]

Woman suffrage was strategically useful to progressive Democrats. They believed that young men would vote progressive, but Texas men were volunteering or being drafted into military service for World War I. The women's vote helped replace the soldiers' vote. Progressive Democrats had been trying unsuccessfully to break the hold of boss rule in South Texas by making citizenship a requirement for voting, but they lacked the votes to do so. Allowing women primary suffrage tested how they would vote and in what numbers, while also countering the votes of Mexican and German immigrants in the primary. The South Texas political bosses opposed votes for women and did not register or encourage female immigrants under their influence to vote. Most importantly, allowing white women to vote prevented other groups from being the deciding factor in the party split, and white women were seen as preferable to black or brown voters who might otherwise decide the election.

As the campaign revved up, Ferguson publicly addressed the partial enfranchisement of Texas women:

> Don't you understand me, though, that I have succumbed to the passions of the hour, that I am taking any back water now, simply because the Legislature has made it possible for the ladies to vote. But more than three years ago, when the politicians of Texas were playing hide and seek with that great question, when you could not get them to give an honest expression to the good ladies upon that question, in more than four public speeches, at four different places in Texas, one principally in Waco, I declared that if the women wanted to vote, let them vote; that if women wanted more power you might just as well give it to her, because she was going to have it any way. But I said that I wanted the women to decide the question. I did not want to . . . lead her against her will to the ballot box. . . . Understand, when I say "woman" I mean that in a democratic sense. I mean the great majority of women. I do not mean these women who are running around over the country making woman suffrag-

ists *foot and block*. . . . I am talking, as I say, in a democratic sense, about the great majority of the women, not the favored few, that class of women who would rather raise trouble than to raise a family.[28]

Ferguson was a consummate politician. He hid behind the idea that he would support woman suffrage if women proved they wanted it. However, women who wanted and worked for the vote disqualified themselves from being the type of women Ferguson would grant suffrage. In contrast, the Hobby campaign published fliers instructing women how, when, and where to vote, reiterating that Hobby gave woman the vote, Ferguson fought it, and reminding them of Ferguson's actions in Saint Louis. The war of words got heated. Ferguson argued against his detractors, "They say that Ferguson was indicted, but so was Jesus Christ." In response, the Hobby campaign pointed out that Pontius Pilate found nothing wrong with Jesus, which was not true of Ferguson. One senator introduced Hobby by comparing him to Moses. The Ferguson campaign replied, "According to the 25th chapter of the Leviticus, Moses was a socialist, ruled forty years and never reached the promised land."[29]

Behind the scenes of the campaigns, Cunningham anticipated a legal challenge to the primary suffrage law. Supporters wrote warning her of danger, "We hear persistent rumors, as no doubt you have, that at the last minute the Ferguson forces will go into the courts and by way of injunction attempt to prevent the women from participating in the primaries." Cunningham's solution was a Legal Defense Committee comprised of pro-suffrage attorneys willing to defend the law pro bono. In July, T. N. Jones wrote Cunningham that he was concerned about the outcome of injunction proceedings if they were submitted before a Ferguson appointee in Tarrant County. He conferred with Crane, the attorney who prosecuted Ferguson, and they suggested that Judge Frank A. Williams lead TESA's defense of the law. Cunningham appealed to Williams, who accepted the position.[30]

Cunningham sent telegrams to all of the proposed committee members requesting their counsel. She was assured quickly of their services. Speer replied, "This partial franchise is only half a loaf (war bread at that) and I am extremely anxious that it not be taken away from the women upon any pretext; it is a weapon by which they will be able to demand and receive the full franchise in a little while; and I for one am anxious to see them wield this weapon for all it is worth." By mid-July, Cunningham had put together a formidable defense.[31]

Cunningham informed the Hobby campaign about the Legal Defense Committee. As requested, J. A. Elkins of the Hobby campaign lent his services. He believed the challenge to the bill would come after the election, seeking to have the women's votes thrown out as unconstitutional. The committee organized a meeting at the Hotel Galvez in Galveston, Texas, on July 20, 1918. They drafted a press statement, effectively informing Ferguson and his allies that defenses were ready should they try a last-minute or postelection challenge to the law. Crane also issued his opinion to Texas newspapers on Ferguson's ineligibility for office.[32]

Legal defenses were in place, but for the primary suffrage deal to remain successful, Texas suffragists had to deliver a large bloc of votes to Hobby. It was not just their reputation on the line. If Ferguson won, he could have overturned primary suffrage as easily as it was passed. It was an ideal victory for a one-party state, but also an easily reversible one. Additionally, Ferguson opposed the federal woman suffrage amendment, nicknamed the "Susan B. Anthony Amendment," which subsequently passed Congress and moved on to the states for individual ratification. For Texas to be one of the four crucial southern states to ratify the amendment, suffragists had to carry Hobby to a win.

The primary suffrage law exempted women from the poll tax in 1918, but it required women living in towns of 10,000 people or more to register. Additionally, women were subject to a literacy test hidden within the primary suffrage law. It called for women to appear "personally, at the office of the tax collector ... [and] personally fill out, with her own hand, in duplicate, or upon a form and stub, the form of registration receipt." This is the only literacy test in Texas history. For men, the poll tax receipt did not even require a signature. This portion of the law was questioned and the attorney general clarified that women were indeed required to fill out the form in their own hand. Speer wrote Cunningham that he believed the attorney general's ruling to be in error: "Where a woman appears in person before the collector, signs and swears to the certificate, she is a qualified voter." Despite Speer's reservations, women were required to fill out their own registration forms.[33]

The women only had a seventeen-day registration window. Cunningham and TESA organized a registration campaign using their county chairpersons. They encouraged all women, even those outside the required areas, to register, lessening the chance that the women would be turned away on primary election day. Potter informed NAWSA, "All active suffragists in the state are filling speaking engagements in many counties for the cause of good government in Texas. We want to give Ferguson such a drubbing that he will never be able to lift his head again."[34]

TESA had to work to counter the view progressives gained of Hobby when he was Ferguson's lieutenant governor. League instructed suffragists to "emphasize the importance of centering on Hobby in the political cricis [sic] that faces us just now. We are for good Government and for keeping out of office all those men who will not live up to the required standards; and for Governor that man is Ferguson." Mrs. J. S. Sweeney wrote TESA requesting the issuing of a circular informing the public that Hobby supported suffrage as early as 1915. She added, "While Gov. Hobby and I are [related], I have had unfavorable feelings toward him, for being on the ticket with Ferguson and too he was an antiprohibitionist, though I never knew of him doing anything especially in favor of liquor. Good people sometimes get in bad campaigns and sometimes later they see their mistakes." Cunningham replied that she would consult the Hobby campaign, and if they approved, would produce the requested circular.[35]

Suffragists were not the only ones trying to establish Hobby's suffrage record. James T. Denton telegrammed Cunningham, asking for the "full and exact language of WP Hobbys letter in 1914 favoring equal suffrage." League replied that TESA did not give out copies of their records "upon unexplained requests." As the telegram came from Temple, and TESA had an old letter from Denton on *Ferguson Forum* letterhead, she posted the letter care of *Ferguson Forum*. Denton promptly replied, "in view of the standing *that I ought to have* in your circles, any request for information or facts of a public nature that I might make ought not to need 'explaining.'" However, he explained that the governor has said the letter exists but did not produce a copy, "Governor Hobby's opponents assert that [his statement was] untrue—that there never was such a letter. What's the reply?"[36]

Under the instructions of TESA and the Hobby campaign, clubwomen and suffragists respectively or together formed Hobby Clubs and led registration campaigns. Hobby Clubs answered to the Hobby campaign and were formed specifically to encourage men and women to register and vote for Hobby. Suffrage leagues advocated for woman suffrage and usually affiliated with TESA. They encouraged people to register and vote for Hobby and other politicians who supported woman suffrage. In 1918, the groups shared the same goal and strategies, but which group formed where depended on the local political situation. Nannie Webb Curtis, concerned that pro-Ferguson husbands would not allow their wives to vote if they joined a Hobby Club, formed a "Democratic League." J. M. Andrews tried to organize a suffrage club, but some of the women did not want to be called suffragists. Instead, they called themselves the Wharton County Hobby Club. TESA's Edith League replied, "so long as cooperation in the matter of registering, and then voting in the Primary Election, July 27th, is what is desired you did the correct thing."[37]

A Mrs. George Langley wrote Cunningham about her organization: "We call ourselves the Hobby Club now as we want every woman to know we will not have Ferguson. . . . [We will] go in a body to register that the Ferguson men may see we mean business." Langley also noted that men in town "who would not think of suffrage when I [championed it] last winter, are now saying well done. Funny, isn't it?" Knowing that women could bring the candidate they supported to victory swayed the men. When the dominant party split, women were seen as the least threatening group to deliver the deciding vote. County chairperson Mrs. D. N. Stowe reported that local clubwomen organized twenty-three Hobby Clubs in her county. She noted that the number of women registered to vote closely aligned with the membership of the Hobby Clubs and concluded, "I feel confident that nearly all who registered will vote for Gov. Hobby. . . . I think we shall give Hobby and [decency] a good vote on July 27th."[38]

While supporting Hobby, TESA maintained calculated separation between themselves and the official Hobby campaign. They did not issue Hobby campaign literature, instead instructing supporters to write directly to the Hobby campaign. After the election, Cunningham maintained, "Our organization has never officially endorsed Governor Hobby, either before his election or since. As between himself and Mr. Ferguson, even leaving out the question of the latter's impeachment, our women would naturally have voted for Hobby because of Ferguson's speech against Suffrage in Saint Louis. Those of us who heard it, and I was one, are not likely to forget it." Cunningham never forgot Ferguson's actions in Saint Louis, but she did more to elect Hobby than she later let on. She even drafted letters and sent them to the Hobby campaign for printing on campaign stationery.[39]

Cunningham declined the Hobby campaign's request to move her TESA office in Galveston to Austin or Dallas so the two entities could more closely coordinate their campaigns. When the Women's Committee for the Hobby Club of Galveston secured an office on the same floor as Cunningham's TESA office, TESA kept clear the dividing line. League wrote a Galveston suffrage supporter, "the rush of getting important letters and papers out to the various County Chairpersons for Hobby Clubs through the state prevented earlier reply." She admitted to spending her time working with local Hobby Clubs, and yet she noted, "we have had our phone (891) move[d] into that room, which is two doors distant us. It was impossible to secure a separate phone, and we thought that the Women's Comm. of Hobby Club needed a phone more than we did just at this time. This in explanation of 891 now being the phone to call for Miss Hill, and why I am unable to answer." During World War I, there was a delay when ordering new phone lines as government offices had priority. While League was sending correspondence to Hobby Clubs, she could not have it appear that she, as an employee of TESA, was answering the Hobby Club phone. When the 1918 primary concluded, TESA took custody of the phone and the number 891 again.[40]

Many women wrote TESA asking who they should vote for or which candidates supported woman suffrage. TESA repeatedly instructed suffragists to avoid "anyone who is supporting Mr. Ferguson in his unlawful candidacy" and informed women as to the track record of particular candidates on woman suffrage and sometimes prohibition. The campaign was more anti-Ferguson than pro-Hobby. Cunningham argued,

> In my estimation the most important [political issue] before us today is that of the candidacy of Mr. Ferguson, in defiance of law, and order, and the Constitution. . . . Mr. Ferguson's efforts to get himself reinstated embraces the election of a favorable legislature and of Judges Spann, (of Temple), and Harvey to the Supreme Branch of the State, so I trust that the women will be on guard and not vote for any men in the Legislature who are not thoroughly reliable.[41]

While they campaigned against Ferguson, TESA also used the war effort in their rhetoric. Servicemen were absolutely disenfranchised in the Texas constitution. German and Mexican immigrant workers could vote, while enlisted men could not. Suffragists encouraged women to vote in 1918 to counter the immigrant vote and the loss of servicemen's votes. Suffragists capitalized on conservatives' reluctance to support the draft, fearing the resultant expansion of the federal government. They argued that votes for women was a war measure and encouraged women to vote to "elect All-American men who will stand behind our boys at the front." A political cartoon showed soldiers voting above the caption, "The solider votes 'yes' on woman suffrage so that his wife and mother may guard his interest back home while he is 'over there.'" The Hobby campaign also issued literature connecting Ferguson with the German-American Alliance under investigation in Washington, DC.[42]

Even while the Hobby campaign and some suffrage literature used anti-immigrant messages, several TESA county chairmen expressed the desire and willingness to register Latinas. Lenore Hise wrote to League, "our county is not very populous therefore it will not be a very large task to get the women to register. It will require some effort to find the Mexican women that can vote and get them to register." Hise left League to assume that she would put in the effort. A Mrs. Wilmer Threadgill of Laredo, wrote League, "since time is passing so rapidly, and since we have quite a problem on our hands with regard to the Mexican women, who will not vote unless we organize them, we would like to get busy at once." The following month Threadgill explained in a letter to Cunningham that she preferred to concentrate her work in the city:

> Laredo is the only large town in Webb County, for this is a ranch, Mexican country. The near-by villages are populated by Mexicans who do not speak English for the most part. I would be glad to be County Chairman for you, but I think I could do more effective work as City Chairman for the reason explained. . . . I should look after these surrounding villages incidentally.

However, Threadgill planned on visiting the villages as opposed to ignoring them. Cunningham routinely emphasized that county chairmen were to adjust campaign plans according to local needs and her reply to Threadgill reiterated this.[43]

Louise Dietrich of El Paso informed TESA, "We are organizing the Negro women and Mexican who are not affected by the Thomason Law, and we are going to impress upon them the sacredness of the ballot given them and that it is not for sale." Progressives regularly accused persons of color of being easily bought by liquor interests. While Dietrich pledged to register black and Latina women, she warned, "Owing to the fact that over one half of the poll taxes in El Paso co. are held by Mexicans you can see that every other part of the state will have to get votes enough to offset these." Dietrich detailed her plan, "I have 14 other towns [than El Paso] with 802 voters (white) and 257 Mexicans.... I have arranged for meetings in these towns and will have some speaker talk in Spanish to the Mexicans, altho [sic] everyone who know them well say they will not vote for the amendment." Although Dietrich believed that the Mexican vote controlled by boss rule would go for Ferguson, she still worked to register black and Latina women, even using translators when necessary.[44]

Historian Bruce Glasrud notes that World War I "strengthened the objective of black Texas women to acquire the power of the ballot," particularly after seeing black men drafted into military service at a higher percentage than whites. In 1918, Mrs. E. Sampson of El Paso wrote directly to NAWSA requesting recognition of her suffrage club. Sampson was black. Catt sympathized with Sampson, "I am sure if I were a colored woman, I would do the same thing they are doing." However, because of conservative rhetoric that linked woman suffrage with increased black voting, it would have been detrimental to TESA for NAWSA to recognize a black suffrage club in Texas. While woman suffrage removed one barrier between women of color and the ballot, it did not lead to black women's enfranchisement. Most progressive Democrats supporting woman suffrage also supported the disenfranchisement of black men and women through the poll tax and the all-white primary and the disenfranchisement of Mexican immigrants by ending noncitizen voting. Cunningham responded to Sampson, citing the uniqueness of the request and leaving the decision for the state convention. This delay tactic saved face but did not stop black women from registering to vote.[45]

When a group of African American women in Houston tried to register and were denied, they returned and presented the registrar with a letter from the National Association for the Advancement of Colored People (NAACP) threatening a lawsuit. They were allowed to register. In Orange, Texas, the registrar was sued for not registering black women. Cunningham asked for details of the case, concerned that it was actually an antisuffragist effort to get a court ruling against primary suffrage. Glasrud notes that despite registering, "few [black women] voted in the primary election," as the all-white primary usually prevented their participation.[46]

Officially, the primary suffrage bill did not limit voting based on race, as the all-white primary and the poll tax were expected to legally limit nonwhite voting. However, tax collectors viewed the law through their own prejudices and advertised it as such:

> By authority of a ruling of the attorney general of Texas, all white women who reside outside of Waco were not required to register, and therefore all white women in McLennan County residing outside of Waco, over the age of 21 on or before July 27th, 1918, and who are citizens of the United States, and who have resided in Texas one year and in McLennan county six months may vote at the primary election, regardless of whether or not they registered.

While this tax collector's ad suggests that only white female citizens were to benefit from primary suffrage, the actual law did not limit suffrage based on race or citizenship status.[47]

Cunningham wrote to TESA suffragist Jane McCallum about the hard work that summer made sweeter by being able to register to vote herself. Approximately 386,000 Texan women registered to vote in seventeen days, or as Cunningham put it, "enough to make Ferguson sick." Hobby won the governorship by more than 300,000 votes, giving him a 2 to 1 margin over Ferguson. Ferguson argued that women's votes were unconstitutional but estimated he earned less than 10 percent of them. A Victoria County paper reported, "If Ferguson's claim . . . is correct, without the women voting in this county Hobby's vote would have been less than 549 to 742 or more for Ferguson, which would have given Ferguson a majority of at least 149." Newspapers ran the numbers for their counties, reporting the actual number and estimates of what they would have been without the woman vote, proving its impact. Congratulations poured into Cunningham's office; one correspondent called it the "greatest victory since [the] battle of San Jacinto." The *Woman Citizen* carried an article titled "Who Will Women Remember?" recalling Ferguson's Saint Louis speech of 1916. The article concluded, "When the primary returns were all in, it was found that James E. Ferguson had been defeated. . . . Texas women remembered."[48]

In August, Cunningham wrote Legal Defense Committee member Crane with good news. Ferguson had publicly announced that he would accept the election results as final. Texas women were credited with turning the tide against Ferguson, and politicians took notice of their political power and usefulness when the party divided. In 1918, the Texas Democratic Party unanimously adopted a suffrage plank, endorsing state and federal woman suffrage amendments.[49]

Despite the defeat of a state suffrage amendment in May 1919, the following month the Texas legislature became the ninth state to ratify the "Susan B. Anthony Amendment." Texas women were voters in the one-party state's Democratic Party primary, and the majority of Texas legislators either supported woman suffrage or were too concerned for their office to speak out against these new voting constituents. Either way, Ferguson's impeachment and his subsequent 1918 campaign opened a political door for Texas suffragists to negotiate partial suffrage, which in turn helped pave the way to remove sex-based suffrage restrictions nationwide. On August 26, 1920, the Nineteenth Amendment became part of the Constitution of the United States. Governor Hobby, who owed his office to the Texas women voters, declared September 4, 1920, a holiday on which people should "honor the indomitable spirit of American womanhood."[50]

NOTES

1. Finnigan to Ferguson, June 11, 1914, and G. McKay to Finnigan, June 17, 1914, folder 5, box 3, Jane Y. McCallum Papers, Austin History Center, Austin Public Libraries, Austin, Texas (hereafter referred to as McCallum Papers); Finnigan to Hobby, June 12, 1914, and undated reply on same letter, folder 45, box 5, Minnie Fisher Cunningham Papers (hereafter referred to as Cunningham Papers), University of Houston Special Collections, Houston, Texas; Finnigan to Ferguson, January 8, 1915, folder 6, box 4, McCallum Papers. For this article's title quotation, see MFC to Metcalfe, January 28, 1918; MFC to Metcalfe, February 13, 1918, folder 28, box 5, all in Cunningham Papers.

2. Judith McArthur and Harold L. Smith, *Minnie Fisher Cunningham: A Suffragist's Life in Politics* (New York: Oxford University Press, 2003), 49–50; Bruce Rutherford, *The Impeachment of Jim Ferguson* (Austin, TX: Eakin Press, 1983), 22; Ralph W. Steen, "James Edward Ferguson," *Handbook of Texas Online*; Evan Anders, "Boss Rule and Constituent Interests: South Texas Politics during the Progressive Era," *Southwestern Historical Quarterly* 84, no. 3 (1981): 269–72; Darlene Clark Hine, *Black Victory: The Rise and Fall of the White Primary in Texas* (1979; Columbia: University of Missouri Press, 2003), 86.

3. Glenda Elizabeth Gilmore, *Gender and Jim Crow: Women and the Politics of White Supremacy in North Carolina, 1896–1920* (Chapel Hill: University of North Carolina Press, 1996), 55; McArthur and Smith, *Minnie Fisher Cunningham*, 40, 44, 50; Hine, *Black Victory*, 81–82, 86–87; J. B. Cranfill to Cunningham, May 27, 1916, folder 1, box 12, McCallum Papers.

4. McArthur and Smith, *Minnie Fisher Cunningham*, 50–51; Rutherford,

Impeachment of Jim Ferguson, 22; newspaper clipping, "Women Hiss Texas Executive," and newspaper clipping, *Dallas Evening Journal*, June 16, 1916, "Gov. Ferguson Makes Fight on Suffrage Plank," folder 43, box 5, Cunningham Papers.

5. Mrs. Benigna G. Kalb to Cunningham, June 19, 1916, folder 3, box 13, McCallum Papers; McArthur and Smith, *Minnie Fisher Cunningham*, 51; Cunningham to Mrs. Davis, July 7, 1916, folder 2, box 12, McCallum Papers.

6. Newspaper clipping, June 18, 1916, "Suffragist Says Ferguson's Stand 'Cheap Politics'"; newspaper clipping, *Dallas Evening Journal*, June 17, 1916; "'We Will Nail Ferguson to the Cross,' Declares Advocate of Suffrage"; newspaper clipping, *Galveston Daily News*, June 18, 1916; "Declares Ferguson Starts His Funeral," folder 43, box 5, Cunningham Papers; Cunningham to J. W. Butler, July 26, 1916, folder 6, box 11, McCallum Papers.

7. ER Cheeseborough to Cunningham, August 2, 1916, folder 6, box 11; Cunningham to Armstrong, August 7, 1916, folder 4, box 11; Cunningham to Mrs. Leslie Adkins, August 12, 1916, folder 4, box 11; Cunningham to Finnigan, August 11, 1916, folder 5, box 12, all in McCallum Papers.

8. Rutherford, *Impeachment of Jim Ferguson*, 1–2; Will C. Hogg to Potter, June 25, 1917, folder 23, box 2, Cunningham Papers.

9. Ellis to J. W. Canada, June 8, 1917, folder: Correspondence: Governor's Attack, box 2P374; Cunningham to Ellis, August 30, 1917, folder: Minnie Fisher Cunningham, box 2P363, A. Caswell Ellis Papers (hereafter referred to as Ellis Papers), Dolph Briscoe Center of American History, University of Texas, Austin, Texas.

10. Cunningham to Ellis, June 18, 1917; Ellis to Mrs. McAllister, June 14, 1917, folder: Correspondence: Governor's Attack, box 2P374, all in Ellis Papers.

11. Vinson to Ellis, July 16, 1917; J. C. Terrell to Ellis, July 18, 1917, folder: Correspondence: Governor's Attack, box 2P374, all in Ellis Papers.

12. Cunningham circular, July 21, 1917; League to Mr. R. B. Alexander, August 9, 1917, all in folder 8, box 63, McCallum Papers.

13. Rutherford, *Impeachment of Jim Ferguson*, 1; Cunningham to Fuller, July 27, 1917; Cunningham to Jess Baker, July 28, 1917; Cunningham to Mrs. Althea Jones, July 28, 1917; Cunningham to Mrs. Canfield, July 28, 1917, all in folder 8, box 63, McCallum Papers.

14. Rutherford, *Impeachment of Jim Ferguson*, 9–10, 23; Ellis to Dr. W. S. Sutton, August 6, 1917, folder: Ellis, A. C. Campaign Material, newspaper history of Ferguson Fight, Clark Lecture Notes, box 2P30, Ellis Papers; Cunningham to Mrs. A. E. Waters, August 7, 1917, folder 8, box 63, McCallum Papers.

15. Rutherford, *Impeachment of Jim Ferguson*, 47–63; Cunningham to Dr. John C. Granbarr, August 22, 1917, folder 8, box 63, McCallum Papers.

16. League to Engle, August 26, 1917, folder 8, box 63, McCallum Papers.

17. Rutherford, *Impeachment of Jim Ferguson*, 65–71; Ellis to William Clancy

Langdon, August 29, 1917; Vinson to Ellis, September 15, 1917, folder: Correspondence: Governor's Attack, all in box 2P374, Ellis Papers.

18. Rutherford, *Impeachment of Jim Ferguson*, 73, 91–92, 100–101, 109–14; T. H. Shelby to Ellis, September 1, 1917, folder: Ellis, A. C. Campaign Material, newspaper history of Ferguson Fight, Clark Lecture Notes, box 2P30, Ellis Papers; Walter L. Buenger, *The Path to a Modern South: Northeast Texas between Reconstruction and the Great Depression* (Austin: University of Texas Press, 2001), 177.

19. Cunningham to Potter, September 26, 1917, folder 23, box 2, Cunningham Papers; Cunningham to Capt. Geo. E. B. Peddy, August 20, 1917, box 63, folder 8, McCallum Papers.

20. League to Engle, August 26, 1917, folder 8, box 63, McCallum Papers; Mary E. Gearing to Mrs. Ellis, December 21, 1917, folder: Ellis, A. C. Campaign Material, newspaper history of Ferguson Fight, Clark Lecture Notes, box 2P30, Ellis Papers.

21. Ellis to Maud Wood Park, January 31, 1918, folder: Ellis, A. C. Campaign Material, newspaper history of Ferguson Fight, Clark Lecture Notes, box 2P30; Ellis to President Wilson, December 14, 1917, folder: Suffrage, Ellis, all in Ellis Papers, box 2P92; McArthur and Smith, *Minnie Fisher Cunningham*, 40, 49; Ralph W. Steen, "James Edward Ferguson," and William P. Hobby Jr., "William Pettus Hobby," *Handbook of Texas Online*; Hine, *Black Victory*, 1.

22. Potter to Cunningham, February 17, 1918; Edith H. League to Potter, January 21, 1918, folder 23, box 2, all in Cunningham Papers.

23. Eleanor Flexner, *Century of Struggle: The Woman's Rights Movement in the United States* (1959, 1975; Cambridge, MA: Belknap Press of Harvard University Press, 1996), 72; Marjorie Spruill Wheeler, "Introduction: A Short History of the Woman Suffrage Movement in America," and Judith N. McArthur, "Minnie Fisher Cunningham's Back Door Lobby in Texas: Political Maneuverings in a One-Party State," in *One Woman, One Vote: Rediscovering the Woman Suffrage Movement*, ed. Marjorie Spruill Wheeler (Troutdale, OR: New Sage Press, 1996), 17–18, 297; McArthur and Smith, *Minnie Fisher Cunningham*, 52–53. See also, *How Did Texas Women Win Partial Suffrage in a One-Party Southern State in 1918?* Documents Selected and Interpreted by Judith N. McArthur (Binghamton: State University of New York at Binghamton, 2006), in Women and Social Movements Database.

24. MFC to Metcalfe, January 28, 1918; MFC to Metcalfe, February 13, 1918; Metcalfe to Cunningham, March 26, 1918, folder 28, box 5, all in Cunningham Papers. See also, McArthur and Smith, *Minnie Fisher Cunningham*, 61–62; Buenger, *Path to a Modern South*, 175.

25. MFC to Finty, January 28, 1918, folder 24, box 5; Potter to Cunningham, March 13, 1918, folder 24, box 2, all in Cunningham Papers.

26. Potter to Cunningham, March 14, 1918, folder 24, box 2, Cunningham Papers; General Laws of Texas, Act 1918, 35th Legislature, 4th Called Session, Chap. 34.

27. MFC to Kate Gordon, February 16, 1917, folder 24, box 5, Cunningham Papers.

28. Transcription of Ferguson speech, May 22, 1918, folder 42, box 5, Cunningham Papers. The last line was seen as a dig at Cunningham, who was married but had no children.

29. "Women Can Vote in Texas in July, 1918, How, When and Where They Can Cast Ballots," and "Those Indictments" by Galveston County Club for Election of W. P. Hobby for Governor, folder 49, box 5; newspaper clipping, untitled, folder 50, box 5, Cunningham Papers.

30. Marshall Eskridge to Cunningham, July 16, 1918; Jones to Cunningham, July 9, 1918; Cunningham to Williams, July 10, 1918, all in folder 1, box 5, Cunningham Papers.

31. Cunningham to Crane, Stedman, Ben L. Jones, and Speer, telegrams, July 10, 1918; Ocie Speer to Cunningham, July 13, 1918, all in folder 1, box 5, Cunningham Papers.

32. Cunningham to Walter J. Crawford, July 13, 1918, folder 1, box 5; JA Elkins to Cunningham, July 11 1918, folder 2, box 5; MFC to Perkins, July 22, 1918, folder 1, box 5; newspaper clipping, "Ferguson Is Claimed Ineligible to Serve," May 5, 1918, folder 43, box 5, all in Cunningham Papers.

33. General Laws of Texas Act 1918, 35th Legislature, 4th Called Session, Chap. 34; Jessica Brannon-Wranosky, *Southern Promise and Necessity: Texas, Regional Identity, and the National Woman Suffrage Movement, 1868–1920*, unpublished book manuscript in author's possession, 206; Speer to Cunningham, July 13, 1918, folder 1, box 5, Cunningham Papers.

34. Potter to Park, June 21, 1918, folder 23, box 2, Cunningham Papers.

35. League to Hise, June 27, 1918, folder 48, box 2; Sweeney to Cunningham, May 26, 1918, folder 23, box 2; Cunningham to Sweeney, May 27, 1918, folder 28, box 2, all in Cunningham Papers.

36. Denton to Cunningham, telegram, July 5, 1918; HQ Secretary to Denton, July 8, 1918; Denton to League, July 10, 1918, all in folder 21, box 5, Cunningham Papers.

37. Curtis to Cunningham, May 24, 1918, folder 44, box 5; Andrews to Cunningham, July 3, 1918, folder 30, box 3; League to Andrews, July 10, 1918, folder 30, box 3, all in Cunningham Papers.

38. Langley to Cunningham, July 23, 1918, folder 30, box 3; Stowe to Cunningham, July 20, 1918, folder 8, box 3, all in Cunningham Papers.

39. League to Mrs. J. E. Ellington, July 10, 1918, folder 49, box 2; Cunningham to Virginia Yeager, June 21, 1919, folder 1, box 3; MFC to R. Lee Kempner, May 27, 1918, folder 44, box 5, all in Cunningham Papers.

40. Cunningham to Elkins, June 13, 1918, folder 21, box 5; League to Sweeney, June 20, 1918, and League to L. M. Kelsey, November 27, 1918, folder 28, box 2, all in Cunningham Papers.

41. League to J. C. Llewellyn, July 18, 1918, folder 18, box 3; Cunningham to Mrs. J. S. Bowles, June 11, 1918, folder 51, box 2, all in Cunningham Papers.

42. League to Andrews, July 19, 1918, folder 30, box 3, Cunningham Papers; political cartoon, folder: Suffrage, box 2P92, Ellis, A. Caswell Ellis Papers; League to J. W. Lee, July 9, 1918, folder 30, box 3, Cunningham Papers.

43. Hise to League, June 24, 1918, folder 48, box 2; Threadgill to League, May 8, 1918; Threadgill to Cunningham, June 14, 1918; and Cunningham to Threadgill, July 3, 1918, folder 29, box 3, all in Cunningham Papers.

44. Dietrich to League, undated 1918 letter (response written on May 17, 1918), folder 2, box 3, Cunningham Papers; Dietrich to Jane McCallum, undated, folder 1, box 6, McCallum Papers; Dietrich to Cunningham, undated, folder 2, box 3, Cunningham Papers; Gilmore, *Gender and Jim Crow*, 55. The Thomason Law was aimed at illiterate and non-English-speaking voters. It prevented voters from having undue help filling out a ballot.

45. Bruce Glasrud, "Time of Transition: Black Women in Early Twentieth-Century Texas, 1900–1930," in *Black Women in Texas History*, ed. Bruce A. Glasrud and Merline Pitre (College Station: Texas A&M University Press, 2008), 112; Catt to League, July 17, 1918, folder 10, box 5, McCallum Papers; McArthur and Smith, *Minnie Fisher Cunningham*, 62.

46. Monroe N. Work, ed., *Negro Year Book: An Annual Encyclopedia of the Negro* (Tuskegee, AL: Negro Year Book Publishing, 1916–17), 57–58; Rosalyn Terborg-Penn, *African American Women in the Struggle for the Vote* (Bloomington: Indiana University Press, 1998), 148; Cunningham to Benckenstein, July 17, 1918, box 1, folder 35, Cunningham Papers; Glasrud, "Time of Transition," 114; Brannon-Wranosky, *Southern Promise and Necessity*.

47. Newspaper clipping, *Waco Times-Herald*, July 21, 1918, folder 42, box 3, Cunningham Papers.

48. Cunningham to Jane McCallum, undated (Monday, 1918), folder: Jane Y. McCallum: Women's Suffrage, Correspondence, Letters Received, 1918–1921 & Undated, box 3K84, Jane Y. and Arthur N. McCallum Papers, Dolph Briscoe Center for American History, University of Texas, Austin, Texas; McArthur and Smith, *Minnie Fisher Cunningham*, 64; Buenger, *Path to a Modern South*, 178; newspaper clipping, *Galveston Daily News*, July 28, 1918, folder 50, box 5; newspaper clipping, folder 42, box 3; Mr. and Mrs. Kirby to Cunningham, telegram, July 28, 1918, folder 44, box 5; newspaper clipping, *Woman Citizen*, August 24, 1918, folder 50, box 5, Cunningham Papers.

49. Cunningham to Crane, August 8, 1918, folder 1, box 5, Cunningham Papers; "Democratic Platform Adopted Unanimously at Waco 1918," folder: Suffrage, box 2P92, Ellis, A. Caswell, Ellis Papers.

50. Ruthe Winegarten and Judith N. McArthur, eds., *Citizens at Last: The Woman Suffrage Movement in Texas* (Lufkin, TX: Ellen C. Temple Publishing, 1987), 196.

4

In the Public Eye

Texas Governor James Ferguson's Fight with the Press

Leah LaGrone Ochoa

The 1914 Texas gubernatorial campaign was similar to other campaigns in the late nineteenth and early twentieth centuries. All candidates took to the press to deliver their messages of promised change and reform to the waiting public. Banker, lawyer, and self-proclaimed "man of the rural people," James Ferguson adopted a "folksy" style to appeal to his target audience. Known as "Farmer Jim," he campaigned on the idea that the poor farmers of Texas needed a gubernatorial advocate, and the target audience was eager to have him represent rural life on their behalf. People crowded into venues to hear campaign supporters speak on Ferguson's plans for the people. The *Dallas Morning News* described an event when Senator T. H. McGregor of Austin spoke to an "enthusiastic" audience in Dallas about their role as a "wholesale town built largely on agriculture and other businesses that have a direct connection to the farm," and how they needed a governor like James Ferguson to accommodate their needs. Over "fifteen hundred voters of Dallas" packed into the Majestic Theater to listen to a speech on Ferguson, "and at several different times the cheering was deafening." Farmer Jim's message recognized the needs of the rural "folk" and gained him a popular following. As historians Judith McArthur and Harold Smith highlight in *Minnie Fisher Cunningham: A Suffragist's Life in Politics*, Ferguson "made the farm tenancy problem the centerpiece of his noisy 1914 campaign."[1]

The other frontrunner for the Texas Democratic Party's nomination was Thomas H. Ball of Houston. Ball gained the support of Texas prohibitionists and many of the state's urban progressives. Since prohibition garnered the most attention during the campaign, each candidate employed the participating Texas daily newspapers to construct their public image and outline their stance. The campaign garnered wide press coverage in Texas, and as the candidates toured the state, their speeches landed on the pages of the state's largest media outlets, especially those of the boisterous Ferguson. So began a relationship with the public built on the wrangling of Ferguson with the major daily press of Texas and how the press covered, participated in, and influenced the political and social processes.

As it turned out, campaign disputes were not the only fight the daily press of Texas covered over the following five years in the Ferguson frenzy. The press played a large role in the public's perception of Ferguson's business practices and operations within the state. Ferguson, of course, fought back against all allegations thrown his way, but he was up against powerful Texas names and money that exerted their influence over state operations. Many political officeholders were also businessmen; these businessmen invested in the press, and many of the owners of the Texas press were invested in other businessmen and, more importantly, invested in the University of Texas. This triangulation of power helped propagate the opposition to Ferguson by using the drama that surrounded the governor to stir up emotion, readership, and in turn eventual support for his impeachment.

In his book *First Texas News Barons*, historian Patrick Cox describes the impact the daily newspapers of Texas had on society at the turn of the twentieth century. Cox argues that in the first years of the twentieth century the "small club of Texas newspaper publishers expanded their media holdings and thoroughly asserted their influence over public opinion and policy making." Subsequently, the newspapers played an important role in shaping society and how people interacted with news broadcasted in print. Daily newspapers helped build a group of "urban middle class consumers" and advocated for commercial growth and expansion through a dominance exerted over political powers. Cox highlights the modernization and industrialization of the United States during the early twentieth century and argues that this helped fuel the popularity of daily newspapers because they "served as a reliable vehicle to deliver both news and advertisements to the public."[2]

In Texas, the publishers worked to create their own "publishing enterprises" and expand their influence beyond the urban borders and reach the extensive rural populations. Until after World War II, the majority of Texas residents lived in rural areas. Cox argues that these "news barons," such as A. H. Belo and George Dealey of the *Dallas Morning News* and

Galveston News, William P. Hobby of the *Houston Post*, Jesse H. Jones of the *Houston Chronicle*, and Henry Sevier of the *Austin American*, helped shape the image of the state as a leading competitor in the news industry. Additionally, the news barons also helped shape the opinions of the state's inhabitants—rural and urban—by appealing to the public's taste for drama and ability to participate in politics through the pages of the newspapers.[3]

Ferguson understood politics and the role of the media; he previously worked as a campaign manager for several local politicians in Bell County, ran two of his own successful campaigns for Bell County attorney, and aided in the successful campaign for the governorship of newspapermen Oscar B. Colquitt and lieutenant governor William H. Mayes. He also understood the importance of the press and manipulation of the public attitude when it came to popular political issues. Ferguson appeared especially careful when catering to select audiences, particularly rural Texans, by not taking a firm stance on prohibition and "emphasizing the state of education in Texas and the compulsory attendance laws." Ferguson used his ability to appeal to the rural people as a way to divide the voting classes and emphasized breaking up the elite cliques that formed on the government and business level that essentially ran the politics of the state. The *Dallas Morning News* ran campaign advertisements and articles that detailed Ferguson's travel plans, locations, and speeches across North Texas in his own gubernatorial campaign. His appeal to the public was through his captivating personality and his ability as an orator, which was captured in his "stump speeches"; therefore, the Texas voters elected the forty-three-year-old Ferguson as the successor in a long line of Democratic governors.[4]

After his election in 1914, Ferguson took office in January 1915 to great media fanfare. That month, the *Dallas Morning News* ran articles covering the inauguration, the Governor's Ball, and the residential move of the Ferguson family, spurring the public interest in all the entertainment that surrounds the festivities of a newly elected governor of Texas. Even the national magazine *Harper's Weekly* published an article on Ferguson later that year on a celebratory note. Titled "Governor Jim of Texas," Charles Holman applauded Ferguson for his ability to shift "politics as usual" from a prohibition fight to push legislation in favor of the tenant farmer, whom the state "had wholly neglected." He wrote that during the campaign for governor, "The liquor fight degenerated into a struggle between the extremists who would clear the whole state, and the organized liquor interest, who would maintain their ground." The article pointed to Ferguson's "self-interest" past, pushed readers to have a wait and see attitude, and argued that Ferguson would be the next great leader, possibly in Congress. Or, it stated, that "he may revert to the training of his youth; he may subside to the sphere of mere party politician." For the time, though, Ferguson was celebrated as a champion in the national magazine.[5]

However, when the first initial weeks in office were over and the newness wore away, Texas newspapers got down to the business of reporting the policies that Governor James E. Ferguson planned to roll out over his term in office. In his "first message to the legislature," on January 21, 1915, the *Dallas Morning News* ran every point Ferguson made on the floor and called the platform "well received." Within the text of the article are points six and seven that called for larger appropriations for rural education reform and a combined leadership for Texas A&M and the University of Texas. To put this portion of Ferguson's agenda into context, in the South, the public school systems trailed behind the North, and the tangible evidence resided in the amount per student each region spent on education. In his book *To Get a Better School System: One Hundred Years of Education Reform in Texas*, historian Gene Preuss quotes C. Vann Woodward and his descriptions of the discrepancies in the average expenditures of each southern state's public school system, and put into perspective the lack of funding appropriated to the rural regions. Preuss argues, "Despite the fact that Texas spent more per child per diem than other southern states, it still ranked thirty-eighth in the nation in the number of children enrolled in school, thirty-seventh in per capita expenditures for education, and thirty-fifth in literacy," all before Ferguson took office.[6]

According to the *Dallas Morning News*, Ferguson advocated for reallocating Texas funds to better serve the rural education districts of the state because his own education came from the rural system, so he identified with the people of Texas who were behind the national average in literacy rates, as he claimed. Historian Lewis Gould argued that Ferguson's message to the state legislature, after his election, "pointed to an imbalance in educational emphasis," but his "interest in education changed from sympathy to suspicion when it turned to the state's university system." This suspicion toward academia also manifested into suspicion of the press, since as Ferguson saw it, many of the Texas newspapers favored the University of Texas. Furthermore, a number of the University of Texas faculty also possessed a publishing background that added to the media scrutiny of Ferguson and helped solidify the support of the commercial elites to the university. Also, the dual position of faculty as daily press participants added to the ire Ferguson harbored for the Texas newspapers.[7]

Ferguson advocated for a system that did not favor the urban elite, but instead, allocated expenditures toward advancing rural education, therefore systematically siding with those who supported his rural centered plans. It was this relationship with the university systems and arguments over education appropriations that eventually sparked the media sensation that surrounded Ferguson and his financial controversies, and subsequently, created mistrust among Ferguson, the press, and the media magnates of Texas who aided in his downfall.

Throughout 1915, his first year as governor, the Texas newspapers detailed the events surrounding the fight between Ferguson and the University of Texas. The fight focused on the veto of appropriations of state funds needed to continue the basic function of the university. However, Ferguson's perspective of academia is noted in his own words. In his opinion, the university was run by "disloyal . . . butterfly chasers, day dreamers, educated fools and two-bit thieves." Ferguson's justification for the veto he applied to the appropriations bill was that the university president misappropriated line item funds designated for the salary of employees that they did not hire and funneled it to "other purposes not disclosed to the Appropriation Committee of the Legislature."[8]

Ferguson viewed his position in the governor's office as a platform to break up the cliques that he asserted organized all the University of Texas's affairs. Even though many historians describe Ferguson as a fool who lacked any moral compass, his strategic and focused scuffles with the daily press demonstrate that he understood the underpinnings of the relationship the press had with its readers. Ferguson's downfall started with an error in his judgment that he could take on and win against the entire Texas daily press, the same arrogance that began the battle with the press also became the fuel that continued it.

When Ferguson first aimed his polemics at the University of Texas, he set his sights on acting president William J. Battle, and then on professors A. Caswell Ellis and R. E. Cofer. Nevertheless, historian Lewis Gould argues that one of Ferguson's dominant irritants was William Harding Mayes, a journalism professor at the university. Mayes, after he served as Colquitt's lieutenant governor, took the position as a faculty member,

Portrait of the lieutenant governor of Texas, William Mayes, who resigned from the elected office to accept the position of dean of the newly created School of Journalism at the University of Texas. 1913. Individual portrait from "Thirty-Third Legislature Senate 1913 Senate." Composite photo of Senate members, Senate Chapter 3E.5 Gallery, Third Floor, Texas State Capitol Building, Austin, Texas, under stewardship of Texas Preservation Board. Photo of individual portrait in composite by Jessica Brannon-Wranosky.

founded the University of Texas's journalism department, and served as dean for twelve years. Ferguson regarded Mayes as objectionable because of the political criticisms written about Ferguson's ability as governor, and his push against the University of Texas that were published in the pages of Mayes's paper, the *Brownwood Bulletin*—a newspaper that he owned and edited in Brownwood, Texas. Ferguson complained that the *Bulletin*, "skinned me from hell to [breakfast]." In addition, the University of Texas's paper published out of Mayes's journalism department, the *Daily Texan*, editorialized a severe dislike of Ferguson when they ran an article claiming that people from the fourth ward of Austin would vote for a "Negro postal worker for governor" over Ferguson. Ferguson declared his offense at the article, which he argued showed proof of the university's disloyalty, because "any publication permitted at any institution under the supervision of the faculty, which states that they would rather have a 'nigger' for Governor of the State rather than one which white democrats of the state have put in office, is the most disloyal organization to that extent that could exist."[9]

The fight with the University of Texas that played out in the Texas daily newspapers sparked inquiries into other factions of Ferguson's governorship and created the catalyst that united the state's daily press in their criticism and opposition to Ferguson. Ferguson pushed against a wall of newspaper operators who were connected to the University of Texas and its regents and professors, and in some cases, newspaper operators who were part of the university directly. Ferguson's philosophy, according to his daughter Ouida, was that all stories about him in the press, real or stretched truths, were just "good copy" that did not come to fruition the way he imagined. Once the media attention and fight with the press got started, Ferguson could not control it.[10]

Even after the press storm that surrounded the fight with the University of Texas board of regents died down, the newspapers picked up other claims during the 1916 campaign that questioned the governor's finances. So much so that by June, Ferguson took to the press to defend his character and administration against the charges of financial misconduct. Talks of impeachment resurfaced during this time, but in February 1917 both the *Dallas Morning News* and the *Austin Statesman* ran articles that declared, "The Senate would not investigate any charges against the governor." Gould argues that even after Ferguson's second inauguration, the governor's finances were quietly mopped up with special help from Texas brewers to pay off the debt balance to Temple State Bank for more than $150,000—with the express promise of anonymity. Gould also notes the irony in the new fight between Ferguson and the press, especially since the governor accused the university president of financial misappropriation.

Nevertheless, by March 1917, the *Dallas Morning News* published an article with the headline, "Governor Ferguson Exonerated by Committee and by the House" and wrote that the committee, while finding the governor's financial problems with Temple State Bank and use of state funds for groceries and other household expenses worthy of "criticism and condemnation," came to the conclusion "that said conduct was unjustified and wholly unwarranted, but does not merit the severe pains and penalties of impeachment." However, Ferguson did not view the publications of his exoneration as favorable, but instead, he honed in on the use of the term *impeachment*.[11]

Soon, the financial quibble shuffled out of the limelight and the question of the University of Texas's appropriations and the governor's veto garnered headlines once more. Again, by early 1917, the fight between the regents of the University of Texas and Governor Ferguson ensued, leaving a wake of anger among powerful Texas elites. Ferguson's announcement of allocating funds toward "common education" pitted rural school district proponents against higher education faculty and directors of the University of Texas and shifted the talk for appropriations toward campuses and curriculum. After the appropriation debacle reached its climax, the president of the university, Robert Vinson, reached out to John Lomax, another one of Ferguson's targets, and warned him of impending plans of "Ferguson reopening the whole matter" of an appropriations veto from years earlier.[12]

Lomax served as the secretary of the University of Texas Alumni Association from 1910 to 1925, which eventually became the "Texas Exes." He played an instrumental role in the fight to save the university from the rehashed focus of Ferguson's appropriations veto. Lomax, in an effort to publicize the fight, called the editors of the *San Antonio Express*, the *Dallas Morning News*, and the *Houston Post* and persuaded them to run editorials in favor of the University of Texas. The *Austin Statesman*, and then on following day the *Dallas Morning News*, called the meeting of the board of regents ordered by Ferguson "unlawful" and unnecessary. Furthermore, adding that any veto of the appropriations to the University of Texas, "be a legal nullity, and, in that case, the execution of it could be prevented." Just as in the campaign speeches Ferguson sent to the daily newspapers, and the close coverage of the press on Ferguson's financial turmoil, the public dialogue and debate over the issues that surrounded the University of Texas and the power of the governor positioned the daily press to attract readers and helped increase circulation by contributing and publishing the major, ongoing story. Thereby, the press provided a medium that allowed the public to participate by proxy and aid in the eventual impeachment of the governor.[13]

The battle between the governor and the university often has been categorized as "common folks" versus "the elite" and has emphasized arguments over which services the state should provide through public and higher education. These political issues played a part in the Ferguson impeachment and created opposition that prompted people to choose sides. In Texas, the one-room, one-teacher schoolhouses dominated the public school system and underscored the disparity in funding. In addition, the public universities failed to garner adequate financial support from the state government since many families considered it more of an economic necessity for their children to participate in picking cotton rather than sitting in a classroom. As emphasized in *To Get a Better School System*, progressive reformers wanted increased state funding for schools, and that included more money allocated per pupil, free textbooks, consolidation of local school districts, and better pay for teachers. Ferguson was able, for a time, to capitalize on these public needs with efforts to make the University of Texas the scapegoat for the discrepancy, which also added some public interest to the developing stories.[14]

The media's participation in the fight within all these categories played an enormous role in how the public viewed the feud between Ferguson and the University of Texas, and subsequently, his financial misconduct. It was the Texas press that kept talks of impeachment alive until the final Senate hearing in September 1917 and created a power struggle and a codependent relationship between the public and the press that helped shape reader's opinion of the governor.

Ferguson's fight with the university, and especially the media, continued after he "decided to reopen the whole matter, veto the appropriation, and press again to control the university." The circus that surrounded Ferguson's mistrust of the media heated up to the point where the newspapers fought back against the charges that Ferguson threw at them that claimed the paper's owners and writers accepted bribes. The *Dallas Morning News* ran an article on May 3, 1917, that detailed a statement made by Ferguson before the Senate Committee on Education that attested, "I don't know what they [the *Austin Statesman*] are getting for it, but they are getting paid for it at any rate." The "it" Ferguson referred to were what he considered slanderous articles meant to undercut his genuine concern for education. The *Austin Statesman* responded by writing, "If that charge is true, it is the duty of Governor Ferguson to make public the evidence which moved him to make it and *The News* offers the use of its columns to make it." Texas newspapers continued to follow the controversy that surrounded Ferguson and the University of Texas; however, both Ferguson and people close to the regents used newspaper articles to argue their case for justification of power because the daily press and Ferguson realized they needed to capitalize on the accusations against one another to create doubt among the readers to further each side's agenda.[15]

The articles that questioned Ferguson's motives lasted until the talk of impeachment began. Ferguson condemned Texas newspapers, especially the *Austin Statesman*, for their attempts to churn up talks of impeachment, but Ferguson's losing battle led to increased public support for his indictment and popular mistrust of the governor concerning the misappropriation charge. The *Austin Statesman*, and rerun by the *Dallas Morning News*, quoted Ferguson in a speech given in Plainview, Texas, where he stated, "*The News* has been condemning me in their editorial columns and saying that I ought to be impeached and banished." The *Statesman* fired back by pointing out that the word *impeached* had not appeared and was only used to report on the House Committee proceedings. The *Austin Statesman* went further to assert that Ferguson misconstrued the *News*'s support for an agricultural school in West Texas and wrote, "*The News* began to advocate the establishment of an agricultural college in West Texas before the people of the State had heard of Governor Ferguson."[16]

Throughout Ferguson's quarrels with the university, the media helped fuel and participated in the debate by questioning the legality of the governor's dealings with the University of Texas. More pressing was the legal use of funds and incurred debt that the governor owed Temple State Bank. This was evident in the publicity assault waged by prohibitionists, Texas suffrage campaign workers, and other prominent Texas clubwomen. The most damning assault came from Houston millionaire and leader of the Texas-Exes, William C. Hogg. In his chapter detailing this war of press bulletins, Gould points to the fact that by June 1917, Hogg "set his lawyers to work on precedents for impeachment proceedings, conferred with Joseph D. Sayers and Lomax about reaching out to the newspapers, and helped compose a series of broadsides against the governor." Hogg wrote publications that were printed in national papers about the struggle, calling Ferguson a "crack-head with a swagger frankness mistaken for courage and a large stock of chicanery." In addition, many of the major daily newspapers began running the same articles and advertisements that focused on Ferguson's fight with the University of Texas.[17]

By July 1917, the *Houston Chronicle* published a five-part series on the "differences between Ferguson and the University of Texas" with the final headline titled, "The Peoples' University—Shall It Be Destroyed?" The purpose of the segment was to detail the legality of the governor's fight against the University of Texas Board of Regents while adopting Ferguson's language to appeal to the people. The series ended with the question, "Will the Governor be allowed to violate the constitutional law, which he has sworn to obey, and destroy an institution designed by the fathers and necessary to the educational system and progress of the state?" The *Houston Chronicle* ran the series as full-page editorials listing the support of both the University Ex-Students' Association and the University Citizens Committee.[18]

Also in July 1917, the *Dallas Morning News* ran the same series of full-page pieces titled advertisements that pitted the governor against the university. The paper quoted Ferguson as saying, "There are too many people going hog wild about higher education." In addition, the headline matter-of-factly read "Governor Ferguson Vs. The University of Texas" while calling out all of Ferguson's charges against the university as a set of untruths that needed to be quashed in favor of an "investigation." The advertisements aimed their questions at the general public and stated, "The people of Texas should demand that Governor Ferguson assemble the Legislature in a special session, and that he lay before the body the charges of 'gross irregularities' which he has mentioned in his veto message, and in the public utterances which he is reported to have made." The fight was now firmly front and center in the Texas press, and both sides issued a public en garde as the feud drew more attention.[19]

The goal of the daily press with their editorials and advertisements was to unite the professional and commercial community by capitalizing on the reader's interest in the feud in opposition to Ferguson's ability to also unite and inspire his supporters, therefore highlighting their power to influence the public. At the same time, it is important to note that Ferguson did not have a platform without the daily press, but it was his nature to seek attention, and so he could not or did not bring himself to shy away from their limelight either. Gould argues that Ferguson took his case to the people of small towns stating, "They [the University of Texas] are denouncing me because they say I am ignorant and illiterate." But when asked by the *Dallas Morning News* about his plans for the university, he said, "I do not care a damn what becomes of the University. The bats and owls can roost in it for all that I care."[20]

As the Ferguson versus the university campaign picked up steam, the

Texas newspapers once again picked up the talk of impeachment. After word spread that Chester Terrell of San Antonio wrote to the Speaker of the House, Francis O. Fuller, asking for a special session to address the charges of misconduct, impeachment talk mounted in the daily press. Fuller was at the center of the West Texas A&M debacle where votes were cast in favor of placing the university in Abilene. Ferguson wanted Abilene as the official site, Lieutenant Governor Hobby and the commissioner of agriculture voted for different cities; however, Fuller was the deciding vote. After Abilene won, Fuller denied casting his vote for Abilene and siding with Ferguson. Ferguson charged back at Fuller's denial by stating that he specifically discussed the vote with Fuller, and Fuller confided to him that he voted for West Texas A&M to be placed in Abilene. Gould writes that after Fuller was backed into a corner he "began intense discussions of impeachment with Hogg and other anti-Ferguson forces," including a comparison of notes with lieutenant governor William P. Hobby of the alleged misdeeds of the governor.[21]

While Fuller in a statement given to the press avowed he had nothing to do with the indictments or the call to order of the House, the state legislators began to assemble. Historian Patrick Cox argues that Will Hogg and university friends "spent a long hot summer working in Austin to counter the governor's attacks and coordinate the impeachment movement." He also asserts that Speaker Fuller called the special legislative session, and in a "counter move, Ferguson called the special session himself to consider the universities appropriations," although it was to Ferguson's detriment.[22]

Gould argues that according to Hogg's diary, Hogg "urged Fuller to call the House members to session," but Fuller did not act until July 23—on the same day that Hogg arranged for Fuller and Hobby to meet and compare notes on the university events. This was within days of when Hogg gave a speech in Dallas at a special event luncheon covered in the *Dallas Morning News*. The article detailed Hogg's stance on the Ferguson impeachment issue and called for many more to join the fight in the anti-Ferguson campaign. Hogg told the members of the University of Texas Ex-Students' Association at the luncheon that, "Insomuch as the opposition to Governor Ferguson's personal and official performances has developed into impeachment proceedings involving his University attitude and action simply as incidents, we must maintain the integrity of the Ex-Students' Association by continuing to fight." He added at the end of the speech,

"The Governor's audacity in announcing for a third term would excite one's admiration rather than pity, if it were not sheer despair: If it were not the arrogant hope of an individual who can do no wrong." Hogg's leadership and the methods he used to spearhead the impeachment talk centered on funneling the energy of University of Texas supporters; he also encouraged the major newsmen of the state to organize as part of a media campaign, and once the media campaign against Ferguson began, it snowballed into a major source of entertainment.[23]

While Ferguson toured Texas to speak to the rural constituents about the negative light the Texas press cast upon him, the newspapers continued to circulate talk of impeachment. The *San Marcos Times* wrote, "The man could not run the great institution himself, so he destroyed it," as the correlation of the university and misconduct circled around the talks of impeachment. Even though the *Houston Post*, the *Dallas Morning News*, and the *San Antonio Express* ran some of the most disparaging editorials against Ferguson, Ferguson also found little support among the rural newspapers. The big Texas daily newspapers, though, Ferguson charged, set in motion the talk of impeachment and set the stage for legislative inquiries into his finances, even after the financial charges were laid to rest, much like how Ferguson rehashed the appropriations veto. Again, the major daily press used the expanded interest in the story of the Ferguson fight to unite the business community in opposition to Ferguson in favor of supporting the university.[24]

Once the impeachment trial got underway, the headlines previously dedicated to political, humanitarian, and military stories on World War I gave way to front-page headlines about Governor Ferguson. The *Houston Chronicle* ran broad headlines that read, "More American Troops Die" but that in equally attention-grabbing sensation, on the same page read, "Governor Replies to Indictments" and "9 Counts in Indictments against Gov. Ferguson Charging Misuse of Funds." The headlines and articles detailing the charges and impeachment trial against Ferguson continued to warrant front-page placement throughout Texas newspapers. Then, by the beginning of August 1917, the impeachment trial headlines detailing the charges and testimony in the legislative proceedings appeared every day.[25]

The *Austin Statesman*, accused by Ferguson as leading the sensational reporting and having the most anti-Ferguson stories, publicized the impeachment events in meticulous detail. On August 2, 1917, the *States-*

man detailed the motions of the convening Texas legislature and the resolutions that passed in the case of the governor's possible transgressions. They wrote that "it was resolved that the hearing shall be conducted and evidence submitted upon not only such matters as may be charged specifically but on other matters involving the official integrity of Governor James E. Ferguson." And question his integrity they did. In the same issue, the *Statesman* ran a small article out of the *Galveston News* that argued, "The horse which Governor Ferguson now bestrides is several hands less high than the one he mounted when he vetoed all but a fraction of the appropriations for the University." The author added, "When one recalls that Governor Ferguson could have vetoed as many of the items in the University's appropriation as he chose, and thus reduced it to whatever total he might have thought fit, the explanation which he now gives to his actions lacks something of being quite plausible." The power of the Texas press helped provide the public with a unique opportunity to peer inside the halls of the state legislature and follow the daily soap-opera-like drama.[26]

The entertainment value of the impeachment trial continued throughout the month of August. On August 4, 1917, the *Houston Chronicle* detailed a "list of prominent men" expected to testify to the validity of the charges against the governor. Then, on August 6, the *Chronicle*'s top headline declared, "The Governor Declines to be First to Testify." On the same dates that the *Statesman* began detailing the charges, the *Dallas Morning News* published articles that also supplied extensive details on the House proceedings and noted, "Within fifteen minutes after the House had convened today Speaker Fuller, in his own behalf and under oath, filed charges against Governor James E. Ferguson, asking that they be investigated to determine whether or not the House will present a bill of impeachment to the Senate."[27]

In the same publication, the *Dallas Morning News* also detailed the "Text of the Speaker's Charges against Governor Ferguson" that outlined in eight different subheadings every incident or unlawful act the governor committed. The charges started with misappropriation of state money that ranged from "the purchase of groceries and gasoline; that the committee appointed by the House of Representatives found that he did so," to detailing the incidents with the University of Texas, including the veto of appropriations and the charges against the faculty. In this section of the article, the editorial argued "the governor in his public speeches and public warnings declared to the people of Texas that the faculty of the University of Texas are grafters and [corruptionists], that they are liars and that they are disloyal to their government." In addition, it was added that "the faculty, in justice to themselves and to the institution which they serve and to the people of Texas whose money supported and maintained the institution, applied to the Senate of Texas for a full and fair investigation" to clear their names from the charges Ferguson made, thereby making Ferguson the aggressor. The emphasis of "disloyalty" by the Texas press coincided with the push against the German population of Texas; Ferguson argued they politically supported their native country during World War I, and therefore, were "disloyal" to the Texas government. Ferguson continued to use loyalty as a slogan to garner support for his stance against the daily press and the University of Texas, claiming that they proved their disloyalty with all the organized trouble they created behind the scenes. But the public continued to soak up the drama by purchasing the newspapers that lambasted him, further contributing to the campaigns on both sides.[28]

When the Texas House investigations switched from the problems between Ferguson and the university to the charges of the debt Ferguson incurred at Temple State Bank, the *Houston Chronicle* ran multiple front-page articles detailing the spectacle. Their lead article used specific phrasing that highlighted the fact that "Testimony Ends with Ferguson Maintaining Secrecy about Loan," when asked what entity paid off his debt to the bank. Furthermore, they ran an article that discussed the citation issued to the Temple State Bank president, T. H. Heard, "for failing to turn over to a receiver certain money said to be on deposit in the bank and belonging jointly to parties to a suit now pending in the courts of Harris County." This suit consisted of tracks of land purchased and sold by Ferguson. Any news related to Ferguson, whether or not it was directly part of the official charges, ended up as a source of scrutiny. By August 25, 1917, all the major newspaper outlets in the state published articles, similar to that of the *Dallas Morning News*, titled, "Governor Ferguson Impeached by House on Twenty-One Counts." The *Dallas Morning News* version ran two pages worth of details about each charge, the discussion of that charge by House members, and how each member voted.[29]

The state Senate officially took over the case and the media frenzy that once again ensued quenched the thirst of the public courtroom news devotees. Several papers ran editorials arguing for and against the key points, or insults, Ferguson lobbed at the university regents and other Texas officials, and they published rebuttals from key members of the institution. Other newspapers reprinted the transcript of the trial, point by point, and eventually took the "Ferguson Speech" as a script of the court proceedings and published articles that read like the House and Senate legislative journals, allowing the public to virtually sit through the impeachment trial. On August 28, the *Dallas Morning News* published the "Rules of the Ferguson Trial," and the next day, the article "Senate Begins Trial of Ferguson Today" published every detail of the lawyer's arguments that represented each side and the names of witnesses who began their testimony. By the time the Senate convened, the trial began, and Ferguson chose to testify in his own defense, the major news outlets latched on to every word he expressed on the floor. The *Dallas Morning News* article on the day Ferguson took the stand stated that "[he] occupied the stand all today, testifying in answer to the articles of impeachment returned by the house, and being tried by the Senate.... At one point in today's testimony Governor Ferguson called upon the Almighty God to strike him dead if the statements he was making were not true." The following day the *Dallas Morning News* posted two pages worth of questions sent up to Ferguson from the Senate floor, complete with Ferguson's answers. Whether the people of Texas agreed with Ferguson's responses on putting the university in a "proper place" or "letting the regents know he would not be bullied," they had a front seat from which to decide for themselves if he was guilty on the misuse of power and funds and other charges brought up against him.[30]

Then, by the end of September, the *Dallas Morning News* published, "Judgment was voted by the Senate of Texas to remove James E. Ferguson from the office of Governor of Texas and disqualifying him from holding any office of honor, trust, or profit under the State." They continued by adding, "The Senate court adjourned *sine die*, ending the most dramatic and momentous session of the Senate in the history of the State." The conclusion of the controversy left the participants so exhausted that one Austin journalist noted, "All of us here felt rather dazed at the realization that it had finally ended, and that the days of strenuous news chasing were over." The dramatic case fascinated readers, reporters, and the public as information rushed in, from weekly reports to daily, sometimes multiple articles, in all major Texas newspapers and rural bulletins. The newspapers led the media frenzy that surrounded Ferguson's fall from the governor's chair. However, in less than four months posttrial, the public had a new venue in which to participate in the ongoing Ferguson drama.[31]

This case was so dramatic and sensational that a motion picture that depicted the impeachment events traveled throughout the state. The Hippodrome Theater House in Dallas offered moviegoers a chance to watch the Ferguson impeachment rather than just read about it in daily articles. By March 1917, the *Dallas Morning News* published an article that stated, "A treat was offered moving picture fans in the presentation in 'The Impeachment of Governor Ferguson' last evening." The author also noted the picture's seeming impartiality in the "data regarding the University, and Governor Ferguson's fine farm and stock ranch man that came to help him." The film review concludes, "There are no fake scenes in the six reels, all being from actual happenings." Subsequent advertisements of the impeachment film drew viewers to the theater that played the picture on a continuous loop, every day—the entire day—from March 24 through March 30 in Dallas.[32]

After the conclusion of the trial and the announcement of impeachment, Ferguson told the press he would most likely resign before any impeachment took place, but he made no mention of future plans. His intentions were to defy the ban the legislature had placed on him from occupying any government office, but one of many problems with organizing a new run for office was his soured relationship with the state's press. Ferguson vocalized his mistrust for the "big Dailies" that endorsed his enemies throughout the impeachment trial; therefore, he decided to start his own publication to get his version of events to the public.[33]

Ferguson did not see the events unfold in the same manner as the daily press. After the impeachment proceeding finalized and the Senate submitted their verdict in the last weeks of September 1917, Ferguson retreated to Temple, Texas, to create his own publicity outlet. By November of the same year, the *Ferguson Forum* adopted a newspaper outline and began as volume 1, number 1, to detail events as perceived by the former governor and aimed at winning back the support of his followers where the Texas papers created doubt. With the creation of the *Ferguson Forum*, Ferguson aimed to compete with the daily press that he argued did not represent him fairly. His own publication allowed him to control and circulate this argument throughout the state. This was also Ferguson's attempt to join the media elites he disdained and criticized, but he also wanted the opportunity to communicate his stance to the masses on an equal level.[34]

The *Forum* also served as vindication for Ferguson as a way to create a source of income to make up for, as his friends indicated, the fact that he felt "the state had made him the victim of ghastly and conscienceless persecution in the course of which it has stripped him of all that he had." As a way to combat this public humiliation, Ferguson argued that it was entirely within his right and reason, or "ethical and moral right," to establish a source of income that brought in as much money as possible—"as long as he made it within the law." After his impeachment, Ferguson's legal expenses, campaign expenditures, and ongoing personal debt problems led to the creation of the *Ferguson Forum* as continued utilization of his name to generate interest from his constituents.[35]

In his first issue of the *Ferguson Forum*, Ferguson printed the entire front page as a rebuttal to the newspaper articles he perceived as manipulative and guilty of appeasement to the university crowd during the entire length of his terms as governor. The first headline read, "Ferguson's Veto Message of University Appropriation," written by Ferguson, who referred to himself in the third person and argued that the purpose of the publication was "in order that the public may be fully informed as to the reasons to that veto which caused the impeachment, the veto message is here reproduced in full, together with a sample of over a thousand letters received by Governor Ferguson commending his action in vetoing said appropriation." The entire article, which continued into page three, recounted his view of the appropriation bill, conversations and statements by and to him, and his account of the protest that took place outside the state capitol organized by the student body of the university. He wrote:

> This parade marched down the walk in front of the capitol, and in about fifteen or twenty minutes returned by the same route to the capitol, and came directly in front of my office, where I was then conferring with the board of regents, and in turn exhibited said banners directly in my face and within twenty feet of where I and the board were conferring, and while said banners were being flaunted in my face, various students of the university called to me in divisive tones to read the banners. And said body of students remained in front of my office window for twenty-five or thirty minutes, and the howling and yelping was of such a degree that further deliberation of myself and the board of regents was absolutely prevented.[36]

His account of the events that surrounded the University of Texas was just a stepping-stone for his rebuttal to the media frenzy that took over the impeachment proceedings. In addition to his account of the university-versus-Ferguson events, on the front page of the first volume was a letter penned to his constituency titled "A Statement to the Citizenship of Texas," where he argues that "necessity is the mother of invention"; therefore, it was necessary that he create the journal because "self preservation is the first law of nature, and these time honored truth's apply to newspaper difficulties as anything else." He continued to argue his stance and used sensational phrases, including "submarined by the Texas Legislature" and the "big daily newspaper used as an insidious weapon to accomplish this purpose," and he pointed out that the "big daily" newspapers did not give the same attention to the "ranks of organized labor." He stated his intention clearly to use the *Ferguson Forum* as the "destroyer of newspaper submarines" with the analogy complete with a reference to the German submarines, the enemies of the United States during World War I. Again, Ferguson was among the early politicians to capitalize on the popularity of his name and curiosity that surrounded his governorship so that he could remain in the public eye. He used the *Ferguson Forum* in the same manner that modern-day discredited politicians use a myriad of media outlets to resurrect their own lives and careers.[37]

The subsequent *Ferguson Forum* volumes appeared to operate as a regular newspaper, with articles on the Great War, government policy, even wedding announcements and other social events. Nevertheless, under the facade of a daily press, the resentment toward his treatment by the big newspapers, particularly the *Austin Statesman* and the *Dallas Morning News,* filtered into almost every page. By the third publication, Ferguson's hatred of the *Dallas Morning News* was tangible. He accused the paper of strategically withholding pertinent news that exonerated him "because the press was against him" and because they were "sore" at him for "vetoing a bill put through by the legislature that prevented them from being sued in the county where they might . . . libel the character of any citizen." He continued to state that the paper "was determined not to give Ferguson any publicity that might enlighten the people" to the charges brought against him in the courts.[38]

His fight with the *Dallas Morning News* centered on his claim that the paper took the side of the university and did not give him a fair shake or space in the paper to publish his side of the story. In an article, Ferguson published a correspondence between himself and the paper about a press release he wanted printed on the front page. The *Dallas Morning News* replied that they intended to mark the press release an "advertisement," edit it to take out incriminating remarks about the penitentiary system, then charge $95 to place the ad on an inside page. Ferguson was furious at the slight and took this as proof of the cahoots that formed between the university regents and the Texas newspapers.[39]

Ferguson continued to appeal to the rural population, and to keep up his "Farmer Jim" persona, with his articles on land prices, special seed, and "the best way to make hogs fat." However, Ferguson routinely used his front page to entice this same group of Texas citizens to keep abreast of his intentions on rejoining the political circles with headlines that read, "Ferguson's Candidacy for Governor Stirs Interest among Texas Politicians," and "Ferguson Sure of Election as Texas Governor." In this same publication, he assured his readers that the plot against him by the legislators, the university, and the Texas press had "absolutely failed and the readers are sure to rebuke and punish his accusers and slanderers." He wanted his constituents to trust and accept that he fought for their interests.[40]

In the book *Minnie Fisher Cunningham*, historians Judith McArthur and Harold Smith argued that even as Ferguson "defiantly declared himself a candidate for governor in 1918 . . . 'Farmer Jim' was still popular with rural voters." In Ferguson fashion, he announced his candidacy in the first issue of the *Ferguson Forum* of the new year. On January 3, 1918, the headline read, "Ferguson Sure to Have Name on the Ticket," and it was accompanied by a cartoon of political elites dancing around a burning Statue of Liberty with the caption, "when the political teachers, lawyers and preachers, get their foul hands upon the judicial branch of government the witch-fires start burning in the Temples of Justice and these polished prostitutes of learning, justice and mercy begin a war-dance around the Statue of Liberty which, for barbarianism, cunning and cussedness would awe a savage, subdue a criminal and shame the Devil."[41]

In the next five issues he detailed exactly who the political enemies were and how he aimed to expose their political corruption. In no uncertain terms, Ferguson intended to use his *Forum* to fight against the *Austin Statesman* and the *Dallas Morning News* and the academics he argued created his predicament. By August 1918, the headline read, "200,000 Liars Running Loose in Texas." The article detailed how the "howl of the political crook" took the shape in the articles of the big city newspapers. He accused the aforementioned large newspapers—and included the *Houston Post*, *Chronicle*, and the *San Antonio Express*—of "pretending to be high class newspapers," but, he stated, the reality was that "they produced lies in almost every issue of their slander sheets."[42]

The fight continued in the form of Ferguson's weekly publication and lasted until 1927, where both James Ferguson and his wife, Miriam, used the funds generated through the sales of the newspaper to further their political campaigns. This included selling advertisement space to corporations that wanted to appease him, since he orchestrated deals with the state Highway Department and his former railroad commissioner that proved quite lucrative. Nevertheless, his circulation topped at no more than 20,000 subscriptions, including the fact that practically all state employees subscribed to the *Forum* while Miriam Ferguson was governor.[43]

Ferguson created his own outlet of media hype to combat what he saw as inflammatory propaganda launched by the Texas press as an assault on his character. Nevertheless, Ferguson slowly ran out of the time, money, and star power that appealed to Texas voters. Historian Dewey Grantham referred to Ferguson as a Texas "political demagogue" who, after he failed to relaunch his political career, "used his wife as his political proxy." Ferguson essentially did the same with the *Ferguson Forum*, by using the pages as a political platform to launch his comeback tour as a political contender and have a format to express his ideas, since he routinely articulated his disgust with the big city Texas newspapers and the university academics, and how they railroaded him out of the governor's office.[44]

Throughout the entire impeachment debacle, a media-centered war surrounded the governor, the University of Texas, and the Texas newspapers. Both sides played to their readership and catered to the notion that the main platform of the contest encompassed the underlying issues of rural folks versus the urban elite. Many of the elites connected to the university and political offices had newspaper publishing backgrounds and enough knowledge to understand the power of the press and public reactions to sensational headlines. Ferguson adopted these same methods to launch his media tirades that appealed to his anti-academia camp. The media fight between Ferguson and the daily press, including the creation of the *Ferguson Forum*, further illustrates the financial and political conflict in the traditionalism and modernization that existed in Texas during the early twentieth century, and continued to remain an issue for generations. Nevertheless, all media outlets that surrounded the political bout allowed the public a front row seat to view the contenders of the largest conflict and media spectacle in Texas history.

NOTES

1. Editorial, "McGregor Arraigns Ball at Majestic," *Dallas Morning News*, July 22, 1914; Judith McArthur and Harold Smith, *Minnie Fisher Cunningham: A Suffragist's Life in Politics* (New York: Oxford University Press, 2005), 49.

2. Patrick Cox, *The First Texas News Barons* (Austin: University of Texas Press, 2005), 3. For more information on the power and influence of the Texas daily newspapers see pages 18–23.

3. Cox, *The First Texas News Barons*, 3–6; Curtis Bishop and R. L. Schroeter, "Austin American-Statesman," *Handbook of Texas Online*, accessed February 16, 2016, http://www.tshaonline.org/handbook/online/articles/eea11.

4. Ralph W. Steen, "Ferguson, James E.," *Handbook of Texas Online*, accessed September 5, 2015. Last modified on June 12, 2010, http://www.tshaonline.org/handbook/online/articles/ffe05; George P. Huckaby, "Colquitt, Oscar Branch," *Handbook of Texas Online*, accessed September 5, 2015. Last modified on June 12, 2010, http://www.tshaonline.org/handbook/online/articles/fc032; Carol O'Keefe Wilson, *In The Governor's Shadow: The True Story of Ma and Pa Ferguson* (Denton: University of North Texas Press, 2014), 12; editorial, "Ferguson Speaks at the Majestic Theater," *Dallas Morning News*, June, 14, 1914; editorial, "Ferguson Speaks in Greenville," April 1, 1914; editorial, "Ferguson Addresses Crowd at Bay City," June 23, 1914; Jack Elton Keever, "Jim Ferguson and the Press, 1913–1917" (master's thesis, University of Texas, 1965), 41–50. Many of the Ferguson campaign speeches across Texas include his stance to veto any legislation on prohibition both pro and anti that comes across his desk. He argues that the state needs a break from prohibition talk.

5. Charles W. Holman, "Governor Jim of Texas," *Harper's Weekly*, September 18, 1915, 279–80.

6. Editorial, "Governor Ferguson Urges Legislation," *Dallas Morning News*, January 21, 1915; Gene Preuss, *To Get a Better School System: One Hundred Years of Education Reform in Texas* (College Station: Texas A&M University Press, 2009), 15.

7. Lewis Gould, *Progressives and Prohibitionists: Texas Democrats in the Wilson Era* (Austin: Texas State Historical Association Press, 1992), 187; James Ferguson, *Ferguson Forum*, vol. 1, no. 7, December 30, 1917, 1.

8. Patrick Cox, "Governor Jim Ferguson and His Battle with Eugene C. Barker," *The Texas Book Two: More Profiles, Histories, and Reminisces of the University*, ed.

David Dettmer (Austin: University of Texas Press, 2012), 135; Gould, *Progressives and Prohibitionists*, 190.

9. Gould, *Progressives and Prohibitionists*, 193, 196–97; "Mayes, William Harding," *Handbook of Texas Online*, accessed September 7, 2015. Last modified on June 15, 2010, http://www.tshaonline.org/handbook/online/articles/fma89; "Investigation by the Board of Regents of the University of Texas of Certain Members of the Faculty," *Bulletin of the University of Texas*, no. 59 (Austin: University of Texas Press, 1916), 47; *Daily Texan*, December 3, 1916.

10. Keever, "Jim Ferguson and the Press, 1913–1917," 35 and 63.

11. Editorial, "Ferguson Defends His Administration," *Dallas Morning News*, June 25, 1916; Associated Press, "Senate Will Not Investigate Charges against the Governor," *Dallas Morning News*, February 15, 1917; Gould, *Progressives and Prohibitionists*, 202; editorial, "Governor Ferguson Exonerated by Committee and by the House," *Dallas Morning News*, March 16, 1917.

12. Gould, *Progressives and Prohibitionists*, 186, 202.

13. Wayne Gard, "Lomax, John Avery," *Handbook of Texas Online*, accessed September 7, 2015. Last modified on June 13, 2012, https://tshaonline.org/handbook/online/articles/f1007; editorial, "No headline," *Austin Statesman*, May 28, 1917; editorial, "A Conference with the Regents," *Dallas Morning News*, May 29, 1917.

14. Preuss, *To Get a Better School System*, 36–38.

15. Gould, *Progressives and Prohibitionists*, 202; editorial, "As to Some Critics of the News," *Dallas Morning News*, May 3, 1917.

16. Editorial, "News/Opinion—No Headline," *Dallas Morning News*, June 20, 1917.

17. Gould, *Progressives and Prohibitionists*, 207.

18. Editorial, "The Peoples' University—Shall It Be Destroyed?" *Houston Chronicle*, July 5, 1917. The preceding four articles appeared June 27, June 29, July 1, and July 4.

19. "Advertisement," *Dallas Morning News*, July 4, 1917. The same advertisements and dates coincided with the articles that ran in the *Houston Chronicle*.

20. Gould, *Progressives and Prohibitionists*, 208.

21. Ibid., 209–10.

22. Editorial, "Leaders Gathering at State Capitol," *Dallas Morning News*, July 30, 1917; Cox, "Governor Jim Ferguson and His Battle with Eugene C. Barker," 139.

23. Gould, *Progressives and Prohibitionists*, 211; editorial, "Will Hogg Speaks at Luncheon Here," *Dallas Morning News*, July 29, 1917; William H. Mayes was the owner and editor of the *Brownwood Bulletin* and the dean of the College of Journalism at the University of Texas. Lieutenant Governor William P. Hobby was also manager and part owner of the *Beaumont Enterprise* until he was elected in 1914. See William P. Hobby Jr., "Hobby, William Pettus," *Handbook of Texas On-*

line, http://www.tshaonline.org/handbook/online/articles/fh004, accessed October 25, 2015. Uploaded on June 15, 2010.

24. Gould, *Progressives and Prohibitionists*, 207.

25. All articles appeared as editorials and front page headlines, *Houston Chronicle*, Saturday, July 25, 1917.

26. Editorial, "Urges Change in Resolution for Investigation," *Austin Statesman*, August 2, 1917; Associated Press, "The Governor's Veto Stand," *Austin Statesman*, August 2, 1917, via *Galveston News*.

27. Editorial, "Numerous State Officials Will Give Testimony," *Austin Statesman*, August 4, 1917; editorial, "Governor Declines to Be First to Testify," *Austin Statesman*, August 6, 1917; editorial, "Speaker Fuller Files Thirteen Charges against Gov. Ferguson," *Dallas Morning News*, August 2, 1917.

28. Editorial, "Text of Speaker's Charges against Governor Ferguson," *Dallas Morning News*, August 2, 1917; Walter D. Kamphoefner, "The Handwriting on the Wall: The Klan, Language Issues and Prohibition in the German Settlements of Eastern Texas," *Southwestern Historical Quarterly* 112, no. 1 (2008). For further information on anti-German sentiment and German American activity in World War I Texas, see James Bernard Seymour, "War within a War: The Effects of the Great War on the Social Progressivism in Texas" (PhD diss., Texas A&M University, 1997), passim.

29. Editorial, "Testimony Ends with Ferguson Maintaining Secrecy about Loan," *Houston Chronicle*, August 22, 1917; Associated Press, "Temple State Bank President Cited by Court," *Houston Chronicle*, August 22, 1917; editorial, "Governor Ferguson Impeached by House on Twenty-One Counts," *Dallas Morning News*, August 25, 1917.

30. Editorial, "Senate Begins Trial of Ferguson," *Dallas Morning News*, August 29, 1917; editorial, "Ferguson on Stand in His Own Behalf," *Dallas Morning News*, September 18, 1917; editorial, "Ferguson Concludes Direct Testimony," *Dallas Morning News*, September 19, 1917.

31. Editorial, "Lieutenant Governor Hobby Probably Will Take Oath as Governor of Texas Today," *Dallas Morning News*, September 26, 1917; Gould, *Progressives and Prohibitionists*, 219; quoted from Edmunds Travis to John H. Kirby, October 10, 1917, John H. Kirby Papers, University of Houston Special Collections, Houston, Texas.

32. Advertisement, "Zep's Last Raid at the Hippodrome," *Dallas Morning News*, March 24, 1918. According to the *Dallas Morning News* archives, advertisements for the impeachment trial film ran at the Hippodrome Theater for the following six days, "continuous from 11 am to 11 pm," *Dallas Morning News*, March 24–30, 1918.

33. Editorial, "To His Future Plans," *Dallas Morning News*, September 23, 1917.

34. Gould, *Progressives and Prohibitionists*, 219.

35. Dewey W. Grantham, *The Life and Death of the Solid South: A Political History* (Lexington: University Press of Kentucky, 1992), 83.

36. James Ferguson, *Ferguson Forum*, vol. 1, no. 1, November 19, 1917, 1, 3; Texas Christian University Archives and Special Collections houses the *Ferguson Forum* on microfilm, beginning with the first issue in November 1917 through December 1923.

37. James Ferguson, *Ferguson Forum*, vol. 1, no. 1, November 19, 1917, 1.

38. James Ferguson, *Ferguson Forum*, vol. 1, no. 3, November 22, 1917, 1.

39. Ibid.

40. James Ferguson, *Ferguson Forum*, vol. 1, no. 7, December 20, 1917, 1.

41. McArthur and Smith, *Minnie Fisher Cunningham*, 61; James Ferguson, *Ferguson Forum*, vol. 1, no. 9, January 3, 1918, 1.

42. James Ferguson, *Ferguson Forum*, vol. 1, no. 40, August 8, 1918, 1.

43. Norman Brown, *Hood, Bonnet, and Little Brown Jug: Texas Politics, 1921–1928* (College Station: Texas A&M University Press, 1984), 277–88.

44. *Ferguson Forum*, https://www.tshaonline.org/; Grantham, *Life and Death of the Solid South*, 9.

5

Fergusonism, Factionalization, and Thirty Years of Texas Politics

Mark Stanley

In the thirty years following the impeachment of governor James E. Ferguson, Texas Democratic Party politics were among the most factionalized of any southern state. Under any one-party system, that party has to account for the entire spectrum of political opinion. At its purest, politics consists of two sides: liberal and conservative. Rapid growth and impending modernity resulted in a corresponding growth among various interest groups. Texans divided among many competing interests, including urban and rural, industrial and agricultural, rich and poor, and black and white in addition to the traditional left and right. Thus Texas politics of the period was far from pure. This state of affairs contributed to a subtle undercurrent of divisiveness and rancor that flowed continually until it broke surface, often violently. The impeachment of Governor James E. Ferguson was an example of this phenomenon and was a consequential moment in Texas political history. In this case, Texas's two main political factions, the conservatives and the progressives, were in open conflict. It was long in coming, and it was part of a protracted breakup that ultimately drove Texas conservatives into the open arms of the Republicans.[1]

Ferguson's election as governor in 1914 came amid a struggle between conservatives and progressives for control of the Democratic Party of Texas. One polarizing issue rose above all others to divide them—prohibition. It became a major campaign issue, one near and dear to the hearts of liberals. Texas progressives committed themselves to nominating a prohibitionist candidate. So popular was this reform that the executive committee of the prohibition Democrats was swamped by potential candidates and forced to resort to an "elimination" process to pare down the field.

The committee eventually settled on Thomas Ball, a former congressman from Houston. Ball, an attorney, had the added advantages of being an active prohibitionist and having the countenance of a statesman with his flowing white hair and beard. Unfortunately, Ball had the disadvantage of having represented both railroads and large corporations in the course of his legal practice. Many viewed him as a "tool of the plutocracy." In Texas's political environment, with its large number of disadvantaged and disaffected working people, it was a critical failing.[2]

Meanwhile, some conservative Democrats also advocated an elimination process to choose their candidate by calling a convention for that purpose. "Farmer Jim" Ferguson, as he soon became known, would have none of it. Ferguson suggested the elimination convention was merely a means of removing the "true democracy" of Texas from the political process in order for "bosses" to keep control for themselves. In his first speech of the campaign, Ferguson promised to seek legislation to limit rent rates for tenant farmers. It became the central component of his campaign and was very astute. At the time, Texas was mostly rural and the majority of its farmers were tenants. Thus this one campaign promise had the potential to appeal to a large section of the electorate. But it would likely not be enough to get him elected on its own. He knew he would need some support among middle-class, progressive-minded voters. Consequently, Ferguson argued that his controversial anti-tenancy program would have the added benefit of curbing "radicalism" and "socialism" among tenant farmers. In a move clearly aimed at southern business progressives, the candidate suggested it was time to elect a "successful businessman," such as himself, as governor. Jim Ferguson had carefully put together a winning coalition of poor white farmers, conservatives, and a number of business progressives. In the July primary election, the deciding election, Ferguson defeated Ball by a 237,062 to 191,558 votes.[3]

By 1916, factional discord within the Democratic Party of Texas was reaching a crescendo. Texas progressives were increasingly influential, with one of their own, "Colonel" Edward M. House, serving as one of President Woodrow Wilson's key advisors. Meanwhile, conservatives sought to maintain overall control of the party. As Texas Democrats met for their state convention in the summer of 1916, both sides believed that theirs would prevail. Some observers rightly noted that Democrats seemed to be a "party made of irreconcilable differences." The struggle for control of the party soon centered on control of its message via the platform. Many Texas progressives favored neutrality in the ongoing World War I, support of Wilson's administration, woman suffrage, and most importantly prohibition. Conservatives, of course, favored practically none of that. The progressives had a rude awakening as the platform committee came under control of conservatives. Moreover, the "committee" consisted mostly of archconservative former United States senator Joseph Weldon Bailey and Governor Ferguson, who were observed "in their shirt sleeves working together" to draft the platform. It was a simple platform of just four planks: support for the Wilson administration, support for Ferguson's administration, opposition to woman suffrage, and opposition to national prohibition.[4]

With the support of the sitting governor, titular head of the party, and with the convention controlled by conservatives, the Ferguson-Bailey platform was adopted by the convention delegates. It was a bitter loss for the progressives. No doubt dejected and defeated, they released a minority report that ironically contained fourteen points in support of Wilson and his reforms, especially woman suffrage and prohibition. Having lost this round, Texas progressives did not give up. There were scores to be settled, and settle them they would. Many progressives likely could not shake the image of Ferguson and Bailey working to destroy their idealistic program. Ferguson was likely quite happy with himself. In fact, his actions at the 1916 Texas Democratic Party Convention, as well as those at the subsequent Democratic National Convention, played a major role in creating the coalition of progressives and suffragists that secured his impeachment the next year.[5]

For all of his failings, Ferguson was a talented and effective politician. Elected in 1914, and then reelected in 1916, he appealed to what was probably Texas's largest political faction—poor, white farmers. "Farmer Jim" was himself, by vocation, a banker who also happened to be an attorney. Nevertheless, Ferguson carefully cultivated the perception among his key supporters, farmers, that he was one of them despite being firmly in the camp of the establishment. Once in power, Ferguson regarded himself as a free agent, independent of oversight either legislative or electoral. Just as he had cultivated a coalition of supporters to get elected, as governor, Ferguson seemingly cultivated another coalition of opponents from varying factions. This was his eventual downfall. Moreover, Ferguson actually created a new faction that turned out to be one of the most formidable arrayed against him. In his efforts to pander to his rural constituencies,

Ferguson often advocated rural education at the expense of higher education—especially the University of Texas. In what became known as Ferguson's "War with the University of Texas," he directly took on the school's administration. The confrontation became more than the governor bargained for.[6]

Founded in 1883, the University of Texas (UT) was the state's first public university; it also included a law school. From the beginning, UT had a reputation for the "tradition of academic freedom" and excellence. Naturally, the school could count among its supporters the large cadre of alumni and members of the Ex-Students' Association commonly known as the "Texas Exes." By Ferguson's time, many among the state's educated professionals, who tended to be progressives, called UT their alma mater. These businessmen, physicians, and attorneys all had an interest in protecting the school. No doubt many of them held seats in the legislature. It was Ferguson's distrust of academics and bias against the university that got him in trouble with UT supporters. In his first term, Ferguson got into a dispute with acting UT president William J. Battle over several line items of the budget. The governor grudgingly signed the appropriation bill but pointed out to regents several items he disliked. It would not be so easy next time. Ominously, Ferguson told one regent that UT was run by a "clique" that he was determined to purge.[7]

Here started Ferguson's war against UT. His sights first set upon Battle, who had resisted the governor's attempts at itemization of the university budget. The confrontation between the two men ruined any chances of Battle's permanent appointment. The board of regents began looking for a university president; meanwhile, Ferguson identified several faculty members he wished fired—mostly because he suspected them of being prohibitionists. When the board of regents hired Robert E. Vinson as university president, without having consulted the governor, and without firing the objectionable faculty members, Ferguson was infuriated. Vinson visited the governor and discussed the firings and asked about "specific charges." Ferguson banged his fist on the desk and demanded the men "had to go." Eventually, Ferguson did charge that Battle had misled him about the budget and accused the faculty members of padding their expenses. The regents reviewed the charges, investigated them, and concluded they were not substantial enough to warrant firings. At this point, Ferguson became convinced that the regents were also part of the "clique" and could not be trusted.[8]

University supporters sensed the danger and rallied to meet the challenge. Disparate factions that might not have normally aligned began to coalesce against Ferguson. In January 1917, Governor Ferguson personalized the conflict by appointing cronies to vacancies on the University of Texas Board of Regents. President Vinson astutely made overtures to key Texas progressives soon after his appointment. In a letter to former Texas House Speaker, future governor, and UT law school alumnus Pat M. Neff, Vinson wrote, "I . . . believe that, with the continuance of your cooperation, we may together labor for the advancement of the university." It was likely one of many such letters. Moving the university forward against Ferguson's opposition would be difficult. Meanwhile, university officials worked behind the scenes to shore up support from legislators while assuring them they would support intense scrutiny of school finances. Finally, one university supporter and legislator, Representative O'Banion, turned the tables on the governor by suggesting that *his* finances should be investigated—not the university's. By this time, questions had arisen over Ferguson's business dealings and especially overdrafts written to his own Temple State Bank. Of course, these investigations widened and eventually led to the impeachment proceedings against Ferguson.[9]

Ultimately, it was the governor's decision to defund the University of Texas in June 1917 that brought down the wrath of his opponents. At the time, Ferguson fell back on his populist roots and appealed directly to his largest constituencies, rural people and farmers. The governor asserted that he believed the state university should not be run by "educated highbrows" to the exclusion of the people who pay for it. It was good politics, but it was not enough. By this time, Ferguson's enemies list was much longer than his friends list and included university students, university alumni, many attorneys, progressive politicians, and prohibitionists and woman suffragists who remembered Ferguson's role in removing those planks from the 1916 Texas Democratic Party platform. Furthermore, the governor's enemies had political motivations of their own beyond mere altruism or opposition to corruption. For example, as soon as Ferguson announced his decision to defund the university, the student body president, George E. B. Peddy, organized demonstrations at the state capitol, which Ferguson famously observed through his office window. Peddy himself was an embodiment of the factions opposing Ferguson. At the time, he was a law student at UT. He was elected to the legislature in 1917 and later went into practice. Over the course of the next ten years, he became an operative within the Texas Democratic Party and ran against Earle Mayfield, a known Klansman, for US Senate in 1922. Clearly, Peddy parlayed his involvement in the Ferguson impeachment effort into a political career.[10]

Interestingly, women who could not yet vote constituted some of the most effective opposition to Ferguson. They played leading roles in two of the largest factions facing the governor—prohibitionists and suffragists. Nannie Webb Curtis, president of the Women's Christian Temperance League of Texas, rallied her organization's members against the "liquor domination" of the University of Texas. It was the suffragists who were most calculatingly political during the impeachment episode. Minnie Fisher Cunningham, president of the Texas Equal Suffrage Association (TESA), recognized Ferguson as the biggest impediment to woman suffrage in the state through his power of veto. In a letter to Carrie Chapman Catt, president of the National American Woman Suffrage Association (NAWSA), Cunningham wrote, "it seemed to me a chance of a lifetime to break the power of corrupt politics ... when they [legislators] phoned me ... to come to Austin to swing the women's end of it. I came." However, it was more than merely breaking corruption that motivated her. Cunningham explained that if the impeachment were successful, the new governor, William P. Hobby, would be obliged to call a special session of the legislature to reinstate university appropriations as well as various officials fired by Ferguson. Cunningham wrote, "It seems to me a wonderfully opportune moment to ask them to put through our primary suffrage bill." It was to be a quid pro quo.[11]

When the inevitable impeachment proceedings began, the House of Representatives visitors' galleries were "crowded," no doubt with observers from the various anti-Ferguson factions. The House eventually voted twenty-one articles of impeachment against Ferguson. On September 23, 1917, the Senate found Governor Ferguson guilty of eleven charges ranging from diversion of state funds to coercion of state officials (UT Board of Regents) and removal of regents without sufficient cause. Observers in the gallery were respectfully quiet as the vote was taken. "Bedlam" broke out when the vote was completed as Ferguson's opponents gleefully filed out of the building. Three days later, the Senate formally removed the governor from office and banned him from holding public office. Meanwhile, the same day, Ferguson released to the press a resignation letter dated two days prior and announced his intent to run for governor again based on the assertion that since he was no longer governor, the impeachment and ban did not apply. Obviously, the tactic failed; Ferguson became the only Texas governor ever impeached, and he never held office again—though he tried. Soon after the impeachment, Texas women received the right to vote in the state's Democratic primaries, just in time to vote for Governor Hobby. Within less than two years, Texas ratified both the Eighteenth Amendment, which instituted Prohibition, and the Nineteenth Amendment, giving women full voting rights.[12]

To a great extent, the 1920 gubernatorial contest sought to decide whether the progressive or conservative factions controlled the Texas Democratic Party. This race was both bitter and contentious, pitting four progressive candidates against a conservative candidate, none other than Joseph Weldon Bailey, for the party nomination and certain subsequent election in the fall. By 1920, Bailey had been out of office for several years, and though still influential as evidenced by his role in the 1916 state democratic convention, he was largely out of touch with Texas. In many ways, the 1920 elections were seen as a referendum on both progressivism and the administration of President Woodrow Wilson, especially in Texas. Generally, Bailey denounced the administration and its policies, while progressives praised it. Bailey had also been opposed to woman suffrage, and newly enfranchised women were not about to forget it. In the end, division within the party, the accompanying disorder, and probably Texas tradition made it possible for "charismatic personalities" like Bailey to gain popular attention among conservatives. Texas progressives needed only to sort through their four candidates to find a similar charismatic personality. In any case, the scene was set for a battle royal to determine the next governor of Texas.[13]

It was former Texas Speaker Pat M. Neff who rose to the top of the pack among progressives. He had taken a twenty-year break from state politics and had most recently led a successful prohibition campaign in his hometown of Waco in 1917. When Neff began his campaign for governor, he ran an independent campaign. His main advantages were having been out of state politics during the Ferguson impeachment and a well-acknowledged skill for oratory. According to Neff, "No one solicited me to run for governor. I did not ask permission of anyone to get into the race" and added, "no publicly recognized political leader had any interests . . . in me. No business interests had any concern." Neff was his own man, having no campaign manager or headquarters. He traveled the state taking his message into the "hearts and homes of the people." The tactic of making a direct appeal to Texas's disaffected voters, while portraying himself as an "outsider," was a brilliant tactic. Moreover, his independence allowed him to maintain the appearance of being "above" politics. In the heavily factionalized, toxic atmosphere that pervaded state politics in the wake of the Ferguson episode, it was probably his greatest asset.[14]

During most of the election campaign, the ratification of the Nineteenth Amendment was ongoing. Women were an increasingly important part of the electorate that also happened to be a key faction of the party. Bailey, of course, ignored them. The progressives, instead, actively courted them. Minnie Fisher Cunningham supported Robert Thomason, a legislator and attorney from Bailey's hometown of Gainesville. Cunningham took out an advertisement in the *Dallas Morning News* that offered a side-by-side comparison of Thomason and Neff. Neff, while friendly and sympathetic to the suffragists, had not publicly supported ratification of the suffrage amendment. Nevertheless, Neff had kept in close contact with various women's organizations in the state and generally tried to appease them. In one letter Neff wrote, "I am exceedingly anxious to be honored by receiving, not only your vote, but your active support" and "have at all times been in favor of women's suffrage." Neff apparently gave private assurances of his support for woman suffrage but was unwilling to do so publicly. The support of women was crucial to Neff's election—and he knew it. However, Neff also knew the race was likely to be tight and might hinge on bleeding off votes from conservatives.[15]

Bailey ran on the key conservative principles of fiscal responsibility, states' rights, and resistance to progressivism. His opening speech of the campaign laid his conservatism bare for all to see. Bailey said, "Times may change, and men may change with them, but principles never change; they are as immutable as truth and justice, they are the same today as they were yesterday, and they will be the same tomorrow as they are today . . . these prophets of a new cult, proceeded to substitute Progressive policies for Democratic principles." The passage neatly encapsulated the notion of conservative resistance to change. At the same time, it almost seemed like a formal declaration of war against progressivism. Moreover, it is indicative of the deteriorating condition of intraparty relations since the Ferguson impeachment. Bailey put progressives on notice that he intended to give the electorate a clear choice—if nothing else. In the end, Bailey and his conservative policies became the central issue in the campaign.[16]

On March 6, a mass meeting of "Woodrow Wilson Democrats" assembled in Dallas at City Hall Auditorium. The meeting of up to 1,200 included many of Texas's most prominent progressive politicians and activists, including Governor William Hobby and former Texas attorney general Martin M. Crane. The four progressive faction candidates for governor, Benjamin F. Looney, Dwight Lewelling, Robert Thomason, and Pat Neff, appeared. Others included clubwoman and suffragist Anna Pennybacker, Texas League of Women Voters president Jessie Daniel Ames, and former Texas Equal Suffrage Association president and national League of Women Voters leader Minnie Fisher Cunningham. Generally, participants at the meeting gave high praise to Wilson and his administration and condemned Bailey. In a speech by fellow attorney and longtime friend of Neff, Cullen Thomas, the progressives answered the call to arms. Thomas said, "We delight to call ourselves Progressive Democrats. We stand arrayed against the Bourbon Democrats, who never forgot the old and never learn the new. We know we live in a new day and we won't spend our time groping in graveyards." Thus the lines of battle were drawn clearly between the two factions.[17]

The advent of Texas primary woman suffrage did not bode well for Bailey. In fact, the entire campaign did not go well for Bailey. In the county nominating conventions held in the early May, Bailey's support was found to be "negligible." County conventions across Texas sent delegates to the state convention that supported the Wilson administration and presumably progressive faction policies—Bailey was on the wrong side. Even Bailey's home of Cooke County, and even the very precinct he lived in, rejected him. The effect was such that Bailey returned to Washington, DC, where he lived most of the time, no doubt to confer with his friends there and to lick his wounds. At this point, Bailey probably should have surmised the probable outcome of his endeavor, but he refused to give up. The campaign continued, and the Texas Democratic primary was held on July 25. The race between Neff and Bailey was close; most reports during the next week gave Bailey a slight lead. Final figures released by the Texas Election Bureau on August 6 gave Bailey a lead of just 1,852 votes over Neff, with Bailey receiving 152,173 votes and Neff 150,321. The results put Bailey and Neff in a runoff election. Ultimately, Neff defeated Bailey by 73,325 votes. The progressives had won, and the conservatives lost. Nevertheless, the rift between progressive and conservative Texas Democrats continued.[18]

Despite the impeachment, Ferguson continued to be a force in conservative politics, and his supporters remained a sizable faction within the party. Neff was elected to two terms, equaling a total of four years in office. During much of his tenure, the newly arisen Ku Klux Klan became a political faction unto itself and was a constant enemy of progressive reform. According to historian Charles C. Alexander, "To the Klan, reform meant preserving or restoring the status-quo. To reverse changes wrought by progressive reform, as well as the shift from rural values to urban values." He adds, that in the case of Texas, "people ... were ready to adapt the Klan to their own needs and use it as a shortcut to political and moral renovation, to the reestablishment of law and order." To the notion of rolling back progressive reform, conservatives and the Klan most certainly agreed. Many conservative Texans harnessed the Klan to advance their agenda, and Jim Ferguson was most certainly among them. By 1924, the Klan's influence on politics was unquestioned, with the organization actually endorsing candidates. This was the case in the governor's race when Dallas Grand Dragon Zeke Marvin endorsed a fellow Klansman, Judge Felix D. Robertson. Ferguson, who had been plotting his return to politics since his impeachment, likely saw this political environment as a golden opportunity. In January 1924, Ferguson announced his candidacy for governor and stated that, in the event his name was not placed on the ballot, his wife would run.[19]

Ferguson's opponents mounted legal challenges to his candidacy. The case went all the way to the Texas Supreme Court. The justices upheld Ferguson's impeachment on all counts and further endorsed the Senate's verdict as both legal and final. Thus, Miriam A. Ferguson became the first woman to run for the highest office in the state when the Texas Democratic Party officially placed *her* name on the ballot instead of her husband's. She had little preparation, having never held office and, in fact, previously showed little interest in public affairs. Mrs. Ferguson's chief interest in running seemed to be her desire to clear the family name in the wake of the impeachment. It was widely asserted that she was nothing more than a surrogate for her husband. What ensued was yet another complicated democratic gubernatorial primary. There were four candidates. Two were conservatives, Robertson and Ferguson; two were progressives, T. W. Davidson and Lynch Davidson, both of whom had served in the legislature. On election day, no one candidate had a majority. The two leading candidates were Robertson and Ferguson who would meet in a runoff. Many voters considered it an awful choice—either a Klansman or a woman whom they viewed as a proxy for a man barred from holding office. There was no progressive candidate. In the final runoff, the Fergusons won by 127,588 votes. Texas elected its first female governor. "Ma" Ferguson, as she was often called, served two nonconcurrent gubernatorial terms, 1925–27 and 1933–35.[20]

Meanwhile, the 1922 US Senate race against the ailing and elderly incumbent Charles A. Culberson also highlighted the factionalization of the Texas Democratic Party. At the root of this conflict was the Ku Klux Klan's foray into organized politics. After defeating Culberson and others in the state Democratic Primary, the subsequent runoff pitted Earle B. Mayfield, a Klansman, against Jim Ferguson. The main issue of the campaign was the Klan and Mayfield's membership in it. Although Mayfield had reportedly quit the Klan, he was, nevertheless, its endorsed candidate. Many feared that the Klan could co-opt control of the Democratic Party. As the Texas Democratic Party Convention approached, one of the proposed agendas included an "anti-Klan" plank. The fight over the plank constituted an all-out war between progressive and conservative Texas Democrats. Through the next few days, the Resolutions Committee debated the anti-Klan plank and eventually drafted a weak version. When the issue went to the floor of the convention, debate was closed by a vote of 691 to 135. Thus the convention rejected the anti-Klan plank. The action caused uproar on the floor of the convention and probably strengthened the resolve of progressives.[21]

In addition to their rejection of the Klan, progressive Democrats also refused to accept its candidate for the Senate. Just days after the close of the party convention, progressives began to search for an independent candidate to face Mayfield in the election. They chose Harris County assistant district attorney George E. B. Peddy. In a surprise move, Texas Republicans removed their own candidate for Senate and replaced him with Peddy. The fusion candidacy was controversial, and the ensuing contest marked one of the messiest episodes in Texas political history. Part of this controversy centered on the "primary pledge" that bound those voting in the primary to support the party's candidate in the fall election. Some said that voters should adhere to their pledges, others said voters should not be obligated to vote for someone they did not support. The contest between Mayfield and Peddy was hard and bitter. Both sides challenged the legitimacy of the other's candidacy. Both filed suit to have the other's name removed from the ballot, and Mayfield's case went to the Texas Supreme Court. Just four days before the election, the court ordered the secretary of state to postpone the printing of ballots. By Election Day, the issue remained unsettled, and it was not clear whose name would be on the ballot. Voters were upset and confused. Eventually, election officials certified Mayfield as the winner. Despite this, the legality of Mayfield's candidacy remained in the courts for over a year. Senate leaders refused to seat Mayfield until the following December. Even then, many of Texas's Democratic establishment politicians avoided contact with the state's newest United States senator.[22]

Factional discord within the Texas Democratic Party continued through the rest of the 1920s—although its nature began to change. After several bitter gubernatorial showdowns, neither faction seemed able to gain overall control. Both sides resorted to using wedge issues, such as woman suffrage, prohibition, "Fergusonism," radicalism, socialism, or the Klan to pit the various subfactions against one another for their own purposes. Such tactics were often effective in winning elections. But electoral success did not always translate into successfully enacting policy. Many on both sides became frustrated and began looking for other options. For the first time, Texas Democrats began to seriously question the efficacy of the "primary pledge." In 1928, when the Democratic National Convention nominated Governor Al Smith of New York for president, it was too much for many Texans to bear. Smith, an antiprohibitionist, Catholic, and "Yankee," drew transfactional opposition from Texas Democrats. Many establishment democrats did the previously unthinkable and actively campaigned for the Republican nominee, Herbert Hoover. Former governor Oscar B. Colquitt formed the "Hoover Democrats." Many rank-and-file Democrats followed Colquitt's lead. In the fall election, Hoover defeated Smith in Texas by a margin of 367,036 to 341,031 and became the first Republican presidential candidate to carry the state since Reconstruction. More importantly, for the first time, the factionalism of the party threatened to tear it apart.[23]

As one would expect in the course of a nasty breakup, even late into the 1930s many of the participants had hard feelings. The various bitter electoral confrontations began to take their toll. Maintaining a facade of unity and harmony became increasingly difficult. One such effort at keeping up appearances makes this apparent. In 1937, the former governor, Neff, struck upon the idea of gathering all of the living former governors in one place at one time. The ex-governor was respected by most within the party for his impartiality. The occasion was the grand reopening of Mother Neff State Park, the land for which his family donated, following extensive improvements by the Civilian Conservation Corps. In a letter to Jim Ferguson, Neff wrote, "If I remember correctly, the former governors of Texas have not for the past fifteen years . . . assembled anywhere at the same time." Neff then appealed in a spirit of reconciliation, "It seems to me there should be a common tie that binds together all of those who have served as governor, and this without regards to political views, previous campaigns, political alignment, or 'previous condition of servitude.' We should meet now and then on a common platform." The odds of bringing together old political enemies like Jim Ferguson, Dan Moody, and Bill Hobby were nearly incalculable. As one reads Neff's orchestrations with Ferguson, the book of Matthew can practically be heard echoing in his mind, "Blessed are the peacemakers." Neff wrote all of the former governors, as well as then governor James Allred, and patiently, perhaps even naively, awaited a reply.[24]

A few days later, Neff received a reply from Ferguson. He wrote, "My wife joins me in stating that while we appreciate the high motives which have prompted you in this idea . . . and while we both hold you in high esteem, we do not believe that such a meeting would promote harmony, and very likely would result in a lack of congeniality." Ferguson's sincerity and thoughtfulness here is commendable as he declined Neff's invitation. Former Governor Hobby, wrote that he was in "accord" with Neff's idea and added that he and his wife, Oveta, would attend. Former governor Moody replied the same day as Hobby. Moody wrote, "I sincerely appreciate the invitation. . . . It would, however, be unfair to you for me to accept if all the former governors of this state are to be present." Moody explained, "There is one with whom I have nothing to do and I am pleased that he has nothing to do with me. . . . I am opposed to the things he typifies . . . and avoid any and all contacts with him." He could not even mention Ferguson's name. Of course, it was Moody who had handily defeated Miriam Ferguson in 1926 by a near two-to-one margin. Yet after her defeat, the Fergusons remained in Austin, and Jim Ferguson spent his time publicly criticizing and mocking Moody's gubernatorial actions. Neff's meeting of the governors never materialized. Much like the factions they represented, Moody and Ferguson could not bury the hatchet long enough to keep up appearances for the good of the party. Many appreciated and admired

Neff's high-mindedness, but few were able to emulate it—especially when it came to politics. It was not the last time Neff played peacemaker in a warring party.²⁵

The crisis of the Great Depression mitigated much of the partisan conflict during the 1930s, but it did not remove it all together. Naturally, Texas progressives supported the New Deal, as it was the ultimate expression of their ideology. Conversely, the New Deal was highly controversial among conservatives both nationally, and certainly, in Texas. Opposition to the New Deal by southern conservative Democrats was a persistent problem for President Franklin D. Roosevelt. This phenomenon led to the rise of a small but vocal cadre among the Texas congressional delegation known as the "Texas Regulars" who continually voted against the president's policies. Many Texas Democrats supported Roosevelt's vice president, "Cactus" Jack Garner, also of Texas, to succeed the president in 1940. Garner, though part of the administration, had come to oppose New Deal policies. Likely in an effort to counter Garner's effect, during March 1939, First Lady of the United States Eleanor Roosevelt toured Texas speaking in various locales, including Baylor University's Waco Hall. Pat Neff, by that time Baylor University president, introduced Roosevelt to the audience of more than 2,500 Texans. The fact that her speech that night focused on the topic of "Peace" in hindsight places the events occurring one year later in the exact same building in stark contrast. By late 1939, Garner announced that he would accept the Democratic nomination for president if it were given to him. In this political environment, Franklin D. Roosevelt's decision to run for an unprecedented third term sparked anew open warfare between the conservative and progressive wings of the Texas Democratic Party.²⁶

The Texas Democratic Convention of 1940 was held in Waco on the Baylor University campus in Waco Hall. As Democrats gathered, signs of discord between Garner and Roosevelt supporters soon became apparent. "Third termers" were led by San Antonio mayor Maury Maverick, who asserted that Garner should withdraw and stated that the convention would most likely be "stampeded" in Roosevelt's direction. Meanwhile, Myron Blalock, a state Democratic operative and Garner supporter, termed any idea of his candidate's withdrawal as "ridiculous." When the convention met, the result was at best a melee and at worst a riot. Waco police and state highway patrolmen were called to the convention hall to break up fistfights. Police took away "bottles or anything else that could be used as weapons." Meanwhile, delegates in the convention hall shouted

First Lady of the United States Eleanor Roosevelt sitting on stage in Waco Hall at Baylor University with Baylor president and former governor of Texas Pat Neff during a March 13, 1939, public event, in which she spoke to an audience of 2,500 Texans. 1939. Photograph courtesy of Pat Neff Papers, the Texas Collection, Baylor University, Waco, Texas.

down presiding officers. At this point, the gavel was handed to perhaps the one person respected enough by both sides to bring the convention to order—former Texas governor Pat Neff. He began by calling on delegates to "be quiet for just a few moments." He then welcomed "the great Democratic convention to Waco," which drew amused laughter. Thus lightening the mood, Neff next presided over a roll-call vote of delegates all in the name of "democracy," or a fair say to all parties. Neff noted, "This is the most fun I've had in twenty years." At long last, the convention went about its business of choosing delegates and instructing them. The instructions were to renew the Roosevelt-Garner ticket and to deny participation of the delegation in any anti-Roosevelt movement at the national convention. Among the delegates chosen was Neff, who was named a Texas delegate-at-large to the coming Democratic National Convention in Chicago after having ably played the role of peacemaker.[27]

When the delegates met in Chicago the following July, it was still not absolutely clear whether or not Roosevelt would actually run for reelection. In a statement read to the delegates by Senator Alben Barkley of Kentucky, the president expressed "no desire or purpose" to run again. This was met by calls of "We want Roosevelt!" Barkley added, "He wishes . . . to make it clear that all of the delegates . . . are free to vote for any candidate." Roosevelt supporters took this to mean they could continue their efforts—and they did. The next day, Democrats renominated Roosevelt by a wide margin on the first ballot. The possibility of the nation's first three-term presidency was highly controversial. Many Texas Democrats threatened to support the Republican nominee, Wendell Willkie. A group from Corpus Christi even advocated a fusion ticket with Willkie at the head of the Democratic ticket. The movement for Willkie thus posed the possibility of greater fracturing of the party as well as erosion of support for its candidates. In the fall election, Roosevelt defeated Willkie by some 600,000 votes. Nevertheless, the increasing tendency of otherwise reliable Texas Democrats to vote Republican in presidential elections was one of the greatest dangers to the already fractured party. Furthermore, it was a serious political problem for Democrats throughout the South that was indicative of greater problems ahead.[28]

As the Texas Democratic Convention of 1944 approached, the party was already divided into two factions—one supporting a delegation to the national convention that was instructed to vote for Roosevelt, and another supporting a completely uninstructed delegation. Before the convention even met in Austin, the two factions fought over who would preside over the meeting. When the convention finally began, in the Senate chamber of the state capitol, Roosevelt supporters immediately broke ranks and retired to the House chamber. Meanwhile, former governor Moody presided as temporary chairman of the official convention in the Senate. Party leaders sought to reach some consensus. Moody again called upon Neff to address the convention. Neff admonished the delegates, "Abide by the majority vote when the fight is over. Don't go off a pouting if you lose." Neff left the podium to resounding applause, and the official convention sent an uninstructed delegation that was mostly opposed to Roosevelt's renomination. Meanwhile, the rump convention sent its own delegation supporting Roosevelt.[29]

By 1944, Texas Democrats were deeply split by the direction of their party and nation. The rift that had developed between the two main factions of the party could not be mended by mere oratory or calls for reconciliation. When the Democratic National Convention again met in Chicago, political observers noted a similar split between "liberal New Dealers" and "southern revolters." Many expected Texans to play an important role in the convention, which was expected to choose a new vice president who would likely succeed Roosevelt. This included the delegation of Texas Regulars sent by the convention. Amid their efforts to be seated by convention officials, and to thwart the renomination of Roosevelt, they sent Neff a telegram that read, "We have come home at milking time but we are doing the milking." That was clearly not the case. In the end, as many expected, the New Dealers did the "milking" and renominated Roosevelt for president and nominated Harry Truman for vice president. The Texas Regulars, like southern conservatives elsewhere, went home disappointed and no doubt feeling increasingly marginalized in their own party.[30]

In 1948, Truman was in a political fight for his life. As in Texas, the national Democratic Party was split between liberals who supported the New Deal like Truman, and conservatives who opposed it. This was especially true among southern Democrats. To complicate matters further for the president, many of the latter group turned to the segregationist State's Rights Democratic Party, also known as the "Dixiecrats," led by Strom Thurmond. This outright split, along with strong Republican opposition, made Truman's reelection chances seem slim. For Texans, these political realities were nothing new, as exemplified by the movement for Hoover in 1928 and the melees of the 1940 and 1944 state conventions. The 1948 campaign began in earnest with the rival camps aligning either for or against the president. Texans began the 1948 political season in April, quite naturally, with a kick-off fundraiser. Almost predictably given the state of intrapartisan relations, as well as the widely divergent ideals between the two factions, there was not one but *two* competing fundraisers. Thus the two warring factions met simultaneously in two competing picnics that were referred to at the time as the "battle of the barbecues."[31]

As the date of the barbecues approached, observers noted that "rival democratic [party] factions verbally stoked fires" between them. Woodville Rogers, a San Antonio attorney leading the pro-Truman faction, labeled the wayward conservatives as "bolters." Meanwhile, Jerome Sneed, who represented the conservative faction, harkened back to an earlier factional dispute when he reminded Rogers that he himself had rejected the party's chosen candidate when he refused to support Earle Mayfield for US Senate in 1922 and wrote in George Peddy instead. Rogers replied, "I'm still for Peddy." Clearly, old wounds were slow to heal even as new ones were incurred. Governor Beauford Jester, who had organized the conservative faction's bash in Fort Worth, announced he would make "his major political speech of the year" at their picnic. In a flourish of contemporary conservative states' rights rhetoric, Jester said, "I object to efforts of the national party chairman to destroy the state's self-determination of matters that are within the jurisdiction of the state." He added that he would, "report my thinking on the field of states-rights and comment upon the violence which is being done against those rights by the national headquarters of the Democratic Party." Clearly, Jester conflated partisan politics with constitutional law and failed to recognize that the party actually existed outside, and in addition to, the constitutionally prescribed political process. Interestingly, Jester's rhetoric is clearly recognizable today and is still used; the states' rights argument is an old fallback for conservatives.[32]

Allen Duckworth, a journalist covering the barbecues for the *Dallas Morning News*, astutely noted that, "There is more behind the Battle of the Barbecues than the Truman nomination or party loyalty. It is really the beginning of a movement for the '*outs*' in the democratic leadership to oust the '*ins*.'" In effect, as some of today's tea party conservatives would say, it was time for the alienated "outsiders" to "take the party back" from an unresponsive leadership "elite." By this time, as we have seen, the battle for control of the Texas Democratic Party had been ongoing for more than thirty years. Increasingly, the choice that Texas conservatives faced was ousting party apparatchiks or "bolting." Truman carried Texas in 1948 by a considerable margin, besting the combined votes of Republican candidate Thomas E. Dewey and "Dixiecrat" candidate Strom Thurmond by more than 282,000 votes. After such disastrous results, many conservative Texans began thinking of bolting more and more. "Presidential Republicanism" became increasingly prevalent in later elections.[33]

If the breakup of the Texas Democratic Party could be compared to that of a marriage, Ferguson's impeachment was the first public crack. As for the "Battle of the Barbecues," marital trouble is never more apparent than when both sides attend competing parties. The rest of the story of the political breakup of Texas Democrats is almost famous. Allan Shivers served as governor of Texas from 1949 to 1957 and led the conservative wing of the Texas Democratic Party. He is also widely known for his leadership of "Democrats for Eisenhower" in the 1952 presidential election. Thanks to Shivers's efforts, Eisenhower carried Texas by more than 140,000 votes and repeated the feat by nearly as big a margin in 1956. The widespread acceptance of "presidential republicanism" marked the beginning of Texas's and the South's shift to the Republican Party. In 1960, John Tower became the first Republican elected to the US Senate by Texans since 1870. Many considered it the beginning of two-party politics in Texas. Finally, in 1983 Phil Gramm famously resigned his seat in Congress to which he had been elected as a Democrat, in order to run again as a Republican. He won, of course. In many ways, Gramm exemplified the experiences of many conservative Democrats in Texas. After years of battling with the liberal/progressive party leadership for control, they concluded that "ousting" them was not possible. Therefore, they bolted—not just for one election, but for all of them. Gramm's switch triggered a mass exodus of conservative Texans, and southerners at large, to the Republican Party.[34]

From the end of Reconstruction up to Ferguson's governorship, conservatives dominated the Texas Democratic Party. They were "the establishment." The only real threat to their political domination occurred in the 1890s during the "Populist Revolt" when the People's Party drew off support from disaffected urban workers and farmers. The Democrats put down the revolt by co-opting selected Populist Party policies and instituting franchise restriction. By 1901, the conservatives were largely in control of the party and remained so until the rise of the progressives. As the progressives began to move into the establishment's power structure, they increasingly became the "ins" and the conservatives the "outs." Over the years, there were many struggles between conservatives and progressives for control of the Texas Democratic Party. What ensued was a long, protracted, and sometimes violent, breakup. The 1940 and 1944 Texas Democratic Conventions were heated and bitter, with the 1940 Waco convention resulting in an actual brawl. The increasing frequency of "presidential republicanism" during this period, with Hoover, and then later with Willkie, and finally, Eisenhower, amounted to warnings from conservatives that they may leave the party. When it became apparent to conservatives they had little influence on the party's leadership, they did leave—but their losing streak as "Democrats," it could be said, started decades earlier with the successful impeachment of conservative Democratic governor Jim Ferguson.[35]

NOTES

1. Walter L Buenger. *The Path to a Modern South: Northeast Texas between Reconstruction and the Great Depression* (Austin: University of Texas Press, 2001), 4; V. O. Key Jr., *Southern Politics in State and Nation* (Knoxville: University of Tennessee Press, 1949, 2001), 255, 259.

2. Lewis L. Gould, *Progressives and Prohibitionists: Texas Democrats in the Wilson Era* (Austin: University of Texas Press, 1973), 120–24.

3. Ibid., 125–29, 143.

4. Charles E. Neu, "Edward Mandell House," *Handbook of Texas Online* (hereafter cited as *HOT Online*), accessed June 24, 2015, https://tshaonline.org/handbook/online/articles/fh066; editorial, *Dallas Morning News* (hereafter cited as *DMN*), May 26, 1916; The successful Eighteenth Amendment to the US Constitution, which banned the distribution and sale of alcoholic beverages, was drafted by Texas's US Senator Morris Sheppard. *DMN*, May 24, 1916.

5. "Majority Platform Report Is Adopted," *DMN*, May 25 1916.

6. Norman D. Brown, *Hood, Bonnet, and Little Brown Jug: Texas Politics, 1921–1928* (College Station: Texas A&M University Press, 1984), 4; Ralph W. Steen, "Ferguson, James Edward," *HOT Online*, http://www.tshaonline.org/handbook/online/articles/ffe05, accessed June 25, 2015; Gould, *Progressives and Prohibitionists*, 132, 131–32.

7. William James Battle, "University of Texas at Austin," *HOT Online*, http://www.tshaonline.org /handbook/online/articles/kcu09, accessed July 06, 2015; University of Texas at Austin School of Law website, http://www.utexas.edu/law/about/history.html, accessed July 6, 2015; Gould, *Progressives and Prohibitionists*, 188, 190–91.

8. Gould, *Progressives and Prohibitionists*, 192–94.

9. Ibid., 198; Robert Vinson to Pat Neff, May 25, 1916, Pat M. Neff Papers, Texas Collection, Baylor University, Waco, Texas (hereafter cited as PNP); Gould, *Progressives and Prohibitionists*, 199–200.

10. Gould, *Progressives and Prohibitionists*, 203–5; Richard T. Fleming, "Peddy, George Edwin Bailey," *HOT Online*, http://www.tshaonline.org/handbook/online/articles/fpe13, accessed July 27, 2015.

11. Gould, *Progressives and Prohibitionists*, 206; Minnie Fisher Cunningham to Carrie Catt, in Ruthe Winegarten and Judith N. McArthur, eds., *Citizens at Last: The Woman Suffrage Movement in Texas* (Lufkin, TX: Ellen C. Temple Publishing, 1987), 159–60.

12. Gould, *Progressives and Prohibitionists*, 213; *Fort Worth Star-Telegram* (hereafter cited as *FWST*), August 25, 1917; *FWST*, September 23, 1917; *FWST*, September 29, 1917; Judith N. McArthur, *Creating the New Woman: The Rise of*

Southern Women's Progressive Culture in Texas, 1893–1918 (Urbana: University of Illinois Press, 1998), 138. Texas ratified the Eighteenth Amendment to the US Constitution on March 4, 1918, and ratified the Nineteenth Amendment to the Constitution on June 28, 1918.

13. Brown, *Hood, Bonnet, and Little Brown Jug*, 16–17.

14. Thomas E. Turner, "Neff, Pat Morris," *HOT Online*, http://www.tshaonline.org/handbook/online/ articles/fne05, accessed July 28, 2015; Pat M. Neff, *The Battles of Peace* (Fort Worth, TX: Pioneer Publishing, 1925), 7.

15. Joseph M. Ray, "Thomason, Robert Ewing," *HOT Online*, http://www.tshaonline.org/handbook/online/ articles/fth47, accessed July 29, 2015; *DMN*, July 8, 1920; Neff to Mrs. M. F. Bewley, November 14, 1919, PNP. This was a form letter and there are several examples bearing the same date sent to various Texas clubwomen.

16. "Bailey Announces for Governorship," *DMN*, February 19, 1920.

17. "Bailey Is Denounced by Wilson Democrats," *DMN*, March 7, 1920.

18. "Bailey Strength Found Negligible," *DMN*, May 2, 1920; "Gainesville Is against Bailey," *DMN*, May 2, 1920; "Bailey Convention Vote Is under 100," *DMN*, May 3, 1920; "Bailey Will Not Abandon Contest," *DMN*, May 4, 1920; "Final Figures Give Bailey 1,852 Lead," *DMN*, August 7, 1920; "Neff 241,968, Bailey 168, 635," August 31, 1920.

19. Charles C. Alexander, *The Ku Klux Klan in the Southwest* (Lexington: University of Kentucky Press, 1965), 22–23, 34–35; Brown, *Hood, Bonnet, and Little Brown Jug*, 211–22, 216. Not all Texas conservatives turned toward the Klan. Those already in the Democratic Party power structure, such as James Ferguson and Joseph Weldon Bailey, wielded enough power and influence without the Klan's help. Indeed, "Baileyism" and "Fergusonism" were terms often used in political discourse of the time.

20. Brown, *Hood, Bonnet, and Little Brown Jug*, 218–19, 222–23; John D. Huddleston, "Ferguson, Miriam Amanda Wallace [Ma]," *HOT Online*, http://www.tshaonline.org/handbook/online/articles/ffe06, accessed July 31, 2015.

21. "Democrats Gathering in San Antonio," *DMN*, September 4, 1922; "Resolutions Committee Rejects All Anti-Klan Planks Offered," *DMN*, September 6, 1922; "Platform Is Adopted in Form of Majority Report," *DMN*, September 7, 1922; Brown, *Hood, Bonnet, and Little Brown Jug*, 103. Brown includes an entire chapter, titled "Farmer Jim v. Prince Earle," on this topic.

22. "Party Opponents of Klan Called," *DMN*, September 10, 1922; "George E. B. Peddy Senate Candidate for Independents," *DMN*, September 17, 1922; "Are They Trying to Run Texas Republican Party?" Letter to Editor, *DMN*, September 17, 1922; "Says Primary Obligation Nullified in Law and Equity," Letter to Editor, *DMN*, September 17, 1922; "Mayfield's Name Ordered on Ballot after Ruling by Supreme Court," *DMN*, November 7, 1922; "Official Told to Hold-Up Printing,"

DMN, November 4, 1922; "Voters in Today's Elections and Dissatisfied with Both Big Parties," *DMN*, November 7, 1922; Richard T. Fleming, "Peddy, George Edwin Bailey," *HOT Online*, http://www.tshaonline.org/handbook/online/articles/fpe13, accessed August 31, 2015.

23. O. Douglas Weeks, "Election Laws," *HOT Online*, http://www.tshaonline.org/handbook/online/articles/wde01, accessed July 31, 2015; Nancy Beck Young, "Democratic Party," *HOT Online*, http://www.tshaonline.org/handbook/online/articles/wad01, accessed July 31, 2015; "Texas Vote in Presidential Elections, Primaries: 1848–2008," *Texas Almanac Online*, http://www.texasalmanac.com/politics/prez08.pdf, accessed February 10, 2011.

24. Neff to James E. Ferguson, April 4, 1937, PNP.

25. James E. Ferguson to Neff, April 9, 1937, PNP; Dan Moody to Neff, April 18, 1937, PNP; Elections of Texas Governors, *Texas Almanac Online*, https://texasalmanac.com/sites/default/files/images/uploads/gov1845–2010table.pdf, accessed August 4, 2015.

26. George N. Green, "Texas Regulars," *HOT Online*, http://www.tshaonline.org/handbook/online/articles /wet02, accessed August 3, 2015; Lionel V. Patenaude, "Garner, John Nance," *HOT Online*, http://www.tshaonline.org/handbook/online/ articles/fga24, accessed February 10, 2011; Ellen Kuniyuki Brown, "Eleanor Roosevelt's Texas Tour: The Central Texas Stop," *Baylor Line* (Spring 1999); Scott Sosebee, "The Split in the Texas Democratic Party, 1936–1956 (master's thesis, Texas Tech University, 2000). Sosebee characterizes the state of Texas Democratic Party politics as being a three-sided split between liberals, conservatives, and party loyalists who had yet to take a side. Neff may have been among the party loyalists. However, his later actions suggest he genuinely supported many of President Truman's policies. Lionel V. Patenaude, "Garner, John Nance," *HOT Online*, http://www.tshaonline.org/handbook/online/ articles/fga24, accessed February 10, 2011.

27. "Maverick Men Want Jones Vice-President," *DMN*, May 27, 1940; "Most Tempestuous Scenes of Democratic Conventions in Many Years Enacted at Waco," *DMN*, May 29, 1940; "Texas Delegation Will Back Garner," *Cleveland Plain Dealer*, May 29, 1940; "Session Picks Delegates for Chicago Meet," *DMN*, May 29, 1940. South Texans had a reputation for their ability to gather votes and thus held much influence. For more, see Evan Anders, *Boss Rule in South Texas: The Progressive Era* (Austin: University of Texas Press, 1982). Neff probably had more than his usual peaceful motivations for bringing the violent meeting to order. He was then president of Baylor University and his office was just across the street from the brawl outside Waco Hall.

28. "Roosevelt Declares He Has No Desire to Be Candidate for Third Term—Convention Demands F.D.R. Run Again, Despite Statement," *DMN*, July 17, 1940; "Roosevelt Nominated for 3d Term, Winning 946 Votes on First Ballot," *DMN*, July 18, 1940; "Willkie Movement Casts a Shadow on State Convention," *DMN*,

September 10, 1940; "Keep Willkie as Possibility, Dems Urged," *DMN*, July 6, 1940; Presidential Elections And Primaries In Texas, 1848–2012, *Texas Almanac Online*, https://texasalmanac.com/topics/elections/presidential-elections-and-primaries-texas-1848–2012, accessed August 4, 2015; Key, *Southern Politics in State and Nation*, 278–79, 256. Key referred to the phenomenon of changing sides in presidential elections as "presidential republicanism."

29. John W. McCormack to Neff, November 20, 1940, PNP; Edward J. Flynn to Neff, November 14, 1940, PNP; "Bitter Lines Drawn to Fight for Control of State Convention," *DMN*, May 23, 1944; "Violent Democratic Upheaval Follows Refusal to Bind Electors to Nominee," *DMN*, May 24, 1944.

30. "The When, Who, What and How of the Democratic National Convention," *Kansas City Plaindealer*, July 28, 1944; "Wide-Open Democratic Battle Seen over Vice-Presidential Nomination." *DMN*, July 16, 1944; "Rump Convention" to Neff, July 20, 1944, note attached, PNP. Neff's attachment of a note to the abovementioned telegram is a rare example of a historical figure recognizing the significance of a document and recording its significance for posterity.

31. "Barbecue Factions Go All Out to Attract Big Crowds Tuesday," *DMN*, April 18, 1948. For more on President Harry Truman and the election of 1948, see David McCullogh, chapter 13, "The Heat in the Kitchen," in *Truman* (New York: Simon and Schuster, reprint edition 1993). For more on the Dixiecrat revolt and its origins, see also Kari Frederickson, *The Dixiecrat Revolt and the End of the Solid South, 1932–1968* (Chapel Hill: University of North Carolina Press, 2001).

32. Frederickson, *Dixiecrat Revolt and the End of the Solid South*.

33. "Jester's Speech Will Clarify Stand on Truman, Revolt," *DMN*, April 20, 1948; Presidential Elections and Primaries In Texas, 1848–2012, *Texas Almanac Online*, https://texasalmanac.com/topics/elections/presidential-elections-and-primaries-texas-1848–2012, accessed August 4, 2015.

34. Ricky F. Dobbs, *Yellow Dogs and Republicans: Allan Shivers and Texas Two-Party Politics* (College Station: Texas A&M University Press, 2005), 4–5; Presidential Elections And Primaries In Texas, 1848–2012, *Texas Almanac Online*, https://texasalmanac.com/topics/elections/presidential-elections-and-primaries-texas-1848–2012, accessed August 4, 2015; Susan Eason, "Tower, John Goodwin," *HOT Online*, http://www.tshaonline.org/handbook/online/articles/ftoss, accessed August 4, 2015.

35. Donna A. Barnes, "People's Party," *HOT Online*, http://www.tshaonline.org/handbook/online/articles/wap01, accessed August 6, 2015. For a general discussion of the Populist Revolt and its ramifications in the South, see C. Vann Woodward, *Origins of the New South, 1877–1913* (Baton Rouge: Louisiana State University Press, 1951), chapter 9. For more Texas specific information on the revolt, see Alwyn Barr, *Reconstruction to Reform: Texas Politics, 1876–1906* (Austin: University of Texas Press, 1971), chapters 7 and 10. For more on the ramifications of the poll tax, see Key, *Southern Politics in State and Nation*, chapter 28.

6

The Texas Governor's Impeachment in Historical Memory

Jessica Brannon-Wranosky

Following Governor James Ferguson's impeachment in August 1917, and then his defeat in the Texas Democratic primary the following year, it is likely that many of his political contemporaries expected him to fade from the public mind sooner than later. They were wrong. Instead, the memory of Ferguson's impeachment became a kind of political ghostly warning invoked periodically over the next century as a reminder of the horrors awaiting state leaders if they did not play their cards right. This haunting started almost immediately and sometimes even stretched far beyond the borders of the Lone Star State.

In October 1919, just two years after Ferguson's impeachment, National American Woman Suffrage Association (NAWSA) president Carrie Chapman Catt contacted Texas Equal Suffrage Association (TESA) president Minnie Fisher Cunningham for advice. NAWSA executives relied on their own memory of gubernatorial impeachment events in Texas, relayed to them by TESA leaders, when trying to work around recalcitrant governors in Vermont and Connecticut. In both states, the governors refused to call special sessions, and Catt wired Cunningham asking for reassurance of the process planned in 1917 when Ferguson refused to call a special session of the Texas legislature to discuss his own impeachment. Even though Ferguson did finally call the session himself, the original plan (or at least public political bluff) had been for the Texas Speaker of the House and President of the Senate to do so by forced measures. NAWSA executives were well informed of the process and events that transpired during the campaign and legislative process to impeach Ferguson because of the role a number of Texas suffrage leaders played in the governor's removal from office. During the entire episode, Cunningham often directly reported the details to Catt. National suffragists wanted direct correspondence from Cunningham that Texas legislative leaders considered such a measure to call a special session in 1917 so that suffrage supporters in 1919 could compel action in Connecticut and Vermont.[1]

While it was constitutionally questionable even in Texas whether or not officials other than the governor could call the special session, and each state's laws were what provided for the possibility, suffragists hoped to use the threat to force each governor's hand. Although not immediately successful at reaching their goal, the fact that national women's rights leaders tried to use the public memory of the removal of a governor and their knowledge of the process so soon after the impeachment shows its power in political memory not just as a warning but as a potential tool. The two states subsequently ratified the Nineteenth Amendment after the thirty-sixth needed state, Tennessee, when they did so in September 1920 and February 1921, respectively.

Also during NAWSA's ratification campaigns in 1919 and early 1920, Oklahoma governor James B. Robertson similarly refused to call a special session of the state legislature for fear that legislators would use the opportunity to impeach him. According to NAWSA and Texas suffrage leaders, despite the majority of both houses petitioning for such, agreeing not to charge the state for expenses, and only considering the federal suffrage amendment, the governor still refused. Thus while NAWSA used the threat that other state officials might call special sessions in some states, the Oklahoma governor's fear of a fate similar to Ferguson's kept him from wanting legislators in a special session. The pressure from both internal and external political forces prevailed, and Robertson called the legislature into special session February 23, 1920. Most state legislators voted for the amendment, not surprising because Oklahoma women were voting constituents, and on February 28, 1920, Oklahoma ratified.[2]

Interestingly, two years after ratification, Oklahoma legislators did impeach their governor, John Walton, and in 1929 repeated the act again by removing Henry Johnston from office. Thus the historical memory created fear held by Robertson may have not been as innocuous as some thought. Instead, within a decade Oklahoma held two out of what eventually became by 2009 only eight gubernatorial impeachments nationwide.

Furthermore, out of the eight gubernatorial impeachments in US history, Oklahoma is the only state with more than one.[3]

The memory of James Ferguson's impeachment created gubernatorial fears one could say in a number of ways "closer to home" during the 1920s as well. Governor Miriam Ferguson feared impeachment during her first term as governor because of what happened to her husband in 1917. In ghostly echoes similar to the public charges levied at Jim Ferguson almost a decade before, again illicit financial dealings appeared connected to a Ferguson as governor. Instead of brewers passing bribes through a bank, it was road construction companies laundering kickbacks through the *Ferguson Forum*. As Texas officials investigated the charges against Governor Miriam Ferguson, a number of state legislators called for impeachment charges. In an effort to get a called session, select legislators petitioned Governor Miriam Ferguson to issue a call to discuss the financial effects of tick eradication. Since in Texas a called session can only consider issues connected to the called purpose, state financial expenditures likely could have opened the door to discussions of misappropriated highway funds. In response, the governor "pounded the table with her fist. 'I won't do it,' she [said]: 'They can't make me do it. That's what caused all the trouble for Jim and I'm not going to let them get me in the same mess. They got him to call a special session and bought enough votes to impeach him. There's a lot of money behind this fight on us and they'll do the same thing to me.'" When the grand jury eventually returned without an indictment, Governor Miriam Ferguson was safe from the threat of impeachment.[4]

In death, as in life, the Ferguson's memory continued to bring about the topic of impeachment. After Jim Ferguson died in 1944, Miriam Ferguson lived for another seventeen years. A program from her eightieth birthday in 1955 shows that a strong contingent of the state's political elite lined up to wish her well and celebrate with the governor and her family. Even so, the 1917 impeachment was not far from the public mind. As part of the last words her contemporaries spoke about her life, in a news obituary upon her death in 1961, the *Houston Chronicle* spent the majority of printed space discussing the Fergusons' time in politics and the importance of Jim Ferguson's impeachment.[5]

Even decades after James and Miriam Ferguson's deaths, whenever gubernatorial impeachment proceeding rumors started to spread, previous impeached governors' stories were resurrected, including Jim Ferguson's. The first two gubernatorial impeachments in the United States occurred during Reconstruction. William Holden of North Carolina and David Butler of Nebraska were both impeached in 1871. Butler was eventually exonerated and ran for and won the office again more than a decade later. The third governor forcibly removed from office was William Sulzer of New York in 1913, just four years before Ferguson in 1917. Then there were the two Oklahoma governors, John Walton in 1922 and Henry Johnston in 1929. Another governor was not impeached for almost sixty years. In 1988, Arizona's Evan Mecham was removed from office, followed more than twenty years later by, the most recent member of the group at the time of this book's publication, Illinois governor Rod Blagojevich in 2009. During both Mecham's and Blagojevich's investigations and subsequent impeachments, newspapers around the nation, including Texas, revisited the old stories of the antics that got others previously thrown out of office. In Texas, this brought Ferguson's name up again, and Texan history enthusiasts and newspaper writers exchanged stories about "Farmer Jim" or "Pa" with the public. In these instances, the safe distance of time created almost a celebratory reaction by states' residents who did not have their governor under investigation by remembering when they had and how simultaneously appalling and entertaining it once was.[6]

There have been times in the last century, though, when state officials in Texas have been under investigation for charges similar to those with Ferguson's abuse of office. In these cases, as comparisons were made, Jim Ferguson's impeachment in public memory has held center stage. By the twenty-first century, many among the general population in Texas held little to no knowledge of the reactionary governor who picked continuous fights with the University of Texas, and who had a taste for money and used the political offices with which he was associated for personal gain. Thus at different times when former Texas governor Rick Perry clashed with the Texas legislature over higher education funding or directly with certain university administrators, often someone would rattle the chains of Ferguson's impeachment as a warning.

In 2007, the *Houston Chronicle* ran an opinion piece by former Texas lieutenant governor Bill Hobby (William Pettus Hobby Jr.). In the piece, Hobby issued a warning to Perry. He wrote,

> Special items are covered by a provision in the Education Code that appropriates money for higher education in a lump sum. In other

words, the governor would have to veto an entire university, not just a particular item. Ninety years ago, Gov. James Ferguson did just that. . . . Technically, Ferguson wasn't impeached because of the veto, but the veto was the proximate cause. . . . The Legislature reappropriated the money. My father, who had succeeded Ferguson as governor, signed the bill and all was well. My father beat Ferguson in the next election by a large majority.[7]

Hobby's son spoke out with firsthand familial knowledge of the Ferguson impeachment with a purpose to bring it back into the public memory. He used the anecdote as a political tool like others had before. It was not a celebration, not a commemoration. Instead, ninety years after Ferguson's impeachment, it stood as a warning to the standing governor—do not pick a fight with Texas higher education, do not pick a fight with the Texas legislature. For a governor, it was a losing battle.

Seven years after Hobby's published warning, a grand jury investigation opened into charges that Governor Rick Perry used his gubernatorial power to threaten the state's anticorruption prosecutorial funding. The office was investigating the governor for charges, similar to those against Miriam Ferguson in 1925, that dealt with Perry's administration awarding tens of millions of dollars of no-bid state contracts.[8] In August 2014, the *Texas Tribune* ran an article comparing the charges against Perry to the case of Ferguson in 1917. While Perry finished his final gubernatorial term in January 2015 without impeachment, he was indicted the previous August on abuse of power charges for vetoing most of the budget of the office investigating Perry concerning the no-bid contracts.[9]

Furthermore, the Ferguson impeachment memory remained fresh in the public mind for a number of reasons during the end of Perry's gubernatorial career. In addition to regular comparisons to Perry, facts about Ferguson's impeachment were also publicly invoked in 2014 when select members of the state legislature called for the impeachment of Perry-appointed University of Texas Board of Regents member Wallace Hall on charges that he used his office as regent to target UT president Bill Powers. The *Dallas Morning News* and other media outlets did not waste any time making connections between the twenty-first-century situation with UT and that which led to Ferguson's impeachment trial. Within months, while campaigning for Texas attorney general, Ken Paxton was under investigation for securities fraud, for which he was indicted in August 2015. The press and the public, yet again, resurrected the 1917 stories. In these cases, the discussion of the similarities with Ferguson was less of a warning and more of an effort to figure out what was going to happen. With the memory of the historical 1917 events, Texans knew the end of the story, and state residents wondered if that meant the same for the twenty-first-century officeholders.[10]

The public perception is often that "history repeats itself." Meaning that history holds some sort of predictive power. Actually, history does not repeat itself; different people create different outcomes at different times in different places. Furthermore, while Jim Ferguson was impeached, as long as historical memory continues to exist, a morphing could happen. The historical events will not change, but the human interpretation and emotional reaction still can. Even commemoration, celebration, of certain people and events can hold different meanings for various people. Despite the continued political application of the Texas governor who was impeached over the last century, how that story is remembered and told in the future is still up for grabs.

On the southwest corner of West Eleventh Street and Congress in Austin, Texas, there is a small cluster of state historical markers located near the ruins of the original Texas capitol building. Five of these markers commemorate Texas gubernatorial officeholders—provisional Republic of Texas governor Henry Smith; Reconstruction Era governors Andrew Jackson Hamilton, Edmund Jackson Davis, and Elisha Marshall Pease, and a joint marker shared by governors James and Miriam Ferguson. On the surface, these five markers and the six governors they represent may not seem to have anything in common, but through the lens of remembrance, this lineup could be called, "Gubernatorial Purgatory"—for those whose legacies are forever caught in the winds of public opinion.

The two Reconstruction governors appointed by federal officials, including United States military commanders, and the one Reconstruction Republican elected all have historical markers at this location—Hamilton, Davis, and Pease. Technically, there were five Reconstruction governors prior to Richard Coke, whose election marked the beginning of the end for Reconstruction in Texas. Those associated with federal government placement and congressional Republican support are those whose public memories often were tainted with a particular hatred by white southerners and are those with markers in this locale.[11]

In the same row as the three Reconstruction governors, there is marker for Henry Smith, who was appointed as the provisional governor of the Republic of Texas at the beginning of the Texas Revolution. By January 1836, a rift developed between two factions of the provisional government. When Smith tried to dissolve Texas's provisional government, they in turn impeached him. Yes, another impeached Texas governor and prior to Ferguson by eighty-one years. He is the only one of the five not labeled as "Governor" in the title of the marker, likely because he was neither elected nor a state governor. Not to mention, the memory of the Texas Revolution is at the core of the cultural identity of Texas. Highlighting the enormously dysfunctional revolutionary government fighting over power does not further the traditional celebratory narrative. The placement of historical markers, though, highlights someone for recognition of something they stood for or continue to represent.[12]

Finally, there is the marker with James and Miriam Ferguson, the impeached governor of the state of Texas, and his wife, who often is remembered in history as his political puppet without her own independent gubernatorial legacy. She did not even receive her own marker. The Ferguson marker is not in the line facing the capitol building with

Governor Edward Ferguson and Governor Miriam A. Ferguson Texas Historical Commission historical marker located at the corner of West Eleventh Street and Congress, Austin, Texas, with the Texas state capitol in the background behind the Ferguson historical marker. 2016. Photograph by Elaina Friar Moyer.

the rest, but is located facing away, exactly 180 degrees, from the other four. The Ferguson's marker has its back turned, per se, to the capitol. Memory is more perception than fact, and historical markers are placed without the context of who and why the petition placed them in a given location. Thus, passersby have the free will to wonder. As a group, these five gubernatorial markers are located just outside capitol gates, across the street from the Texas State Capitol Building, as if to mark for eternity their memories are at a safe distance from current policy making.[13]

A lot can happen in one hundred years. The memory of James Ferguson's impeachment has changed in a variety of ways. The threat terrified some in its aftermath, and it was issued as a warning at times. By the late twentieth century, stories of the colorful "Farmer Jim" were often laughed about at a safe distance. As Texans approached the centennial of his impeachment, it appeared as if much of the hate had turned to acceptance. It was not necessarily approval of his actions, but instead, a public understanding that he was likely doing what many in politics did. He just got caught. As long as the remembrance continues, though, the story is not complete. In 2010, the Ferguson's former residence in Temple, Texas, appeared in irreparable condition. Within two years, a benefactor stepped forward and spent more than $300,000 on renovations. Then, in 2014, a Texas Historical Commission marker was dedicated and placed at the site. What looked like a purposeful act of forgetting instead became a resurrection. As such, how memory is reinvented, passed on, celebrated, or even forgotten, cannot be predicted. There may be indicators, but no guarantees.[14]

When Ferguson's contemporaries expected the impeachment to be the end of the story, they were wrong. Even as the centennial approached, the end of the story had not appeared. In August 2015, a new generation of Texans became involved in the passing of Ferguson impeachment stories. A group of Northeast Texas college students traveled to different sites associated with James and Miriam Ferguson. Their purpose was to film a self-produced movie about Ma and Pa Ferguson. As such, the story continues for future audiences and interpretations. Jim and Miriam Ferguson continued to entertain and enthrall, and where there is a good story, a willing audience is usually had.[15]

NOTES

1. Carrie Chapman Catt to Minnie Fisher Cunningham, October 6, 1919; Minnie Fisher Cunningham to Carrie Chapman Catt, October 13, 1919, all in folder 9, box 1, Cunningham Papers, M. D. Anderson Library, Special Collections and Archives, University of Houston, Houston, Texas.

2. Sara Hunter Graham, *Woman's Suffrage and the New Democracy* (New Haven, CT: Yale University Press, 1996), 136–39; folder 32, box 1, Cunningham Papers; Nettie R. Shuler to Mrs. Percy V. Pennybacker, October 29, 1919; Nettie R. Shuler to Mrs. Percy V. Pennybacker, October 30, 1919; Anna J. Hardwicke Pennybacker to Carrie Chapman Catt, November 16, 1919; [Anna J. H. Pennybacker] to Mrs. Frank Shuler, November 24, 1919; all in folder "Suffrage 1919," box 2M12, Pennybacker Papers, Dolph Briscoe Center for American History, University of Texas at Austin.

3. *New York Times*, February 6, 1988; National Public Radio, January 11, 2009, http://www.npr.org/templates/story/story.php?storyId=99227806, accessed October 4, 2015.

4. Norman D. Brown, *Hood, Bonnet, and Little Brown Jug: Texas Politics, 1921–1928* (College Station: Texas A&M University Press, 1984), 291–92; *Dallas Morning News*, November 24, 1925.

5. *Houston Chronicle*, June 27, 1961; Miriam Amanda Ferguson eightieth birthday program, Governors James E. and Miriam "Ma" Ferguson Collection #3795, the Texas Collection, Baylor University, Waco, Texas.

6. *New York Times*, February 6, 1988; National Public Radio, January 11, 2009, http://www.npr.org/templates/story/story.php?storyId=99227806, accessed October 4, 2015; *Texas Monthly*, June 1998.

7. Bill Hobby, "A History Lesson for Gov. Perry's Benefit," *Houston Chronicle*, February 25, 2007.

8. *Houston Chronicle*, January 16, 2015.

9. Associated Press, August 16, 2014, http://bigstory.ap.org/article/texas-perry-indicted-coercion-veto-threat, accessed September 28, 2015; *Texas Tribune*, August 17, 2014.

10. *Dallas Morning News*, May 12, 2014; *Austin American-Statesman*, August 1, 2015; *New York Times*, August 3, 2015.

11. For more information about Reconstruction, Reconstruction in Texas, or historical memory and Reconstruction, see Eric Foner, *Reconstruction, 1863–1877* (New York: Harper and Row, 1988); Randolph B. Campbell, *Grass-Roots Reconstruction in Texas, 1865–1880* (Baton Rouge: Louisiana State University Press, 1997); Carl H. Moneyhon, *Republicanism in Reconstruction Texas* (Austin: University of Texas Press, 1980); Carl H. Moneyhon, *Texas after the Civil War: The Struggle of Reconstruction* (College Station: Texas A&M University Press, 2004);

David W. Blight, *Race and Reunion: The Civil War in American Memory* (Cambridge, MA: Harvard University Press, 2001); *Handbook of Texas Online* (hereafter cited as *HTO*), s.v. "Andrew Jackson Hamilton," https://tshaonline.org/handbook/online/articles/fha33, accessed September 8, 2015; "Elisha Marshall Pease," https://tshaonline.org/handbook/online/articles/fpe08, accessed September 8, 2015; "Edmund Jackson Davis," https://tshaonline.org/handbook/online/articles/fda37, accessed September 8, 2015.

12. *HTO*, "Henry Smith," https://tshaonline.org/handbook/online/articles/fsm23, accessed September 8, 2015.

13. Nancy Baker Jones and Ruthe Winegarten, *Capitol Women: Texas Female Legislators, 1923–1999* (Austin: University of Texas Press, 2010), 78; *Austin American-Statesman*, July 18, 2009.

14. *Austin American-Statesman*, July 18, 2009; Time Warner Cable News, May 25, 2010, http://www.twcnews.com, accessed August 28, 2015; *Killeen Daily Herald*, September 28, 2013; KWTX-TV News, May 2, 2014, http://kwtx.com, accessed October 15, 2015.

15. "Two for One: The Story of Ma and Pa Ferguson," http://www.ntcc.edu/index.php?module=Pagesetter&func=viewpub&tid=50&pid=9, accessed October 25, 2015.

Document 1

Ferguson's Texas Farm Tenant Law

Comment by Kyle G. Wilkison and Katherine Kuehler Walters

By long-established custom, tenant farmers who owned their own plow animals and tools paid a third of the sales of the corn crop and a fourth of the cotton crop in rent. Likewise, tenants who could not supply their own team and tools paid one-half of the sales of each crop and occupied the status of "sharecropper," the next rung down on the New South's mythical "agricultural ladder." Young landless white farmers were expected to begin their working lives as sharecroppers but then inevitably move, by hard work and frugality, into "thirds and fourths" status before ultimately purchasing their own farms. On the other hand, Jim Crow cultural expectations dictated that African Americans might spend their entire lives at the "halves" sharecropper status. But by the time of James E. Ferguson's rise to prominence, African American farmers in Texas found it increasingly difficult to obtain even half-cropper status. An influx of white southerners competing for tenant farms in Texas cotton country—combined with landlord racism—squeezed blacks off the land except as seasonal cotton pickers.[1]

Despite cultural expectations, by 1910 the majority of Texas's white farmers were landless tenants, whether thirds and fourths tenants or half croppers. Moreover, they now began to realize that these were permanent occupations; tenants could not earn sufficient income from cotton to save a down payment for a farm. This assaulted their expectations and masculine identity as good providers. Worse, as a growing population forced ever-fiercer competition for tenant slots, landlords discovered they need not abide by customary rents and began adding on "points" or "bonuses" for the most attractive farms near schools, with the best soil, houses with window screens, or anything else that the market would bear. Increasingly, landlords simply eliminated the "thirds and fourths" arrangement and demanded half the crop regardless of tenant level of contribution to producing the crop.

Not coincidentally, the appeal of democratic socialism grew rapidly among rural Texas voters. After a decade of slow growth, in the election of 1912 the young Socialist Party of Texas quadrupled its last gubernatorial showing for a distant second-place finish. While unlikely that Texas Socialists represented a genuine threat to Democratic Party dominance, a few Democrats did take notice of rural discontent.

James Ferguson successfully rode this discontent into the governor's mansion. Ferguson himself pointed to the rise of Texas Socialists when explaining to urban newspapers his outreach rhetoric to the rural poor majority. His strategy worked. His faux Populist style and promise of state regulation of farm rents overwhelmed the rural poor majority's potential attraction to the critique of capitalism. Discouraged voters among the rural poor majority were accustomed to being assailed as shiftless by conservative Democrats and to being steadfastly ignored by the moralizing progressive/prohibitionists. In the election of 1914, "Farmer Jim" Ferguson stepped into that opening, into the hearts of the rural poor majority and into the governor's mansion by appealing directly to their hurt feelings and powerful cultural precepts. Ferguson told the poor majority that what had befallen them was not their fault (just as it was also not the fault of the system that enriched banker-landlord Jim Ferguson). Instead, individual bad actors among urban-based absentee landlords were to blame. Relief need not come from the sweeping restructuring offered by socialism with its whiffs of modernity, racial and gender equality, atheism, Yankee influence, contempt for the Confederate dead, and rejection of the party of their fathers. Instead, he, "Farmer Jim" Ferguson, would redeem their party and cleanse the corrupt thread of heartless big-city landlords without unraveling the whole fabric of their culture. To the party elite he pointedly warned that the day might come when Texas tenants might resort to the revolutionary tactics of Pancho Villa if they failed to support his relatively painless reform, a state-mandated return to customary rents.

Ferguson promised state enforcement of customary farm rents if elected. That is not what he delivered. His so-called Tenant Law was instead a testimony to the knowing resilience of the economic elite and their understanding of the rural poor majority's political culture. The law, as one state legislator observed, was not "worth the paper it is written on." There were no criminal penalties. There was no state enforcement.

Defrauded tenants had to get a lawyer to file a lawsuit to request relief, an action requiring access to cash as well as the tender mercies of at least one member of the village elite. The law was not enforced and would be dispensed with as unconstitutional by the Texas Supreme Court in the 1929 case *Culberson v. Ashford*.[2]

The overturning of the Land Tenant Law by the *Culberson v. Ashford* ruling in 1929 continues to be somewhat of a historical enigma that historians still have yet to cover. Initiated prior to 1922 in McLennan County, home of both plaintiff and defendant, the case received little media attention until the final ruling. African American tenant farmer Sham Culberson sued his landlord B. G. (Benjamin Goodman) Ashford, a black business owner and land owner who operated a popular café in the black business area of Waco, for charging him more rent than the 1915 law allowed. Despite a tenuous financial position and his inability to read or write, Culberson hired white attorney James E. Yeager, a prominent long-time member of the Waco Bar Association, to ask the court to enforce the Land Tenant Law and award him redress of $100, twice the paid rent. Instead, on June 19, 1929, the Supreme Court of the state of Texas agreed with Ashford's attorney, noted civil-rights activist Richard D. Evans, and ruled that the 1915 amendment to an 1874 law was unconstitutional according to state law and the Fourteenth Amendment of the Constitution of the United States. The law, the court ruled, denied property owner's rights to set price exchange for their property, thus denying them their property without due process. The press was the first to inform Ferguson of the final death of his administration's legacy. In response, he simply informed the reporter of what the law used to be and how landlords could take advantage prior to the amendment's passage in 1915.[3]

LAND TENANT LAW—PRESCRIBING PAYMENT OF RENTALS IN THE MATTER OF AGRICULTURAL LANDS.[4]

S. B. No. 131.] Chapter 38.
An Act to amend Article 5475. of Title 80, of the Revised Civil Statutes of 1911, by adding thereto the following: "Provided, however, that this Article shall not apply in any way nor in any case where any person leases or rents lands or tenements at will or for a term of years for agricultural purposes where the same is cultivated by the tenant who furnished everything except the land and where the land-

lord charges a rental of more than one-third of the value of the grain or more than one-fourth of the value of the cotton raised on said land; nor where the landlord furnishes everything except the labor and the tenant furnishes the labor and the landlord, directly or indirectly, charges a rental of more than one-half of the value of the grain or more than one-half of the value of the cotton raised on said land; and any contract for the leasing or renting of lands or tenements at will or for a term of years for agricultural purposes stipulating or fixing a higher or greater rental than that herein provided for, shall be null and void, and shall not be enforceable in any court in this state by any action, either at law or in equity, and no lien of any kind, either contractual or statutory, shall attach in favor of the landlord, his estate or assigns, upon any of the property named, nor for the purpose mentioned in this Article; and provided, further, that if any landlord or any person for him shall violate or attempt to evade any of the provisions of this Article by collecting or receiving a greater amount of rent for such land than herein provided, shall be collected or received by him upon any contract, either written or verbal, the tenant or person paying the same, or the legal representative thereof, may, by an action of debt instituted in any court of this State, having jurisdiction thereof, in the county of the defendant's residence, or in the county where such rents or money shall have been received or collected, or where said contract may have been entered into, or where the party or parties paying the same resided when such contract was made, within two years after such payment, recover from the person, firm or corporation receiving the same, double the amount of such rent or money so received or collected," and declaring an emergency.

Be it enacted by the Legislature of the State of Texas:

SECTION 1. That Article 5475. Title 80, of the Revised Civil Statutes of 1911, be and is hereby so amended that the same will hereafter read as follows:

Article 5475 (3225). Landlord Shall Have Preference Lien.—
All persons leasing or renting lands or tenements at will or for a term of years shall have a preference lien upon the property of the tenant, as hereinafter indicated, upon such premises, for any rent that may become due and for all money and the value of all animals, tools, provisions and supplies furnished by the landlord to

the tenant to make a crop on such premises, and together secure, house and put the same in condition for marketing, the money, animals and tools and provisions and supplies so furnished being necc- [*sic*] essary for that purpose, whether the same is to be paid in money, agricultural products or other property; and this lien shall apply only to animals, tools and other property furnished by the landlord to the tenant, and to the crop raised on such premises; provided, however, this Article shall not apply in any way nor in any case where any person leases or rents lands or tenements at will or for a term of years for agricultural purposes where the same is cultivated by the tenant who furnishes everything except the land, and where the landlord charges a rental of more than one-third of the value of the grain and more than one-fourth of the value of the cotton raised on said land; nor where the landlord furnishes everything except the labor and the tenant furnishes the labor and the landlord directly or indirectly charges a rental of more than one-half of the value of the grain and more than one-half of the value of the cotton raised on said land, and any contract for the leasing or renting of land or tenements at will or for a term of years for agricultural purposes stipulating or fixing a higher or greater rental that [*sic*] that herein provided for, shall be null and void, and shall not be enforceable in any court in this state by an action either at law or in equity and no lien of any kind, either contractual or statutory, shall attach in favor of the landlord, his estate or assigns, upon any of the property named, nor for the purpose mentioned in this Article; and provided, further, that if any landlord or any per-[s]on for him shall violate or attempt to evade any of the provisions of this Article by collecting or receiving a greater amount of rent for such land than herein provided, shall be collected or received by him upon any contract, either written or verbal, the tenant or person paying the same, or the legal representatives thereof, may, by an action of debt instituted in any court of this State, having jurisdiction thereof, in the county of the defendant's residence or in the county where such rents or money may have been received or collected, or where said contract may have been entered into, or where the party or parties paying the same resided when such contract was made, within two years after such payment, recover from the person, firm or corporation receiving the same, double the full amount

of such rent or money so received or collected. All laws and parts of laws in conflict with this Article are hereby expressly repealed.
SEC. 2. The crowded condition of the calendar at this time creates an emergency and an imperative public necessity that the constitutional rule requiring bills to be read on three several [sic] days be suspended, and it is hereby suspended, and this Act shall take effect from and after its passage.
[NOTE.—S. B. No. 131 passed the Senate February 11, 1915, 23 yeas, 4 nays. Passed the House March 3, 1915, 102 yeas, 23 nays.]
Approved March 5, 1915.
Became a law March 5, 1915.

NOTES

1. See Walter Buenger, *The Path to a Modern South: Northeast Texas between Reconstruction and the Great Depression* (Austin: University of Texas Press, 2001); Neil Foley, *The White Scourge: Mexicans, Blacks, and Poor Whites in Texas Cotton Culture* (Berkeley: University of California Press, 1997); Thad Sitton and James H. Conrad, *Freedom Colonies: Independent Black Texans in the Time of Jim Crow* (Austin: University of Texas Press, 2005); Debra Ann Reid, *Reaping a Greater Harvest: African Americans, the Extension Service, and Rural Reform in Jim Crow Texas* (College Station: Texas A&M University Press, 2007); Kyle G. Wilkison, *Yeomen, Sharecroppers, and Socialists: Plain Folk Protest in Texas, 1870–1914* (College Station: Texas A&M University Press, 2008).

2. *Culberson v. Ashford*, 118 Tex. 491, 18 S.W. 2d 585 (1929).

3. Ibid.; *Tigner v. First National Bank of Angleton*, 153 Tex. 69, 264 S.W.2d 85 (1954); *Fifteenth Census of the United States, 1930*, McLennan County, Texas, National Archives and Records Administration, Washington, DC: National Archives and Records Administration, 1930, database online, Ancestry.com, accessed April 6, 2016; Benjamin Goodman Ashford, World War I Draft Registration Cards, 1917–1918, Ancestry.com, accessed March 28, 2016; Lois E. Myers, "Landmarks of Waco History: Bridge Street, 1900–1950 Continued," Baylor University Institute for Oral History: Our Research, accessed March 28, 2016; Kneeland Hilburn Clemons, "Oral Memoirs of Kneeland Hilburn Clemons, Series 2, October 21, 1988," interview by Vivienne Malone Mayes, Waco-McLennan County Project, Baylor University Institute for Oral History, transcript, http://digitalcollections.baylor.edu/cdm/ref/collection/buioh/id/1600, accessed April 6, 2016; Katherine Kuehler Walters, "The Great War in Waco, Texas: African Americans, Race Relations, and the White Primary, 1916–1922" (master's thesis, Southwest Texas State

University, 2000), 83–88; Ida Carey and R. Matt Abigail, "Evans, Richard D." in *Handbook of Texas Online*, http://www.tshaonline.org/handbook/online/articles/fev26, accessed April 5, 2016; *San Antonio Express*, October 26, 1922; *Amarillo Globe-Times*, June 19, 1929.

4. For further information about tenant farming and sharecropping in Texas, the Texas Land Tenant Law, or James Ferguson's push for the law, see Norman D. Brown, *Hood, Bonnet, and Little Brown Jug: Texas Politics, 1921–1928* (College Station: Texas A&M University Press, 1984); Lewis L. Gould, *Progressives and Prohibitionists: Texas Democrats in the Wilson Era* (Austin: Texas State Historical Association, 1992); Seth S. McKay, *Texas Politics, 1906–1944* (Lubbock: Texas Tech University Press, 1952); Carol O'Keefe Wilson, *In the Governor's Shadow: The True Story of Ma and Pa Ferguson* (Denton: University of North Texas Press, 2014).

Document 2

Minnie Fisher Cunningham to Carrie Chapman Catt Letter

Comment by Judith N. McArthur

Texas, like all the former Confederate states, was hostile territory for woman suffrage. In no southern state had suffragists been able to persuade the legislature to grant women full voting rights. The National American Woman Suffrage Association (NAWSA) had concluded that it was futile to pursue state constitutional amendments in the South and had directed the Texas Equal Suffrage Association (TESA) and the other southern affiliates to restrict their efforts to more feasible partial measures, such as the right to vote in party primaries (nearly the equivalent of full suffrage in one-party states like Texas) and for presidential electors. But even these limited goals were out of reach as long as James Ferguson, a suffrage opponent, wielded the governor's veto.

Ferguson's troubles provided an unexpected political opportunity for the suffrage movement, and TESA president Minnie Fisher Cunningham spent most of the summer of 1917 working for his impeachment. Publicly, she helped lead the Woman's Campaign for Good Government, a coalition of women's organizations that publicized Ferguson's misdeeds and urged progressive women to pressure their legislative representatives to bring charges against him. Privately, she collaborated with anti-Ferguson legislators at the capitol to build a pro-impeachment majority, sharing the TESA's files on the backgrounds and voting records of each member.

Cunningham's hope, expressed in the letter below, that progressive women could "get most anything we ask" from the men in power in return for their pro-impeachment campaign turned out to be overly optimistic. Her more politically astute prediction—"perhaps we can prove to them that they need us even if they do not want us!"—came true less than a year later. Ferguson's defiant post-impeachment run for reelection in 1918 against acting governor William Hobby gave the suffragists their opportunity. Cunningham made a quiet bargain with key Hobby supporters in the legislature: in return for a primary suffrage bill, the TESA would mobilize the female vote behind Hobby. On March 26, 1918, Hobby signed a bill permitting women to vote in primary elections, and a vigorous pro-Hobby campaign by progressive women helped Hobby defeat Ferguson by a wide margin in the July primary.

202 San Antonio St.
Austin, Texas,
July 31, 1917
Mrs. Carrie Chapman Catt, Pres.,[1]
National American Woman Suffrage Assn.,
171 Madison Ave.,
New York City.
My Dear Mrs. Catt:

The Texas suffragists need some expert advice right now, and I am hoping you will be good enough to give it to us.

We are again in the throes of endeavoring to impeach our Governor, and he has been indicted by the grand jury of Travis County (where the Capitol is located) for embezzlement of funds and eight other kinds of law breaking. The House has been called by the Speaker to prefer impeachment charges. Besides the technical grounds for impeachment, he has really done some of the most shocking and outrageous things imaginable, including an attempt to discharge from the University all professors who are prohibitionists, regardless of the distinguished service of any them, and appointing on the exemption boards such men as are known to be unfit. The whole state is mightily aroused. But so great is the power of the liquor machine here, we are none of us sure of conviction.

Looking the whole thing over, it seemed to me the chance of a lifetime to break the power of corrupt politics in Texas so when they phoned me please come to Austin and swing the women's end of it, I came.[2] We came into the campaign just at the time when everybody was worn to a frazzle and feeling discouraged and beaten; and our interest and enthusiasm and the immediate success of our first bits of work seemed to put new life and vigor into the men who were working. And now, even though we are afraid to say it out loud, it looks like we will WIN. The men are tremendously grateful as well as not a little surprised at the effectiveness of our work, and I believe we can get most anything we ask of them if we do win.

This leads me to my need of advice. After we get impeachment, the Lieutenant Governor will call a special session of the Legislature and endeavor to right certain wrongs that have been done these men in the University and provide for the carrying on of that institution (Ferguson having vetoed the appropriation for the next two years' work).

It seems to me a wonderfully opportune moment to ask them to put through our primary suffrage bill. What do you think, Would you advise it, Our situation in Texas is a serious one.—with the exemption boards planning to exempt Antis and send Pros to war; with the alien voting even though not a citizen of the United States;[3] and with our boys disfranchised under the constitution when they become United States soldiers even if they happen to be training in their home town. And perhaps we can prove to them that they need us even if they do not want us!

That is the political situation. Now, our private Suffrage situation is of course money. We owe the National our entire pledge, and we owe about a thousand dollars beside. And we wonder if you would think it advisable to "go to it" in spite of our crippled financial state. I have not breathed a word of this idea to any except my two closest advisers, so there would be no backing up to do if you think best not to undertake it,—but please let me hear from you at once. A telegram just yes or no would answer the purpose and not give anything away.

Very truly yours,
President.
MFC-EHL
Address us here at Austin, Texas, 2002 San Antonio Street.

NOTES

1. Content of letter published courtesy of University of Houston Special Collections. Minnie Fisher Cunningham to Carrie Chapman Catt, July 31, 1917, Minnie Fisher Cunningham Papers.

2. Cunningham refers here to the Woman's Campaign for Good Government (WCGG), started by a small group of Austin suffragists, including Professor Mary Gearing of the University of Texas. At Gearing's request, Cunningham joined the WCGG leadership and helped recruit a dozen women's organizations as mem-

bers. The WCGG produced a multipage dossier of Ferguson's transgressions and mobilized two thousand women to disseminate the information in a public awareness campaign and urge the Speaker of the Texas House of Representatives to call a special legislative session to consider impeachment charges. After the Speaker complied, the WCGG wrote and distributed 100,000 copies of a one-page "dodger" to hand out in legislative districts where support for Ferguson persisted. It listed the charges against him enumerated in the Speaker's call and urged constituents to press their legislators to vote for impeachment.

3. Like several other states at the time, Texas allowed (male) aliens who had filed a declaration of their intention to seek citizenship to vote in all elections. Suffragists found it particularly galling that they, as US citizens, were disenfranchised, while unnaturalized men, who tended to be antisuffragists, enjoyed full voting rights. Most were also antiprohibitionists and Ferguson supporters, which added to progressive women's resentment.

Document 3

Pat M. Neff to William Pettus Hobby Letter

Comment by Ricky Floyd Dobbs

Bad blood from the Ferguson impeachment continued into the succeeding decades. It blended with later controversies within the Texas Democratic Party and influenced electoral calculus into the 1940s. Evidence of this emerges in a cycle of letters from and to former governor and Baylor University president Pat M. Neff in early 1937.

Neff served as governor from 1921 to 1925, taking office in the immediate shadow of the Ferguson impeachment. He stood for progressive causes such as prohibition, women's public participation in law, and against the demagogic style of Joseph W. Bailey, along with Ferguson, a hated enemy of the state's progressive Democrats. Although Neff's allies worked to keep Ferguson off the 1922 Democratic US Senate primary ballot (a race that led to the election of Ku Klux Klan candidate Earle B. Mayfield), Neff himself had worked alongside Ferguson in 1924 for an uninstructed Texas delegation to the Democratic National Convention. Earlier, Neff disappointed many by failing to criticize directly the Ku Klux Klan, but in 1924, he and Ferguson undermined the Klan's favored Democratic presidential contender, William Gibbs McAdoo.[1]

In 1916, Neff's beloved mother, Isabella, had deeded a six-acre parcel along the Leon River in Bell County to the state of Texas; the former governor added another 259 acres in 1934. The land became the first Texas state park—Mother Neff State Park. From 1934 to 1937, Civilian Conservation Corps workers developed park facilities—buildings, campsites, and roads. Neff attempted to organize a gathering of all living former governors for the opening intended for Mother's Day 1937. He planned a postevent banquet on the Baylor campus for his guests, about thirty miles north of the park.[2]

In his invitation to the Fergusons, Baylor's president explained that he wanted a meeting without rancor, relying upon Mother's Day to "mallow our memories." Neff stipulated that he would cancel the gathering if a former governor could not show, as it "would be a reflection, in my opinion, on the absentee." The Fergusons declined the invitation because they feared it would result in "a lack of congeniality" for reasons Farmer Jim told Neff he would explain "fully" when next they met.[3]

Neff's predecessor as governor and successor to Ferguson, *Houston Post* publisher William P. Hobby, accepted the spirit of the invitation and agreed to attend. Based upon the evidence, it appears that the sitting governor, James V. Allred, was also prepared to attend. Nevertheless, the Fergusons' refusal in addition to the refusal by former governor Dan Moody forced Neff to retract the invitation to all the others while expressing hope that the group event could come to pass in the future.[4]

Dan Moody's polite, but firm, response declined Neff's invitation. While not stating Jim Ferguson's name outright, the correspondence from Moody to Neff detailed the problems between Moody and the Fergusons, and even further the Texas Democratic Party factions as a whole. Moody wrote,

> It would, however, Governor, be unfair to you for me to accept if all former Governors of the state are to be present. There is one with whom I have nothing to do and I am pleased that he has nothing to do with me . . . I am opposed to the things he typifies in the public life of the state and I, therefore, avoid any and all contacts with him where I can in decency do so. I know that people by the thousands differ with me in this viewpoint, but it is my viewpoint.[5]

As attorney general, Moody investigated irregularities in the state highway department during Miriam Ferguson's first term as governor (1925–27). The controversy led to calls for Miriam Ferguson's impeachment. In response, James Ferguson counterattacked against her critics, including Moody, whom he accused of wanting to be governor himself. Ferguson's criticism of Moody had been very pointed and personal during both the controversy over highway contracts in 1925–26 and in the gubernatorial campaign of 1926. Jim Ferguson accused Moody's wife, Mildred, of "running him with a rolling pin." Even so, Moody rode the tide of anti-Ferguson sentiment to victory in the August 1926 Democratic gubernatorial runoff. The two couples behaved badly toward one another at Moody's January 1927 inaugural. Miriam Ferguson's farewell address at the ceremony included swipes at the incoming chief executive, including, "whether you like it or not, he is now your governor." Ten years later, it turned out, the hostility remained.[6]

As mentioned in the following letter, the "more than half of the seven of us" that Neff referred to was undoubtedly Dan Moody, Jim Ferguson, and Miriam Ferguson. Neff was visibly disappointed and anxious at the extreme spite presented by the former Texas governors. Politically cautious, well connected, and experienced, and as such unlikely naive, Neff's attempt at this public event likely marked part of his efforts to heal the broken Texas Democratic Party—the same party that, less than two years later, broke into a brawling fight on the Baylor University campus. While the grudges between Moody and Ferguson may have been personal, they were also part of the era's political polarity that created such drastic electoral swings from one gubernatorial term to the next.

The Fergusons continued to influence state politics into the late 1940s. Ma Ferguson served another term as governor from 1933 to 1935. With her husband's backing, she ran for a third term as governor in 1940, only to be buried by the incumbent, W. Lee O'Daniel. She still managed to poll 100,000 votes. James Ferguson died in 1944. In 1948, Miriam Ferguson's endorsement provided Lyndon Johnson assistance in narrowing the margin in an uphill US Senate race against Coke Stevenson. Even in the 1950s, her political clout led hundreds, including Governor Allan Shivers and Senator Lyndon Johnson, to attend her eightieth birthday party.[7]

Dan Moody went into private practice in Austin but remained active behind the scenes in Texas politics. Although many conservative and dry Texas Democrats broke with the national party in 1928, delivering Texas to Herbert Hoover, Moody refused to oppose the national ticket. He took part in the Texas Democratic Party's internal squabbles during the 1930s and 1940s, opposing the New Deal and Franklin Roosevelt. He ran against incumbent W. Lee O'Daniel and James V. Allred for US Senate in 1942. Moody represented Coke Stevenson during the legal case emerging from the contested 1948 Senate election. In 1952 and 1956, he supported Republican Dwight D. Eisenhower for president, but many other Texans did as well. In 1960, he voted for Richard Nixon and opposed the national Democratic ticket of John F. Kennedy and Lyndon Johnson.[8]

After finishing his term as governor in 1920, William P. Hobby returned to the newspaper business and direct leadership of the Beaumont *Enterprise*, which he had owned since before his election as lieutenant governor in 1914, and soon purchased the Beaumont *Journal*. After assuming the presidency of the Houston *Post-Dispatch* in 1924, which he purchased in 1939 as the *Post*, he sold the Beaumont papers. While Hobby never again sought public office, he and his family remained in the public eye and politically active throughout the twentieth century. After the death of his first wife, Willie Chapman Cooper Hobby in 1929, he married Oveta Culp Hobby in 1931. A former parliamentarian of the Texas House of Representatives, she came from a politically active family and had political and business aspirations of her own. Among her most known public accomplishments, Oveta Hobby served as the organizer and first commanding officer of the Women's Army Auxiliary Corps, later renamed the Women's Army Corps, from 1941 to 1945. The Hobbys had two children. Their son, William "Bill" Pettus Hobby Jr., served as lieutenant governor of Texas from 1973 to 1991, longer than any previous lieutenant governor in the state's history.[9]

April 20, 1937
W. P. Hobby[10]
Houston, Texas
Dear Governor Hobby,
I wish to thank you a thousand time[s] for your acceptance of my invitation to be with us at Mother Neff State Park on Mother's Day. I was especially delighted to know that Mrs. Hobby[11] was willing to come with you on the occasion.
   I stated, however, in my invitation that it was not my intention to have this meeting unless all of those who had served in the governor's office would agree to be present. Believe it or not, and and [sic] as it may seem, more than half of the seven of us who have thus served declined to be present if it was understood that all of those who have served in the office were to be present at the same time. Therefore, the meeting will not be had. This I deeply regret.
I am going to renew the invitation, however, next

year[12] with the hope that time will make possible the gathering at one time and one place all of those who have been honored in Texas with the governor's office.

I am in hopes that no publicity will be given to this matter because I am so ashamed of it that I do not want to be even the medium of revealing to the people of Texas the situation as to those who have served as governor.

Thanking you again for the fine spirit in which you accepted the invitation, and with the best of all good wishes to you and to Mrs. Hobby, I am
Yours in friendship and esteem
until the last Roundup,
[Pat M. Neff]

NOTES

1. Norman D. Brown, *Hood, Bonnet, and Little Brown Jug: Texas Politics, 1921–1928* (College Station: Texas A&M University Press, 1984), 13–14, 67–72, 105, 107, 198–99; Lewis L. Gould, *Progressives and Prohibitionists: Texas Democrats in the Wilson Era* (Austin: University of Texas Press, 1974), 271–73; George Norris Green, *The Establishment in Texas Politics: The Primitive Years, 1938–1957* (Norman: University of Oklahoma Press, 1984), 13; "Pat Morris Neff," *Handbook of Texas Online*, https://tshaonline.org/handbook/online/articles/fne05, accessed October 24, 2015.

2. "Mother Neff State Park," https://tshaonline.org/handbook/online/articles/gkm02, accessed October 24, 2015. On Neff's relationship with his mother, see Brown, *Hood, Bonnet, and Little Brown Jug*, 12.

3. Pat Neff to James Ferguson, April 6, 1937, and Ferguson to Neff, April 9, 1937, Pat M. Neff Papers, Texas Collection, Baylor University, Waco, Texas (hereafter referred to as Neff Papers).

4. William Hobby to Neff, April 10, 1937; Neff to Hobby, April 19, 1937; Neff to Allred, April 24, 1937, and Allred to Neff, April 29, 1937, all in Neff Papers.

5. Dan Moody to Neff, April 10, 1937, Neff Papers.

6. Brown, *Hood, Bonnet, and Little Brown Jug*, 285–95, 305–31, 340.

7. Ibid., 434; "Miriam A. Ferguson," *Handbook of Texas Online*, https://tshaonline.org/handbook/online/articles/ffe06, accessed, October 24, 2015.

8. "Daniel James Moody," *Handbook of Texas Online*, https://tshaonline.org/handbook/online/articles/fm019, accessed October 24, 2015; Brown, *Hood, Bonnet, and Little Brown Jug*, 410, 415–16, 420–22; Green, *Establishment in Texas Politics*, 39–42, 115.

9. "William Pettus Hobby," *Handbook of Texas Online*, https://tshaonline.org/handbook/online/articles/fh004, accessed, October 24, 2015; "Oveta Culp Hobby," *Handbook of Texas Online*, https://tshaonline.org/handbook/online/articles/fh086, accessed, October 24, 2015; Office of the Lieutenant Governor: Records of William Pettus Hobby, Jr., Texas State Library and Archives Commission, Austin, Texas.

10. Content of letter published courtesy of Texas Collection, Baylor University. Pat Neff to W. P. Hobby, April 20, 1937, Neff Papers.

11. "Mrs. Hobby" referred to in this letter was Oveta Culp Hobby.

12. Technically, Mother Neff State Park opened for public use in 1937, but the dedication event did not occur until 1938. On Mother's Day, May 14, 1938, an estimated more than one thousand people attended the official ceremony opening the park. As part of the Neff Papers in the Texas Collection at Baylor University, there are two scrapbooks highlighting different aspects of Mother Neff State Park, including pieces sent by visitors of the park to Neff at different times.

Ferguson's Impeachment

A Selected Bibliography

Jessica Brannon-Wranosky and Bruce A. Glasrud

Alexander, Charles C. *Crusade for Conformity: The Ku Klux Klan in Texas, 1920–1930.* Houston: Texas Gulf Coast Historical Association, 1962.

Alter, Judy. *Miriam "Ma" Ferguson: First Woman Governor of Texas.* Austin: State House Press, 2006.

Anders, Evan. "Boss Rule and Constituent Interests: South Texas Politics during the Progressive Era." *Southwestern Historical Quarterly* 84, no. 3 (1981): 269–92.

———. *Boss Rule in South Texas: The Progressive Era.* Austin: University of Texas Press, 1982.

Anti-Saloon League. *The Brewers in Texas Politics.* 2 vols. San Antonio: Passing Show Printing, 1916.

[Barker, Eugene C.], comp. *Ferguson's War on the University of Texas: A Chronological Outline: January 12, 1915, to July 31, 1917*, inclusive. Austin: Ex-Students Association of the University of Texas, 1917.

Barr, Alwyn. *Reconstruction to Reform: Texas Politics, 1876–1906.* Austin: University of Texas Press, 1971.

Biggers, Don H. *Our Sacred Monkeys; or, 20 Years of Jim and Other Jams (Mostly Jim) the Outstanding Goat Gland Specialist of Texas Politics.* Brownwood, TX: Jones Printing, 1933.

Brannon-Wranosky, Jessica. "Reformers, Populists, and Progressives, 1875–1915." In *Discovering Texas History*, edited by Bruce A. Glasrud, Light Townsend Cummins, and Cary D. Wintz, 243–58. Norman: University of Oklahoma Press, 2014.

———. "Southern Promise and Necessity: Texas, Regional Identity, and the National Woman Suffrage Movement, 1868–1920." PhD diss., University of North Texas, 2010.

Brown, Norman D. *Hood, Bonnet, and Little Brown Jug.* College Station: Texas A&M University Press, 1984.

Buenger, Walter L. *The Path to a Modern South: Northeast Texas between Reconstruction and the Great Depression*. Austin: University of Texas Press, 2001.

Calbert, Jack Lynn. "James Edward and Miriam Amanda Ferguson: The Ma and Pa of Texas Politics." PhD diss., Indiana University, 1968.

Cox, Patrick. "Farmer Jim and 'The Chief': Governor Jim Ferguson and His Battle with Eugene C. Barker and the University of Texas." In *The Texas Book Two: More Profiles, History, and Reminiscences of the University*, edited by David Dettmer, 133–40. Austin: University of Texas Press, 2012.

Davis, Clare Ogden. *The Woman of It*. New York: J. H. Sears, 1929.

DeShields, James. *The Fergusons, "Jim and Ma": The Stormy Petrels in Texas Politics*. Dallas: Clyde C. Cockrell, 1932.

Dobbs, Ricky. *Yellow Dogs and Republicans: Allan Shivers and Texas Two-Party Politics*. College Station: Texas A&M University Press, 2005.

Ewing, Cortez A. M. "The Impeachment of James E. Ferguson." *Political Science Quarterly* 48, no. 2 (1933): 184–210.

Frederickson, Kari. *The Dixiecrat Revolt and the End of the Solid South, 1932–1960*. Chapel Hill: University of North Carolina Press, 2001.

Gantt, Fred, Jr. *The Chief Executive in Texas: A Study in Executive Leadership*. Austin: University of Texas Press, 1964.

Glasrud, Bruce A. "Time of Transition: Black Women in Early Twentieth-Century Texas, 1900–1930." In *Black Women in Texas History*, edited by Bruce A. Glasrud and Merline Pitre, 99–128. College Station: Texas A&M University Press, 2008.

Gould, Lewis L. *Progressives and Prohibitionists: Texas Democrats in the Age of Wilson*. Austin: University of Texas Press, 1973.

———. "The University Becomes Politicized: The War with Jim Ferguson, 1915–1918." *Southwestern Historical Quarterly* 86 (October 1982): 256–76.

Green, James R. *Grass Roots Socialism: Radical Movements in the Southwest, 1865–1943*. Baton Rouge: Louisiana State University Press, 1978.

Guzman, Jane Bock. "Yet Another Look at the Fergusons of Texas." *East Texas Historical Journal* 44, no. 1 (2006): 40–48.

Haley, J. Evetts. *George W. Littlefield, Texan*. Norman: University of Oklahoma Press, 1943.

Hendrickson, Kenneth E., Jr. *The Chief Executives from Stephen F. Austin to John B. Connally, Jr*. College Station: Texas A&M University Press, 1995.

Hill, Larry D. "Texas Progressivism: A Search for Definition." In *Texas through Time: Evolving Interpretations*, edited by Walter L. Buenger and Robert A. Calvert, 229–50. College Station: Texas A&M University Press, 1991.

Hill, Larry D., and Robert A. Calvert. "The University of Texas Extension Services and Progressivism." *Southwestern Historical Quarterly* 86, no. 2 (1982): 231–54.

Hine, Darlene Clark. *Black Victory: The Rise and Fall of the White Primary in Texas.* Columbia: University of Missouri Press, 1979.

Huddleston, John D. "Ferguson, Miriam Amanda Wallace [Ma]." *Handbook of Texas Online.* http://www.tshaonline.org/handbook/online/articles.

Humphrey, Janet G. *A Texas Suffragist: Diaries and Writings of Jane Y. McCallum.* Austin, TX: Ellen C. Temple, 1988.

Jackson, Pearl Cashell. *Texas Governors' Wives.* Austin, TX: Steck Publishers, 1915.

Journal of the House of Representatives of the Second Called Session of the Thirty-Fifth Legislature of Texas August 1, 1917–August 30, 1917. Austin, TX: Von Boeckmann-Jones, 1917.

Key, V. O., Jr. *Southern Politics in State and Nation.* New York: Alfred A. Knopf, 1949.

Lomax, John A. "Governor Ferguson and the University of Texas." *Southwest Review* 28, no. 1 (1942): 11–29.

Luthin, Reinhard H. "Mr. and Mrs. James E. Ferguson: 'Pa' and 'Ma' of the Lone Star State." *American Demagogues: Twentieth Century.* New York: Beacon Press, 1954.

Maxwell, Robert S. "Texas in the Progressive Era, 1900–1930." In *Texas: A Sesquicentennial Celebration,* edited by Donald W. Whisenhunt, 173–200. Austin, TX: Eakin, 1984.

McArthur, Judith N. *Creating the New Woman: The Rise of Southern Women's Progressive Culture in Texas, 1893–1918.* Urbana: University of Illinois Press, 1998.

———. "Minnie Fisher Cunningham's Back Door Lobby in Texas: Political Maneuverings in a One-Party State." In *One Woman, One Vote: Rediscovering the Woman Suffrage Movement,* edited by Marjorie Spruill Wheeler, 315–32. Troutdale, OR: NewSage Press, 1995.

McArthur, Judith N., and Harold L. Smith. *Minnie Fisher Cunningham: A Suffragist's Life in Politics.* New York: Oxford University Press, 2003.

McArthur, Judith N., and Harold L. Smith, eds. *Texas through Women's Eyes: The Twentieth-Century Experience.* Austin: University of Texas Press, 2010.

McCaleb, W. F. "The Impeachment of a Governor." *American Political Science Review* 12 (February 1918): 111–15.

McKay, Seth S. *Texas Politics, 1906–1944.* Lubbock: Texas Tech University Press, 1952.

Nalle, Ouida Ferguson. *The Fergusons of Texas; or, "Two Governors for the Price of One."* San Antonio, TX: Naylor, 1946.

Patteson, Nelda. *Miriam Amanda Ferguson: First Woman Governor of Texas.* Smiley, TX: Smiley, 1994.

Paulissen, May Nelson, and Carl McQueary. *Miriam: The Southern Belle Who Became the First Woman Governor of Texas.* Austin, TX: Eakin Press, 1995.

Pool, William C. *Eugene C. Barker: Historian*. Austin: Texas State Historical Association, 1971.

Porterfield, Nolan. *Last Cavalier: The Life and Times of John A. Lomax*. Urbana: University of Illinois Press, 1996.

Rutherford, Bruce. *The Impeachment of Jim Ferguson*. Austin, TX: Eakin Press, 1983.

Sallee, Shelley. "'The Woman of It': Governor Miriam Ferguson's 1924 Election." *Southwestern Historical Quarterly* 100 (July 1996): 1–16.

Schmelzer, Janet. *Our Fighting Governor: The Life of Thomas M. Campbell and the Politics of Progressive Reform in Texas*. College Station: Texas A&M University Press, 2014.

Sibley, Marilyn McAdams. *George W. Brackenridge: Maverick Philanthropist*. Austin: University of Texas Press, 1973.

Sosebee, M. Scott. "The Split in the Texas Democratic Party, 1936–1956." Master's thesis, Texas Tech University, 2000.

Stanley, Mark S. "Portrait of a Southern Progressive: The Political Life and Times of Gov. Pat M. Neff of Texas, 1871–1952." PhD diss., University of North Texas, 2011.

State of Texas. *Proceedings of Investigation Committee, House of Representatives Thirty-Fifth Legislature: Charges Against Governor James E. Ferguson Together with Findings of Committee and Action of House with Prefatory Statement and Index to Proceedings*. Austin, TX: A. C. Baldwin and Sons, 1917.

———. *Record of Proceedings of the High Court of Impeachment on the Trial of Hon. James E. Ferguson, Governor Before the Senate of the State of Texas. Pursuant to the State Constitution and Rules Provided by the Senate during the Second and Third Called Sessions of the 35th Legislature August 1–September 29, 1917*. Austin: A. C. Baldwin and Sons, 1917.

Steen, Ralph W. "Ferguson's War on the University of Texas." *Southwestern Social Science Quarterly* 35 (March 1955): 356–62.

———. "Governor Miriam A. Ferguson." *East Texas Historical Journal* 17 (April 1979): 3–17.

———. "James Edward Ferguson." *Handbook of Texas Online*. http://www.tshaonline.org/handbook/online/articles.

Texas Legislature. House of Representatives. Committee on investigation of charges against Governor James E. Ferguson: *Proceedings, Investigation Committee, House of Representatives, Thirty-Fifth Legislature. Charges Against Governor James E. Ferguson, Together with Findings of Committee and Action of House, with Prefatory Statement and Index to Proceedings*. Austin: A. C. Baldwin and Sons, contracting printers, [1917].

Texas State Library and Archives Commission. "Portraits of Texas Governors: The Politics of Personality: Part 1, 1915–1927: James E. Ferguson." https://

www.tsl.state.tx.us/governors/personality/index.html#PaFerguson. Accessed October 13, 2015.
———. "Portraits of Texas Governors: The Politics of Personality: Part 1, 1915–1927: Miriam A. Ferguson." https://www.tsl.state.tx.us/governors/personality/index.html#MaFerguson. Accessed October 13, 2015.
———. "Portraits of Texas Governors: The Politics of Personality: Part 2, 1927–1939: Miriam A. Ferguson." https://www.tsl.texas.gov/governors/personality/page2.html#MaFerguson. Accessed October 13, 2015.
Tinsley, James Aubrey. "The Progressive Movement in Texas." PhD diss., University of Wisconsin, 1953.
Vinson, Robert E. "The University Crosses the Bar." *Southwestern Historical Quarterly* 43, no. 3 (1940): 1–13.
Wilkison, Kyle G. *Yeomen, Sharecroppers, and Socialists: Plain Folk Protest in Texas, 1870–1914*. College Station: Texas A&M University Press, 2008.
Wilson, Carol O'Keefe. *In the Governor's Shadow: The True Story of Ma and Pa Ferguson*. Denton: University of North Texas Press, 2014.

SELECT ARCHIVAL COLLECTIONS CONTAINING PRIMARY SOURCE DOCUMENTS AND FILES ABOUT THE IMPEACHMENT AND/OR PERSONAL AND POLITICAL PAPERS OF JAMES AND MIRIAM FERGUSON

Austin, Texas
Austin Public Library
Austin History Center
Jane Y. McCallum Papers
Texas State Library and Archives Commission
Archives and Information Services Division
James Edward Ferguson (Gubernatorial) Papers
Miriam Amanda Ferguson (Gubernatorial) Papers
Records of the Central Investigating Committees of the (Texas) House and Senate, 1917–18
William Pettus Hobby (Gubernatorial) Papers
University of Texas at Austin
Dolph Briscoe Center for American History
Alexander Caswell Ellis Papers
Anna J. Hardwicke (Mrs. Percy V.) Pennybacker Papers
Eugene C. Barker Papers
George E. B. Peddy Papers

James Edward Ferguson Collection
James Edward Ferguson Scrapbooks (From UT President's Office)
Jane Y. and Arthur N. McCallum Family Papers
John Avery Lomax Family Papers
Margaret C. Berry Papers
Martin McNulty Crane Papers
Robert E. Vinson Papers
Robert Lynn Batts Papers
Roy Bedichek Papers
University of Texas Memorabilia
William Clifford Hogg Papers
William James Battle Papers
William Seneca Sutton Papers
Belton, Texas
Bell County Museum
Ferguson Papers
Houston, Texas
University of Houston
M. D. Anderson Library, Special Collection and Archives
Minnie Fisher Cunningham Papers
Lubbock, Texas
Texas Tech University
Southwest Collection/Special Collections Library
William H. Bledsoe Papers
Waco, Texas
Baylor University Libraries
Texas Collection
Governors James E. and Miriam "Ma" Ferguson Collection

Index

The letter *p* following a page number denotes a photograph

Adoue, B., 36
African Americans: JF's failure toward, 3–4, 30, 116; sharecropper status, 168; voting rights, 86; voting rights for women, 24, 102–103
Agriculture Department, Texas, 58, 69
Alcalde, 14
alcohol sales to the military, 21, 23, 45, 60–61, 72, 78
Alexander, Charles C., 144
Allen, Wilbur, 36
Allen, W. P., 27, 35, 39, 67, 72
Allred, James V., 147, 180, 181
Alter, Judy, 6
American, 68
American Party, 3
Ames, Jessie Daniel, 143
Anders, Evan, 85–86
Andrews, J. M., 100
Anheuser-Busch Association, 16, 17
antivice campaign, military training camps, 21, 23, 45, 60–61, 72, 78
Arizona, 161
Armstrong, Tex, 88
Arnold, Kay Reed, 8–9, 53–80
Aubrey, Zoe Rodman, 60
Austin, Charles O., 31, 33
Austin American, 112
Austin Anti-Vice League, 21, 23, 59, 62, 116
Austin Canning Club, 70

Austin Equal Suffrage Association, 59
Austin Statesman, 63, 117–119, 122–123, 128–129
Autrey, R. L., 18

Bailey, Joseph Weldon, 18, 24, 85–86, 88, 137, 141–143, 179
Baker, Newton, 61
Baldwin, A. C., 72, 79
Ball, Thomas H., 2, 17, 18, 110, 136
Barker, Eugene C., 19–20, 23
Barkley, Alben, 150
Battle, William J., 20–22, 24, 26, 114, 138
Battle of the Barbecues, 152
Beaumont Enterprise, 182
Beaumont Journal, 182
Belo, A. H., 111
Benedict, Harry Yandell, 5, 13, 63
Biggers, Don H., 6
Blagojevich, Rod, 161
Blalock, Myron, 148
Bledsoe, William H., 28
Bourbon Democratic machine, 2, 143
Brackenridge, George W., 40, 55–56, 65, 67, 79, 92
Brackenridge, Mary Eleanor, 16, 40, 41, 41*p*, 55, 79
Brady, John, 64, 67, 68–69
Brannon-Wranosky, Jessica, 1–11, 158–165
Brents, William R., 27, 39
brewing industry, 3, 16–18, 21, 35–36, 61, 66

Brown, Norman, 4
Brownwood Bulletin, 24, 114–115
Bryan, E. R., 91
Busch, Adolphus, 16, 17, 19, 61, 63
Butler, David, 161
Butler, J. W., 27, 35, 38
Butte, George C., 42

Campaign Material: Issued by the Headquarters Committee of the Woman's Campaign for Good Government, 72–77
Campbell, Thomas M., 15
canning clubs, 55
Catt, Carrie Chapman, 10, 94, 103, 140, 158–159, 175–177
City Federation of Women's Missionary Societies, 60
Civilian Conservation Corps, 147, 179
Cofer, Robert E., 22–24, 26, 42, 66, 79, 114
Coke, Richard, 163
Colonial Dames, 65, 70
Colquitt, Oscar B., 17, 31, 112, 114, 146
Connally, Tom, 13
Connecticut, 158–159
conservatives, support for JF, 2, 136, 144. *See also* progressives vs. conservatives, Texas Democratic Party
Cox, Patrick, 7, 111, 121
Crane, Martin M., 31–32, 43–44, 91–93, 97–98, 104, 143
Culberson, Charles A., 88, 93, 145
Culberson, Sham, 170
Culberson v. Ashford, 170
Cunningham, A. F., 19–20
Cunningham, Minnie Fisher, 9–10, 16, 22–25, 40, 45, 60, 63–69, 72, 78, 80, 86–104, 140, 142–143, 158–159, 175–177
Curtis, Nannie Webb, 68, 100, 140

Daily Texan, 37, 115–116
Dallas Morning News, 36, 40, 110, 111–113, 116–126, 128–129, 142, 152, 162
Daughters of 1812, 65
Daughters of the Confederacy, 65
Daughters of the Republic, 65
Daughters of the Revolution, 65
Davidson, Lynch, 144
Davidson, T. W., 144
Davis, Clare Ogden, 6, 7
Davis, Edmund Jackson, 163
Davis, Fred W.: Commissioner of Agriculture, 40, 69–70, 72
Davis, Henry Phillip, 29–31
Dayton, George W., 28–29
Dealey, George, 111
Democratic League, 100
Democratic National Convention (1916), 24–25, 137
Democratic National Convention (1928), 146
Democratic National Convention (1944), 86–87, 151
democratic socialism, 169
Denton, James T., 99
DeShields, James, 6
Dewey, Thomas E., 152
Dietrich, Louise, 102–103
Dobbs, Ricky Floyd, 179–183
Domestic Economy department, UT, 54–56, 58, 62–63, 66, 69, 73, 79
Domestic Science Department, UT, 55
Doughty, W. F., 40
draft, WWI, 101–102, 103
Duckworth, Allen, 152

East Texas Normal College (Texas A&M University-Kingsville/Mayo's College), 34
education, higher: 35th legislature

support for, 15; JF on, 15, 19, 27, 34–35, 45–46, 118, 120; land grant normal colleges established, 34; Perry's funding of, 161–162. *See also* University of Texas (UT)
education, rural, 19, 22–23, 55, 62, 113–114, 116–118, 138
Eighteenth Amendment, 45
Eisenhower, Dwight D., 153, 181
election (1914): Bourbon backing, 2; campaign focus, 1; farm tenancy issue, 1, 110, 136; prohibition and suffrage issues, 1, 110–111, 112–113; Texas Democratic Party and the, 2, 17–18, 135–136
election (1916), 24–25
election (1920), 141–143
election (1924), 142–145
Elkins, J. A., 97
Ellis, Alexander Caswell, 22–24, 26–27, 42, 55, 59, 62, 64–67, 69, 72–74, 79, 89–90, 92–93, 114
Ellis, Mary Heard, 22, 59, 62, 67–68, 79, 89
Engle, Lavinia, 88
Evans, Richard D., 170
Ewing, Cortez A. M., 7
Extension Service, UT, 21–23, 26, 54–56, 59–60

Faber, Maurice, 26, 27
"Farmer Jim and 'The Chief'" (Cox), 7
farmers: education for, 22; JF, support for/support of, 17–18, 85, 105, 110, 136–137. *See also* tenant farmers
Farmers Institute, 55, 58, 69–72
Farmers' Union, 18
Farm Tenant Law, 10, 168–173
Federated Women's Clubs, 60, 65, 68
Ferguson, James E. "Pa" (JF): background, 18; election (1914), 1–2, 17–18, 110–113, 135–136; election (1916), 24–25; gubernatorial behavior, offensive, 3–4; historical marker, 164–165, 164*p*; Pa Ferguson, reframing as, 17–18; populist image of, 15, 17–18, 39, 85, 105, 110, 169; press, suspicion of the, 113–114, 118–119, 124, 126, 128–129; scholarship on, 4–6; spoils system of governance, 18; Temple residence, renovation and Historical Commission marker, 165
Ferguson, James E. "Pa" (JF), characteristics: arrogant, 114; charismatic, 1; delusional, 33, 137; demagoguery, 2, 130; megalomania, 21; not a team player, 2; orator, 112; paranoia, 30, 113–114, 118–119, 124, 126, 128–129, 138; persuasive, 1; self-image as above the law, 21, 33, 137; vindictiveness, 18–19, 26, 30, 38, 128
Ferguson, James E. "Pa" (JF), finances: *Ferguson Forum* income, 127, 130; net worth (1914), 18; personal, 32; Texas Brewer's Association loans, 35–36; TSB loan, 28–30, 44, 91–92
Ferguson, James E. "Pa" (JF), impeachment charges: banking law violations, 29–31; embezzlement, 29, 30, 42; excessive commissions to attorneys for State Penitentiary System, 29; public funds, misuse of, 29–31, 42; special interest campaign money, 29; testimony rebutting, 30, 32–33, 92, 125
Ferguson, James E. "Pa" (JF), impeachment of: factors underlying, 1–3, 118; in film, 126, 165; historical memory, effect on other governors,

158–163; Houston Riot during, 4; national politics, effect on, 4, 146–147, 158–163, 179–183; public memory of, 165; scholarship on, 4–6; Supreme Court ruling, 144; Texas politics, effect on, 14, 160–163, 180

Ferguson, James E. "Pa" (JF), post-impeachment: barred from holding office, 1, 45, 79, 92–93, 140–141; governor, 1918 run for, 3, 43, 94, 122, 129, 140–141, 144, 148, 176; Texas lore, favorable standing in, 5, 165; US presidency, run for, 3; US Senate, run for, 3, 179

Ferguson, James E. "Pa" (JF), supporters of: conservatives, 2, 136, 144; farmers, 1–2, 17–18, 85, 105, 110, 112, 135–137; Texans, rural, 1–2, 129, 169

Ferguson, Miriam Amanda, 3, 5–7, 10, 45, 130, 144–145, 147, 160, 163–165, 180–181

Ferguson Forum, 9–10, 94, 99, 126–131, 160

"Fergusonism, Factionalization, and Thirty Years of Texas Politics" (Stanley), 10, 135–153

The Fergusons, "Jim and Ma" (DeShields), 6

The Fergusons of Texas; or, "Two Governors for the Price of One (Nalle), 6

"Ferguson's War on the University of Texas" (Steen), 7

Finnigan, Annette, 85–86

First Texas News Barons (Cox), 111

Fisher, Marion, 78

Fly, Ashley W., 26–29, 35, 39, 41–42, 67

food conservation campaign, 56, 57*p*, 58–59, 69–70

Fourteenth Amendment, 170

Fuller, Francis O., 121
Fuller, Frank, 30, 40, 42, 43–44, 123
Fuller, Oliver Franklin, 90–91

Galveston News, 112, 123
Garner, Jack, 148–149
Gearing, Mary E., 40, 56, 58, 60, 62, 67–69, 78–79
German immigrants, 96, 124
To Get a Better School System (Preuss), 113, 118
Glasrud, Bruce A., 1–11, 103
Goodman, Benjamin G., 170
Gould, Lewis L., 5, 113–114, 116, 119–121
"Governor Ferguson and the University of Texas" (Lomax), 7
"Governor Miriam A. Ferguson" (Steen), 7
Gramm, Phil, 153
Grantham, Dewey, 130
Graves, Ireland, 39
Great Depression, 148
Greater Federation of Women's Clubs, 60
"The Great Texas 'Bear Fight'" (Lundberg), 8, 13–46
Gregory, Thomas Watt, 13
Grubb's Vocational College (University of Texas-Arlington), 34
Gunter, Rachel M., 9, 85–105
Guzman, Jane Bock, 7

Hall, Wallace, 162
Hamilton, Andrew Jackson, 163
Hanger, William A., 31
Harper's Weekly, 112
Harrell, David H., 26–27, 39
Hart, Mrs. Will, 66
Heard, T. H., 124
Henderson, John M., 28

Index

Hill, Miss, 101
Hise, Lenore, 102
Hobby, Oveta Culp, 147, 182
Hobby, William "Bill" Pettus Jr., 161–162, 182
Hobby, William Pettus, 3, 9–10, 15, 40, 44–45, 54, 85, 88, 92, 94–95, 98–102, 104–105, 112, 121, 140, 143, 147, 162, 176, 179–183
Hobby, Willie Chapman Cooper, 182
Hobby Clubs, 99–101
Hogg, James S., 13, 15
Hogg, William C., 13, 17–19, 21, 23, 26–28, 39–40, 42–43, 45, 63–64, 67, 72–73, 79, 89, 119, 121
Holdon, William, 161
Holman, Charles, 112
Hoover, Herbert, 56, 146, 151, 153, 181
Hornsby, J. W., 38
House, Edward M., 136
Houston Chronicle, 112, 119–120, 122–124, 130, 160, 161
Houston Ice and Brewing Company, 18
Houston Post, 36, 61, 112, 117, 122, 130, 182
Houston Post-Dispatch, 182
Hudspeth, Claude, 34

Illinois, 161
"The Impeachment of James E. Ferguson" (Ewing), 7
The Impeachment of Jim Ferguson (Rutherford), 5
impeachments, gubernatorial: 1800s, 164; 1910s-1930s, 161; 1980s, 161; 2000s, 161; of MF, calls for, 160, 180; Reconstruction era, 161. *See also* Ferguson, James E. "Pa" (JF), impeachment of
In the Governors Shadow (Wilson), 6
"In the Public Eye" (Ochoa), 110–131

"James Edward "Farmer Jim" Ferguson's Impeachment and Its Ramifications" (Brannon-Wranosky & Glasrud), 1–11
Jester, Beauford, 152
Johnson, Lyndon, 5, 181
Johnson, W. A., 28, 30
Johnston, Henry, 159, 161
Jones, Jesse H., 112
Jones, Samuel J., 27, 38
Jones, T. N., 97
Journalism Department, UT, 24

Keasbey, L. M., 42
Kelly, Charles Edgar, 35, 39
Kennedy, John F., 181
Knox, Helen, 64
Ku Klux Klan, 3, 5, 7, 140, 144–145, 179

land grant normal colleges established, 34
Land Tenant Law, 168–173
Langley, Mrs. George, 100
Lattimore, Offa Shivers, 27–28, 29
Lawrence, D. H., 27–29, 35
League, Edith Hinkle, 78–79, 92, 99–102
Legal Defense Committee (TESA), 104
Lewelling, Dwight, 143
liquor industry, 16–19, 59
Littlefield, George, 21–22, 27, 39, 66–67, 69, 72
Littlefield, George W., 26
Lochridge, I. P., 26
Lomax, John Avery, 7, 13, 22–24, 26, 36–38, 42, 55, 62, 64, 117, 119
Long, W. R., 26
Looney, Benjamin F., 21, 39, 143
Lundberg, John R., 8, 13–46
Luthin, Reinhard H., 7

Marvin, Zeke, 144
Mather, William Tyler, 22–24, 26, 42, 59, 62–63, 66, 72, 79
Mathis, J. M., 38–39
Maverick, Maury, 148
Mayes, William H., 22, 24, 26, 42, 66, 72, 79, 112, 114–115, 115*p*
Mayfield, Earle B., 3, 140, 145–146, 152, 179
Mayo's College (East Texas Normal College /Texas A&M University-Kingsville), 34
McAdoo, William Gibbs, 179
McArthur, Judith N., 110, 129, 175–177
McCallum, Arthur Newell, 59, 62, 64
McCallum, Jane Yelvington, 23, 59, 62–64, 66–67, 70, 72, 104
McGregor, T. H., 110
McQueary, Carl, 6
McReynolds, George S., 26–27, 67
Mecham, Evan, 161
media: JF impeachment resurrected by the, 160, 162–163; movies, impeachment in the, 126, 165. *See also* press
Metcalfe, Charles B., 94–95
Mexican Americans, 4, 85–86, 102–103
Mexican immigrants, 85–86, 96, 101
Mezes, Sidney, 20, 54–56
Middleton v. Terrell, 31–32
military training camps, antivice campaign, 21, 23, 45, 60–61, 72, 78
military training curriculum, 58
military voting rights, Texas, 101–102
Minnie Fisher Cunningham (McArthur & Smith), 110, 129
Miriam Amanda Ferguson (Patteson), 6
Miriam "Ma" Ferguson (Alter), 6

Miriam: The Southern Belle Who Became the First Woman Governor of Texas (Paulissen & McQueary), 6
Missionary Review of the World, 59
Moody, Dan, 147, 150, 180–181
Moody, Mildred, 180
Moore, Helen, 78
Morris, Charles H., 25, 31
Mother Neff State Park, 147, 179, 182
Mother's Clubs, 59, 65
movies, impeachment in the, 126, 165
"Mr and Mrs. James E. Ferguson" (Luthin), 7

Nalle, Ouida Ferguson, 6, 62, 116
National American Woman Suffrage Association (NAWSA): black suffrage, position on, 103; DNC, role at, 86–88; Ellis involvement, 93; field worker salaries, 79; impeachment, role in, 79, 88, 98–99, 140, 158–159; Nineteenth Amendment and, 93, 95; primary suffrage, support for, 175; ratification campaigns, 159; South Texas campaign, 88; supporters of, 93; war work, 60
National Association for the Advancement of Colored People (NAACP), 103
Nebraska, 161
Neff, Isabella, 179
Neff, Pat M., 10, 139, 141–144, 146–151, 149*p*, 179–183
New Deal, 148, 181
"The News Has Been Condemning Me" (Ochoa), 9–10
New York, 161
Nineteenth Amendment, 45, 80, 93, 95, 98, 105, 142, 159

Index

Nixon, Richard, 5, 181
North Carolina, 161

O'Banion, Madison, 29, 139
Ochoa, Leah LaGrone, 9–10, 110–131
O'Daniel, W. Lee, 181
Oklahoma, 159–160, 161
Our Sacred Monkeys; or, 20 Years of Jim and Other Jams (Mostly Jim) the Outstanding Goat Gland Specialist of Texas Politics (Biggers), 6

Page, Paul D., 28
Parent-Teacher Association, 59
Parker, Edwin B., 13
Patteson, Nelda, 6
Paulissen, May Nelson, 6
Paxton, Ken, 162
Pease, Elisha Marshall, 163
Peddy, George E. B., 37–38, 139, 145, 152
Penn, Mrs. R. L., 70–71
Pennybacker, Anna, 59–60, 62–65, 68, 143
Perry, Rick, 10, 161–162
Pershing, George, 58
Poe, Hosea, 25, 31–32
Polk, Samuel, 26
poll tax, 86, 98, 102–103
Porvenir Massacre, 4
Potter, Elizabeth Herndon, 89, 94–95, 98
Potts, Charles S., 20, 22–24, 26, 66, 93
Powers, Bill, 162
Prairie View State Normal College (Prairie View A&M University), 34
Prather, William, 59
Present Day Club, 60
press: Board of Regents meeting to remove Vinson coverage, 36–38; campaign disputes in the, 111; daily newspapers, popularity of, 111; public opinion, influence on, 111–112, 117–118, 120; publishers, power of, 111–112. *See also* media
press-JF and the: 1915 administration coverage, 113; celebration of, 112–113; control, attempts to, 116; critical coverage, 24, 111; impeachment coverage (1955), 160; JF's understanding of the, 112, 114; vindictiveness toward, 24
press-JF's battle with the: appropriations veto, 114, 117, 123; *Ferguson Forum* and, 126–131; impeachment, role in, 116, 118–119, 121–122; impeachment coverage, 116–117, 122–126; UT battle, coverage of, 114–116, 119–121; UT newspaper, 115–116
Preuss, Gene, 113, 118
primary suffrage, 94–95, 98–99, 103–104, 143, 175–177
Progressive Era, Texas, 15–17
progressives: 1914 campaign, 110; appropriations veto protest, 66; election corruption, attempts to eliminate, 86; ideology, 14; impeachment, role in, 139; primary suffrage, support for, 95–96; suffrage and prohibition, position on, 14–16, 103; Texas Exes, 13–14; voting rights restrictions, 96; women, reaching out to, 54–56; women's war work efforts, 56
Progressives and Prohibitionists (Gould), 5
progressives vs. conservatives, Texas Democratic Party: 1914 election, 2, 135–136; 1920 election, 141–143; 1924 election, 142–145; battle of the barbecues, 151–152;

impeachment, effect on, 45–46; Ku Klux Klan, influence on, 144–145; struggle for control, 135–137, 141–143, 145–153; suffrage and prohibition, positions on, 15–17, 86, 94, 135–136, 142–143
prohibition: 1914 campaign, 110–113; Ellis position, 22; Hobby administration, 15; JF impeachment and, 45–46; JF's position on, 17, 85, 112; liquor industry's fight against, 16; progressives vs. conservatives on, 15–17, 86, 94, 135–136, 142–143; Texas Democratic Party Convention (1916), 137, 139
prohibitionists: alcohol sales to the military, attempts to eliminate, 21, 23, 45, 60–61, 72, 78; impeachment, role in, 139–140; suffragists, alliance with, 16, 22–23; UT faculty, 59, 61; WWI campaign, 58–59
prostitution, 21, 23
Public Discussion division, Domestic Economy department, UT, 55, 60

Ramsdell, Charles W., 23
Republican Party, 152–153
Rich, Jessie, 56
Robertson, Felix D., 144
Robertson, James B., 159
Rogers, Woodville, 151–152
Roosevelt, Eleanor, 149*p*
Roosevelt, Franklin D., 148–151, 181
Rutherford, Bruce, 5

Sallee, Shelley, 7
Sampson, Mrs. E., 103
San Antonio Express, 36, 117, 122, 130
Sanger, Alexander, 27
San Marcos Times, 122
Sayers, Joseph D., 31, 39, 65, 67, 119

Sevier, Clara Driscoll, 68
Sevier, Henry, 112
sharecroppers, 168. *See also* tenant farmers
Shivers, Allan, 152–153, 181
Shuler, Bob, 70
Smith, Al, 146
Smith, Harold, 110, 129
Smith, Henry, 163–164
Sneed, Jerome, 151
Socialist Party of Texas, 169
Speer, Elizabeth, 62, 72, 78, 97–98
Stanley, Mark, 10, 135–153
State Defense Council, WWI, 58
State's Rights Democratic Party, 151
Steen, Ralph A., 7
Stephen F. Austin Normal College (Stephen F. Austin University), 34
Stevenson, Coke, 181
Stowe, Mrs. S. N., 100
suffrage: 1919 referendum, 45; Bailey position, 24; Ellis position, 22; Hobby position on, 15, 85, 94; JF's position on, 15, 85–86, 87–89, 94, 96–97; Mexican immigrant voters and, 86; primary, 94–95, 98, 103–104, 143, 175–177; progressives vs. conservatives on, 15–17, 86, 94, 135–136, 142–143; Texas Democratic Party Convention (1916) platform, 137, 139. *See also specific suffrage groups*
Suffrage Clubs, 65
suffragists: appropriations veto protest, 63–66; impeachment, role in, 45–46, 53, 63–64, 67–73, 137, 139–140; political force of, 16; war work, 60–61
Sul Ross Normal College (Sul Ross State University), 34
Sulzer, William, 161

Susan B. Anthony Amendment. *See* Nineteenth Amendment
Sweeney, Mrs. J. S., 99

Temple State Bank, JF and the: 1916 election, 25; legislative investigation, 7, 25, 28–33; opening by JF, 18
tenant farmers: Farm Tenant Law, 10, 169–173; JF, support for/support of, 1–2, 17–18, 110, 112, 135–136; thirds and fourths status, 168–169
Terrell, Alexander W., 13
Terrell, Chester W., 39, 121
Terrell, H. B., 31
Texans, rural: democratic socialism, appeal to, 169; JF, support for/support of, 1–2, 129, 169; JF's ability to appeal to, 110, 112, 129, 139; newspapers shaping opinions of, 111–112, 122, 130. *See also* tenant farmers
Texas: land grant normal colleges established, 34; Nineteenth Amendment ratification, 105; state historical markers, 163–165, 164*p*; state suffrage amendment, 104
Texas A&M University, 18–19, 22
Texas A&M University-Kingsville (Mayo's College), 34
Texas Agricultural and Mechanical College (Texas A&M University), 18–19
Texas Brewer's Association, 16–18, 21, 35–36
Texas College of Mines (University of Texas-El Paso), 34
Texas Democrat, 22
Texas Democratic Party: 1914 election, 2, 135–136; 1914 primary, 17–18; 1920 election, 141–143; 1924 election, 142–145; political corruption, 85–86; Republican Party, shift to the, 152–153; struggle for control, 135–137, 141–143, 145–153; voter restrictions, 94
Texas Democratic Party Convention (1916), 24, 65, 136–137, 139
Texas Democratic Party Convention (1922), 145–146
Texas Democratic Party Convention (1940), 148–149
Texas Democratic Party Convention (1944), 150–151
Texas Equal Suffrage Association (TESA): antivice campaign, 93; Democratic National Convention (1916), 24–25; DNC suffrage plank and campaign against JF, 24–25, 86–90; Hobby campaign, 9, 94–95, 97–102, 104, 176; impeachment, role in, 67–68, 91–92, 140, 158–159, 175–177; Legal Defense Committee, 97–98; officers, 16, 55, 86; political power, 63; post-impeachment candidacy and, 94; primary suffrage, support for, 9, 98–100, 102–103, 175–177; progressives alliance with, 16; registration campaign, blacks and Latinas, 102–103; reorganization, 16; special session, call for, 90–91; supporters of, 91; Texas Exes alliance, 40; war used in rhetoric of, 101–102; war work, 93
Texas Ex-Students' Association (Texas Exes): 1911 Alumni Association meeting, 13; appropriations veto fight, 39–40, 117; educational focus, 13–14; impeachment, role in, 27, 39–40, 42–43, 64, 67–69, 119–121; officers, 13, 23, 89; power of, 138; progressive politics, 13–14; TESA alliance, 40; as working organization, beginnings, 13

Texas Federation of Women's Clubs, 60
"The Texas Governor's Impeachment in History and Memory" (Brannon-Wranosky), 10, 158–165
Texas legislature (1915) special session, 20
Texas legislature (1917): bill of impeachment, 44, 79, 92–93; on Board of Regents appointments, 35; impeachment hearings and charges investigated, 28–30, 33–34, 42–44, 78–79, 91–92; normal colleges established, 34; Senate resolutions to investigate, 28; special session, 35, 42–43, 70, 78, 90–92, 94, 120–121, 158–160, 177; UT and UT Medical Branch budget, 36
Texas Railroad Commission, 15
Texas Rangers, 4, 42
Texas Regulars, 148, 151
Texas Revolution, 164p
Texas State Archives and Historical Commission, 19–20
Texas State Commission of Insurance, 30
Texas Tribune, 162
Texas Woman Suffrage Association (TWSA), 85
Texas Women's Anti-Vice Association, 60, 66
"Think of the Lives That Might be Saved'" (Arnold), 8–9, 53–80
Thomas, Cullen, 143
Thomason, Robert, 142–143
Threadgill, Mrs. Wilmer, 102
Thurmond, Strom, 151, 152
Tower, John, 153
Truman, Harry, 151, 152
Tucker, J. P., 38, 41

"The University Becomes Politicized" (Gould), 5

University Citizens Committee (UCC), 65, 68, 120
"The University Crosses the Bar" (Vinson), 7
University of Texas (UT): 1915 budget appropriation, 20–21; *Daily Texan*, 115–116; Domestic Economy department, 54–56, 58, 62–63, 66, 69, 73, 79; Extension Service, 21–23, 26, 54–56, 59–60; interests protecting, 138–140; Journalism Department, 24; WWI curriculum, 58, 80
University of Texas (UT) Alumni Association. *See* Texas Ex-Students' Association (Texas Exes)
University of Texas (UT) Board of Regents: attempts to dominate, charge of, 29; mistrust of, JF's, 138; removals/appointments, JF's, 26–29, 35, 38, 41–42, 63, 89, 92, 139
University of Texas (UT) faculty: appropriations veto protest, 64; Busch attempts to fire, 61; dismissals, JF's demand for, 21–26, 36, 62–63, 66–67, 79, 89–90, 138; JF's assessment of, 62; JF's charges against, 62; progressives, 15; prohibitionists, 59, 61; suffrage supporters, 89–90; war work, 79–80
University of Texas (UT)-JF battle: appropriations veto, 37–40, 63–66, 69, 89, 114, 117, 123, 127–128, 139; beginnings, 19; Board of Regents, removals/appointments, 26–29, 35, 38, 41–42, 63, 89, 92, 139; budget line items, 20–21, 138; factors underlying, 15; faculty removals, demand for, 21–26, 36, 62–63, 66–67, 79, 89–90, 138; impeachment and, 45–46; media coverage

of, 114, 117, 123; scholarship on, 5–7; student protests, 37–38; Vinson administration, 21–23, 25–26, 30; Vinson removal, 36–39, 42, 62, 63, 89–90; Winkler appointment, 19–20
University of Texas-Arlington (Grubb's Vocational College), 34
University of Texas Co-op, 62
University of Texas-El Paso (Texas College of Mines), 34
University of Texas Medical Branch, 36
University of Texas Students' Association, 37
UT Reserved Officers Training Corps, 80
UT-TAMC, proposition to unite, 18–19

Vermont, 158–159
Villa, Pancho, 169
Vinson, Robert E., 7, 21–26, 28–30, 36–39, 42–43, 58, 62–66, 80, 89–90, 92, 117, 138–139
voting, Texas: corruption, 86; literacy test, 98; Mexican Americans, 85–86
voting rights, Texas: blacks, 86, 94–96; immigrants, 85–86, 96, 101, 103; military, 101–102; poll tax, 86, 98, 102–103. *See also* suffrage

Wahrmund, Otto, 17, 35*p*, 36
Walters, Katherine Kuehler, 168–170
Walton, John, 159, 161
Ward, John, 41–42
Washington, Jesse, 4
West Texas A&M University, 34, 40, 42–43, 121
West Texas Normal School, 28
white supremacy, 24

white zones, military training camps, 23, 45, 60–61, 72
Wilkie, Wendell, 150, 153
Wilkison, Kyle G., 168–170
Williams, Dan, 37
Williams, Frank A., 97
Wilson, Carol O'Keefe, 6
Wilson, Woodrow, 18, 23–25, 93, 95, 136–137, 141, 143
Winkler, Ernest W., 19–20
Wisconsin Plan, 54
Without Us, It Is Ferguson with a Plurality" (Gunter), 9, 85–105
Woman Citizen, 104
The Woman of It (Davis), 6, 7
"The Woman of It'" (Sallee), 7
women, Texas: Anti-Vice Association, 60, 66; antivice campaign, 72, 78; appropriations veto protest, 64–66; black, voting rights for, 24, 102–103; Domestic Economy department, UT, 54–56, 58, 62–63, 66, 69, 73, 79; Federation of Women's Clubs, 60; impeachment campaign, 54, 67–73, 78–80, 90; progressives reaching out to, 54–56; special training for, 55; UCC division, 67; UT WWI curriculum for, 58; voter registration statistics, 104; voting literacy test for, 98; war work, 54, 56, 57*p*, 58–59, 60–61, 69–70. *See also* suffrage
Women of Texas Protest, 69
Women's Army Auxiliary Corps (Women's Army Corps), 182
Woman's Campaign for Good Government (WCGG): antivice campaign, 78–79; Campaign Material, 72–77; impeachment campaign, 9, 40–41, 68, 72–78, 90, 175–177; suffrage campaign, 78–79

Women's Christian Temperance League, 140
Women's Christian Temperance Union (WCTU), 16, 67–68
women's rights, supporters of, 55
Woodward, C. Vann, 113
Woodward, Dudley K., 67, 68, 72
Wooldridge, A. P., 64
World War I: appropriations veto threat during, 63–66; draft, 101–102, 103; farmers, impact on, 58; food conservation campaign, 56, 57*p*, 58–59, 69–70; State Defense Council, 58; UT curriculum, 58; women's war work efforts, 53–54, 56, 57*p*, 58–59, 60–61, 69–70
Wranosky, Samantha, 10

Yeager, James E., 170
"Yet Another Look at the Fergusons of Texas" (Guzman), 7

www.ingramcontent.com/pod-product-compliance
Lightning Source LLC
Chambersburg PA
CBHW071905090426
42811CB00004B/758